Kabbalah Centre Books

The Zohar *24 volumes by Rabbi Shimon bar Yoḥai, The cardinal work in the literature of Kabbalah original Aramaic text with Hebrew translation and commentary by Rabbi Yehuda Ashlag*

Miracles, Mysteries, and Prayer Volume I and II, Rabbi P. Berg (also available in French, Spanish and Russian)
Kabbalah for the Layman Volume I, Rabbi P. Berg (also available in Hebrew, Spanish, French, Russian, Italian, German, Persian, Chinese and Portuguese)
Kabbalah for the Layman Volume II, III, Rabbi P. Berg (also available in Hebrew, Spanish, French and Italian)
Reincarnation: Wheels of a Soul Rabbi P. Berg (also available in Hebrew, Spanish, French, Italian, Russian and Persian)
Astrology: The Star Connection Rabbi P. Berg (also available in Hebrew, Spanish, French and Italian)
Time Zones: Your Key to Control Rabbi P. Berg (also available in French, Spanish, Hebrew and Persian)
To The Power of One Rabbi P. Berg (also available in Spanish)
Power of the Aleph Bet Volume I, II, Rabbi P. Berg (also available in Hebrew, French and Spanish)
The Kabbalah Connection Rabbi P. Berg (also available in Spanish and Hebrew)
Gift of the Bible Rabbi Yehuda Ashlag, Foreword by Rabbi P. Berg (also available in Hebrew and Spanish)
Zohar: Parashat Pinḥas Volume II, III, Translated, compiled and edited by Rabbi P. Berg (Vols. I and II are available in Spanish)
An Entrance to the Tree of Life Compiled and edited by Rabbi P. Berg (also available in Spanish)
Ten Luminous Emanations Rabbi Yehuda Ashlag, Volume I, II, Compiled and edited by Rabbi P. Berg (also available in Hebrew, 7 volume set)
An Entrance to The Zohar Compiled and edited by Rabbi P. Berg
General Principles of Kabbalah Rabbi M. Luzzatto (also available in Italian)
Light of Redemption by Rabbi Levi Krakovsky

Soon to be Published

Ten Luminous Emanations Volume IV, Rabbi Yehuda Ashlag, compiled and edited by Rabbi P. Berg
Time Zones: Creating Order from Chaos Rabbi P. Berg, Russian Translation
To The Power of One Rabbi P. Berg, French and Russian Translation

BOOKS AND TAPES AVAILABLE
AT BOOKSELLERS AND KABBALAH CENTRES AROUND THE WORLD

The Zohar: Parashat Pinḥas

Volume I

K A B B A L A H

THE ZOHAR PARASHAT PINḤAS

VOLUME I

TRANSLATED AND EDITED BY

RABBI P. BERG

FIRST EDITION
1987
REVISED EDITION
May 1994

0-943688-51-5 (Soft Cover)

For further information:

RESEARCH CENTRE OF KABBALAH
85-03 114th Street, Richmond Hill
NEW YORK, 11418

— or —

P.O. BOX 14168

THE OLD CITY, JERUSALEM

NEW YORK (718) 805-9122
LOS ANGELES (310) 657-5404
FLORIDA (305) 936-0984
MEXICO CITY (525) 589-4464
TORONTO (416) 631-9395
PARIS (331) -43-56-01-38
TEL AVIV (03) 528-0570

PRINTED IN U.S.A.

For the gift of connection
to the Lightforce of healing
for our family and for mankind,
and for the knowledge
of how to use it,
this book is dedicated to

צבי בן שלמה
טובה בת יצחק
והילדים בנימין בן צבי
ורבקה בת צבי

An Important Message to the Reader:

On reading the Zohar you might find it difficult for your mind to grasp its concepts the first time or the fifteenth time for that matter. The way to get the most out of the Zohar is not just by reading it but by "connecting" with it.

This is more than just a configuration of words printed on paper but a vehicle to connect to spiritual energy and higher levels of consciousness. Take each paragraph and meditate on it over and over again. If first you don't understand what you are reading, don't be concerned. Through this approach its inner light will be revealed to you.

Table of Contents

PREFACE 21

INTRODUCTION 27

PARASHAT PINḤAS 63

HEAR MY SON THE INSTRUCTION OF YOUR FATHER 63

1.* *The Light that follows the Righteous* 2. *Open the Gates.*

COMPANIONS LISTEN TO YOUR VOICE 64

3. *She dwells in all* 4. *Turning point of the night* 5. *Strengthened by the Shekhinah* 6. *Death of Zimri and Cozbi* 7. *Soul Transmigration.*

A COMPLETELY RIGHTEOUS AND AN INCOMPLETLY RIGHTEOUS PERSON 65

8. *Who controls our deeds* 9. *The second migration* 10. *Remedy for our sins* 11. *He who is zealous for the Holy name.*

KEEP MY SOUL FOR I AM PIOUS 67

12 . *Midnight is prayertime* 13. *Letters as precious secrets* 14. *Angels of Destruction* 15. *Inheritance for Malkhut.*

THE HEI ADDED TO THE NAME OF JOSEPH AND THE YUD TO PINḤAS 68

16 . *Joseph and Potiphar's wife.*

KEEPER OF THE COVENANT 69

17. *If I forget thee, O Jerusalem* 18. *Joseph's coffin*

* These numbers refer to the paragraph in which the topic is discussed.

19. *Respect for Joseph* **20.** *Pinas's service as High Priest* **21.** *A priest who kills* **22.** *Did Pinas die, or not?* **23.** *Honor of their Master* **24.** *Attire of the Soul* **25.** *Clothing of Evil and Good* **26.** *The parting of Pinḥs.*

FROM ROSH HASHANAH UNTIL THE LAST DAY OF SUKKOTH 73

27. *Secret of Ḥokhmah* **28.** *Order of Unity* **29.** *How to unite the body* **30.** *Rosh haShanah, how it operates for us.* **31.** *The Day of Atonement* **32.** *Sukkoth* **33.** *Shemini Atzeret.*

THE RAINBOW 75

34. *As a Covenant* **35a.** *The significance of the colors* **35b.** *The colors of Malkhut* **35c.** *White is Avraham* **35d.** *White, Red and Green.*

THE FAITHFUL SHEPHERD 78

36. *"Zealous, have I been zealous?"* **37.** *Blessing for the rainbow* **38.** *The secret of Malkhut* **39.** *Exile of the Holy One.*

ROSH HASHANAH MUSAF SERVICE 79

40. *Destruction of the Temple* **41.** *The Rainbow in Exile is Metatron* **42.** *Those who act in God'n way* **43.** *The Name "El"* **44.** *Sons of "Adám".*

LEVIRATE MARRIAGE AND TRANSMIGRATION 81

45. *Marrying a brother's wife* **46.** *Secret of*

Transmigration **47.** *A man without a son* **48.** *"Repentance"* **49.** *Rotation of a soul* **50.** *Four letters of the Tetragrammaton* **51.** *Garment of the letters* **52.** *He who wanders from place to place* **53.** *Divorce and Healing* **54.** *The deceased brother* **55.** *Secret of conception* **56.** *Kabbalistic Pearl* **57.** *Scholars at all levels*

Commentary: On the Sefirot 89

58. *Bird being Ben Yah* **59.** *Six hundred thousand Souls* **60.** *The Circle of Souls* **61.** *Jethro as Cain* **62.** *Rabbi Elazar ben Pedat* **63.** *Letters as related to Sfirot.*

BEFORE THE GIVING OF THE TORAH, THEY DEPENDED ON DESTINY 92

64. *Children, life, and sustenance* **65.** *Significance of the "Hei" in Abraham* **66.** *Study releases one from Cosmic influence* **67.** *Death of the old and rebirth; renewal and the Shema.*

WINE MAKES GLAD THE HEART OF MAN; THE FIR TREES ARE HER HOUSE 94

68. *Wine of the Torah* **69.** *Binah and Malkhut* **70.** *Countenances*

Commentary: Unification of concepts 96

71. *Nadab and Avihu* **72.** *Nadab and Avihu being childless* **73.** *Transmigration into Pinḥas* **74.** *Death of the innocent* **75.** *To condemn a sinner only in Sunlight* **76.** *Proper Tikune* **77.** *The Second Day of Creation* **78.** *The letters Hei, Vav, Yud, and Hei* **79.** *The Water of Nukva* **80.** *The secret of attaining old age* **81.** *What is Binah?* **82.** *Union of Zeir Anpin and Malkhut* **83.** *The Stork.*

FOR THE WIND PASSES OVER IT AND IT IS NOT (PSALMS 103:16) 103

84. *"As for man, his days are as grass"* **85.** *The Holy Wind*
Commentary: The work of Angels. 104

THE FAITHFUL SHEPHERD 105

86. *"Wrath" as an Angel* **87.** *Change your space and your cosmos* **88.** *Demons of destruction*
89. *The body as a house for the Soul* **90.** *The Spirit*
Commentary:The Spirit 106
91. *Change your residence* **92.** *Barreness of the Torah* **93.** *Satan prefers the just* **94.** *Jacob the Righteous* **95.** *Bloodletting* **96.** *The Burden of the Righteous* **97.** *Body and two arms of the Patriarchs*
Commentary:The relation to our anatomy 110
98. *The Exile and Edom* **99.** *Gevurah, how it operates* **100.** *Sins from Jacob* **101.** *Adam haRishon* **102.** *The Patriarchs cleanse our sins*
103. *Greatness of Rabbi Shimon.*

THE PATIENT'S PULSE IN THE EXILE OF EDOM 114

104. *The Reading* **105.** *The Shofar* **106.** *Today and tomorrow is shown through the Shofar*
107. *The Valley of Ono* **108.** *Why the wicked increase in the world* **109.** *Righteous suffer for the generation* **110.** *Pestilence and Disease* **111.** *Atonement for sins* **112.** *The timing is important*
113. *Letting blood and the Righteous.*

NONE OF THE NATIONS SWAY EXCEPT ISRAEL 118

114. *Why Jews sway in prayer* **115.** *Light of a*

Candle **116.** *The flickering Flame* **117.** *Souls of idol worshipers.*

ISRAEL REJOICES IN THEIR MAKER 120

118. *The future of the Accusing Angel*
119. *Rejoicing with the Holy One* **120.** *The Maker.*

THREE CRAFTSMEN: HEAVEN, EARTH, AND WATER 121

121. *The role of Father and Mother* **122.** *The Days of Creation* **123.** *The Fourth Day* **124.** *The Creation of Man* **125.** *A man gives joy to his parents, even in death.*

THE FAITHFUL SHEPHERD — THREE PARTNERS: THE HOLY ONE, BLESSED BE HE, A MAN'S FATHER AND HIS MOTHER 123

126. *The Holy One, and the Soul* **127.** *Time of Redemption.*

BEHOLD I GIVE TO HIM MY COVENANT OF PEACE 124

128. *Rabbi Pinhas ben Yair* **129.** *The letters of the Alphabet* **130.** *Moses and Malkhut*
131. *Covenant of Peace* **132.** *The space of Revealment* **133.** *The Light to Moses.*

WHATEVER YOUR HAND IS ABLE TO DO WITH YOUR OWN STRENGTH, THAT DO (ECCLESIASTES 9:10) 126

134. *The head of the Righteous* **135.** *Awakening of all parts* **136.** *The world depends on speech*
137. *The Shekhina* **138.** *The Righteous shall rise.*

YOUR EYES ARE AS THE POOLS IN ḤESHBON 128

139. *The numerical values*
Commentary: Ḥukhmah and Ḥeshbon. 128

IN THE EVENING SHE CAME AND IN THE MORNING SHE RETURNED (ESTHER, 2:14) 130

140. *The role of the wife* **141.** *Yesod of Zeir Anpin* **142.** *Pinḥas, the Soul raiser.*

A THIRD TEMPLE IS NOT MENTIONED IN THE TORAH 132

143. *The three questions* **144.** *The closeness to Gd* **145.** *Jews forbidden to eat unpurified foodstuff* **146.** *The power of the Holy Name* **147.** *The Exodus from Egypt* **148.** *King Solomon and the building of the Temple* **149.** *The first and the second Temples* **150.** *Clouds of Glory* **151.** *The City of Jerusalem.*

WHY ISRAEL HAS MORE TROUBLES THAN OTHER PEOPLES 135

152. *Israel as the center of the world* **153.** *Heart among the Limbs.*

WHY ISRAEL, WHO DOES NOT PARTAKE OF ANIMALS FOUND DEAD OR NOT RITUALLY SLAUGHTERED, IS WEAK 135

154. *The heart of the matter* **155.** *Why are there no eruptions on the heart?*

NOW THE NAME OF THE MAN OF ISRAEL THAT WAS SLAIN (NUMBERS 25:14) 136

156. *How this should be read* **157.** *Pinḥas, the High Priest.*

WHAT IS NOW FIRST WILL BE LAST AT THE RESURRECTION 137

158. *The donkey of Pinḥas ben Yair* **159.** *Rabbi Shimon and Pinḥas ben Yair* **160.** *Resurrection of the dead; Breath of life to Ezekiel.*

THE RESURRECTION OF THE DEAD 138

161. *Bones and the life in them* **162.** *The future form* **163.** *Job's intention* **164.** *The King's throne* **165.** *Piety of the soul* **166.** *A dream and the Shekhinah*
167. *The Faithful Shepherd.* 140

INTO YOUR HAND I COMMIT MY SPIRIT (PSALMS 31:6) 141

168. *Evil spirits* **169.** *The Letters and sin*
Commentary: Body language 142
170. *Noah and the Dove* **171.** *Evil shall not go unpunished* **172.** *Ignorance and Piety.*

TWO VISIONS 144

173. *Man's death* **174.** *248 parts of the body*
175. *Ascending and Descending* **176.** *In Gd's image* **177.** *Clouds of Glory*
Commentary: What is Malkhut?. 146

ANI AND HU' 152

178. *The Tetragrammaton and Zeir Anpin*
179. *Secret of Ḥokhmah.*

THREE TIMES WAS DAVID CALLED A SERVANT 153

180. *The Sages of the Mishnah* **181.** *Servant of Worship.*

DAVID BECAME POOR, PIOUS AND A SERVANT 154

182. *A servant in worship* **183.** *The letter Dalet* **184.** *Correction of the Three Columns and the worship of the priests* **185.** *Upper Ḥokhmah.*

THE SECRETS OF ELAZAR, YOSSI, YEHUDAH, YUDAI, ABBA AND RABBI SHIMON AND HIS COMRADES 156

186. *A helpmeet*
Comentary: "Ezer" y "Elazar" 157
187. *A perfect throne* **188.** *The secret of El*
Commentary: Aspect of Ḥesed and Gevurah 159
189. *The Tree*
Commentary: Secret of the Central Column. 160

FOR THE LEADER (PSALMS 60:1), GIVE THANKS (I CHRONICLES 16:8). REJOICE, O RIGHTEOUS (PSALMS 31:1); GIVE PRAISE, MELODY, TUNE, SONG, BLESSING, ETC. 160

190. *The nations of the world* **191.** *Rejoicing of the Righteous* **192.** *Mizmor* **193.** *Unity of Tiferet* **194.** *Shushan* **195.** *50 gates*
Commentary: Merit of the Sefirot 164
196. *Letters of the Ḥayyot*
Commentary: "Electrum" 165
197. *The Chariot.*

THE CHARIOT OF METATRON 166

198. *Paradise*
Commentary: Metatron 167
199. *The Sea of Torah* **200.** *Three Letters of the Aleph Beth* **201.** *The letter Aleph*
Commentary: Upper Ḥokhmah and Malkhut 168
202. *Secrets of Zeir Anpin.*

SMOKE ANDFRAGRANCE AND INCENSE 170

203. *The food of the Lord* **204.** *The nostrils*
205. *Wood as a Mitzvah* **206.** *Judgment*
Commentary: To distill Judgment. 170

THREE PRAYERS 176

207. *Abraham, Isaac and Jacob* **208.** *Bride and Groom*
Commentary: Curtain of the Female 177
209. *Memory* **210.** *Hidden sacrifices*
Commentary:The rising of the smoke 179
211. *The heart* **212.** *The arteries of the liver*
213. *Rulership of the heart* **214.** *Offerings of the heart*
Commentary 182
215. *All illness is derived from the liver, from the heart are derived all goodness.*

THE FAITHFUL SHEPHERD: THE SACRIFICES 183

216. *Removal of impurities* **217.** *Nourishment of the Torah* **218.** *Descent of a Lion* **219.** *Bodies of Israel* **220.** *Priest as Brain* **221.** *Holy Malkhut*
222. *The sins* **223.** *Angelic Beings*
224. *Watering of the trees* **225.** *Creatures below*
226. *The radiance of the Lord* **227.** *Life to the world* **228.** *Hokhmah and Binah* **229.** *The Lamb offering at Dusk* **230.** *Idol worshiping*
231. *The Correction* **232.** *Zealousness of Pinḥas*
233. *Killing of Zimri* **234.** *Gd's Camp*
235. *Jacob* **236.** *The setting Sun*
Commentary: Zeir Anpin 192
237. *Daytime Angels*

Commentary: Illumination of mating. 194

THE FAITHFUL SHEPHERD: "COMING UPON" IS APPEASEMENT 194

238. *Words of appeasement* **239.** *Ki va* **240.** *King and Queen* **241.** *Unity of Bride and Groom*
Commentary: "Place" as Malkhut 196
242. *"Man", its meaning*
Commentary: Night and Time 197
243. *Religious Services*
Commentary: The letter "Yud". 200

THE ONE LAMB YOU SHALL OFFER IN THE MORNING 200

244. *Offering at Dusk* **245.** *Concealment of Men and Women* **246.** *Seven days of impurity* **247.** *Drawing from the brain.*

EZEKIEL'S CHARIOT 202

248. *Ezekiel saw the Shekhinah*
Commentary: Numerology and Metatron 203
249. *Ten visions of Ezekiel* **250.** *How prayer is accepted* **251.** *Metatron is the little child*
252. *Color blue as Malkhut*
Commentary: Explanation of Malkhut 207
253. *Power of the sapphire stone* **254.** *Fear of Evil and the color blue*
Commentary: On Harsh Judgment 209
255. *Judgement* **256.** *72 Bridges* **257.** *Six steps to the throne* **258.** *The camp of Israel* **259.** *32 Fringes* **260.** *Four countenances of Metatron*
261. *Garment of Gold* **262.** *Four beings.*

FOUR SHELLS (KLIPPOT) THAT SURROUND FOUR BEINGS 214

263. *The Tree of Life* **264.** *Tohu vaVohu* **265.** *Significance of the teeth* **266.** *The Evil Inclination* **267.** *The lungs*
Commentary: Lion, Ox, Eagle, and Man 216
268. *Four melodies of David* **269.** *72 types of melodies* **270.** *Angels*
Commentary: The actions of the Angels 222
271. *72 Countenanles of the Illumination of Malkhut* **272.** *Four Elements* **273.** *What is Spirit?* **274.** *Ascent and Descent* **275.** *The flight of birds.*

VOICE AND SPEECH 226

276. *Ascending to the lobes of the lung* **277.** *The voice* **278.** *Fine lobes* **279.** *The mouth*
280. *Shema Yisrael*
Commentary: The 245 words of the Shema 227
281. *To understand the voice of the birds*
Commentary: Division of the Partzuf 229
282. *The 18 Blessings*
Commntary: Secret of "Mating" 231
283. *The voice of the beast* **284.** *Meaning of the scroll.*

RECITAL OF THE SHEMA YISRAEL, PHYLACTERIES AND STRAPS 233

285. *72 Links and Knots* **286.** *The Prayer Shawl* **287.** *Beauty as Tipheret* **288.** *The "Dew" of Prayer* **289.** *How to connect to the Phylacteries* **290.** *The fringes*
Commentary: Three Unities 236

291. *The letter Shin* **292.** *Negative and Positive Commandments* **293.** *The Body to the Soul* **294.** *Speech and Voice* **295.** *Malkhut is the Mezuzah* **296.** *Fixed Lengths and widths* **297.** *Phylacteries as an energy channel*
Commentary: Garments of the Priest 241
298. *Transmission from Prayer* **299.** *Man in Perfect Circuit*
Commentary: Managing energy 243
300. *Concepts of Oneness* **301.** *The fingers*
Commentary: Balancing the Central Column 244
302. *The Four Directions* **303.** *Secret of the Rings.*

BOWING AND STANDING UPRIGHT 247

304. *Proclamation of the Lord's Domain* **305.** *Secret of Ḥokhmah* **306.** *Life of the World* **307.** *Four bowings*
Commentary: Joining of Malkhut to Zeir Anpin 250
308. *Secret of the Rings* **309.** *Eye and the thumb* **310.** *Sfirot of the limbs* **311.** *Wings and four faces* **312.** *Faces and Parallels.*

SILENT TIMES AND SPEAKING TIMES 255

313. *Speech and Prayer* **314.** *Control of Hasadim* **315.** *Merit of listening.*

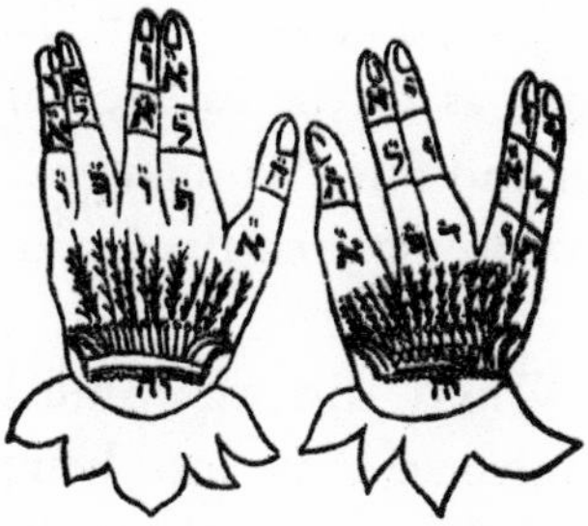

PREFACE

INTO THIS MYSTERIOUS UNIVERSE WE ARE BORN, with no apparent set of instructions, no maps or equations, no signs or guideposts, nothing but our equally unfathomable instincts, intuitions, and reasoning abilities to tell us where we came from, why we are here, and what we are supposed to do. What we do possess—perhaps the key to our survival as a species —is an almost unquenchable need to know. A human being comes into this world with a passionate sense of wonder and inquisitiveness and an equally powerful need for self expression. Yet, somehow these seemingly indelible primal imperatives become eroded, as a rule, after only a few years exposure to modern "reality" and contemporary educational methods.

While there can be no question that we, as a species, have established deep and penetrating channels into the how of things — indeed, it may be said that in some respects we have become masters of material existence — we have, however, made scant headway toward finding the source of the mighty river. Why? In spite of our many stunning scientific achievements, we remain today no closer to uncovering the answer to the ultimate questions as to the essence of existence than we were when First Man and First Woman gazed awe-struck into a clear, starry sky and contemplated the Great Mystery.

Who are we? Where did we come from? Why are we here? Why did the universe come into being? Did life on earth emerge as a matter of chance, or was it the conscious act of a supreme being? Is our suffering a cruel hoax or is it a constituent element of some grand design?

Despite all of our best efforts to arrive at a conclusive understanding of reality, the essential questions concerning the nature of existence remain profoundly impenetrable. That, in itself, is not particularly alarming, what is, to me, unsettling is the fact that today, perhaps as in no other time in history, we, as individuals, seem to be abandoning our one saving grace, our key to survival, our singular claim to fame: the need to know. Increasingly, for the first time in modern history, we as individuals, are failing to meet the challenge to probe life's mysteries. No longer do we feel comfortable attempting to answer the essential questions. We have grown meek, surrendering the investigation,instead, to so-called specialists, consultants, experts, and professionals. To what do we owe this mass flight from meaningful inquiry and personal expression?

For too long — coming on three centuries — the struggle to probe the nature of existence and resolve life's apparent paradoxes has increasingly been considered the exclusive province of specialists. Questions as to the how of things, we relinquish to the scientists, doctors, lawyers, engineers, analysts, and artisans. Why-related questions, such as those addressing themselves to the meaning of life, we leave on the doorstep of the philosophers, psychologists, artists, poets, and theologians. Well, one may argue, this is, after all, the age of specialization. With so much knowledge in the world, so much information, how can the "common" person compete in terms of his thinking with the experts, with their advanced degrees, generous grants and banks of computers, while the common person must make due with seemingly obsolete equipment, reason, hunches, and raw instinct? The question, the kabbalist will tell us, is not so much out-thinking the experts, but rather of simply — at the risk of straining an already dubious idiom — out-knowing them.

Consider the following possibility (though, indeed, in the eyes of certain specialists, the very naming of it is undoubtedly deserving of no less than capital punishment) that the very framework on which the thinking of many so-called scientific authorities is based, the foundation of assumptions, the methods on which their theories and pronouncements have been so painstakingly fabricated, are not, as they would have us believe, infallible.

Could it be that the experts in whom we have placed our absolute faith and trust, have, in certain respects, been acting under a crude illusion? The continuing hostility and dissension among the ranks of the specialists, authorities, and staunch defenders of so-called higher learning should go a long way toward providing evidence in favor of this point of view. In fact, all that the experts can seem to agree on is that they vehemently disagree. Is it conceivable that the entire philosophical edifice upon which science is based is about to topple and that we, the "common man," might perhaps have made a large — even fatal — blunder by relinquishing to its practitioners our most precious gifts, our sense of wonder, our natural curiosity, our need for self expression?

The Zohar's answer to these questions is emphatic in the affirmative. The scientific mind, cannot now and never will — without undergoing a complete metamorphosis — get to the bottom of life's why-related mysteries, for the simple reason that the scientist's dominant how to mode of consciousness is incapable of concocting anything but a how-related construct.

How did it happen? Why? What precisely caused Western man to surrender to others his inalienable right to probe life's most intractable mysteries? No single cause can be named. The reason cannot be pinned on any one source or blamed on any individual. However, if an inventory were to be compiled of people throughout the ages whose philosophies have profoundly affected, for better or for worse, the human psychological condition, the French mathematician and philosopher, Rene Descartes (1596-1650), would be high on the list.

Rene Descartes, the father of modern science, cooked up a theory, the leftovers of which we are still being rehashed to this day. Descartes defined reality as consisting of only that which can be analyzed or explained by the scientific method. By this way of thinking, which is known as the Cartesian paradigm, the world is seen as an immense agglomeration of mass and motion, adhering to mathematical laws. Descartes' paradigm, which has remained the dominant framework of Western consciousness from the seventeenth century to the present, has proved itself to be an excellent tool for answering how-related questions, but it has done nothing with respect to answering those questions that are related to life's greatest mysteries, those based in the question, why?

Why was the world created? Why were we born? Why, in light of our incredible technological strides, our great achievements in medicine, science, psychology, and physics, do we remain in the dark as to the real meaning of our lives?

Unlike the Cartesian paradigm, the Zohar provides a framework for answering life's most profound and perplexing questions. Indeed, the perceptive reader will find in the Zohar satisfactory answers to all of the above questions and many more. Be forewarned, however, that the solutions to life's great mysteries are not served up, so to speak, on a silver platter. Nor are they necessarily easily swallowed, digested, or assimilated. Parashat Pinhas the trilogy of Zoharic texts, translated into English for the first time, are not, as the expression goes, "an easy read." Some paragraphs— indeed, some phrases and sentences — are so densely layered with meaning that the reader might quite literally experience dizziness and fatigue at trying to comprehend them.

Be advised in advance, then, that the Zohar is not for everyone. It will not be appreciated by those who are unyieldingly rational and pragmatic, or those who are so solidly imprisoned in the Cartesian paradigm that to attempt escape would be unthinkable — though both groups will certainly find here much to rail against! Those readers, however, who are eager to accept the challenge of grappling with life's most intransigent mysteries, will, I believe, discover in the multilayered symbolism that makes up Zoharic reality all of the ways and means to do so and will accordingly be rewarded beyond his or her highest expectations.

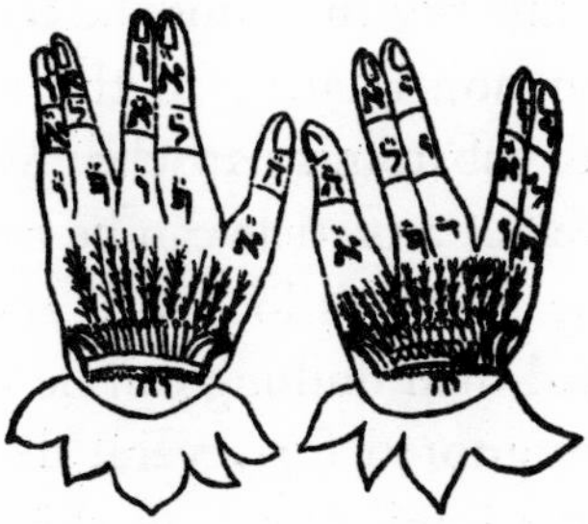

Introduction

TODAY, AS PERHAPS AT NO OTHER TIME IN our history, we are relinquishing a divinely inspired privilege. While science explores the vast reaches of space and invades the privacy of even the smallest subatomic particles, the individual's inborn imperative to probe the depths of mystical experience drifts like a ghost ship on a dark sea of insecurity. The ship is the imprisoned human psyche, enslaved by a dying god, Progress. The sea is the ocean of illusion that we mistake for reality in this modern, high-tech world.

Even as we share this moment, a revolution in the physical understanding of the universe is taking place. Information is beaming in from satellites in space, ingenious theories are being formulated, new scientific breakthroughs are being announced. Yet, ironically, these giant steps forward are being accompanied by a massive retreat in terms of the inner life of man. The more we learn about the physical universe, the less, it seems, we know about ourselves.

At the end of every scientific investigation lies another enigma, an even greater mystery that must be resolved. Consider the paradoxical phenomenon relating to the measurement of the speed and position of subatomic particles. As utterly strange as it may seem, if the speed of a particle can be measured nothing can be known about the particle's location, and, contrarily, if the position is determined then nothing can be known pertaining to its speed. Although ignored for several decades by the mainstream of science, the implications of this discovery are quite astounding. Not only does it defy what we normally consider to be logic, but, more importantly, it demonstrates, among other things, that the scientific method is not, as has been long imagined, infallible.

Does this strange little subatomic anomaly prove that science is a dead end, and that the scientist is engaging in what will ultimately be seen as an exercise in futile self indulgence? Not quite. The scientific method still has applications in what we might call the bigger picture, the world above the subatomic level. It does, however, confirm, as this author believes, that no one has the fast track on the Truth — least of all the scientist — and that it is time to remove science and Descartes' paradigm from the pedestal upon which we have placed them and accept science for what it is: one path among many in humanity's great migration toward renewal and understanding.

The divergent and highly contradictory theories advanced by the various branches of science demonstrate all too clearly that the Cartesian paradigm is inadequate for unraveling life's tangled web of mystery. Little wonder, then, that many people, young and old, have grown disillusioned with the unkept promises of Western science and the civilization based upon it, and have sought refuge in Eastern mysticism and other esoteric traditions, such as Kabbalah, and, indeed, have discovered in the ancient

doctrines answers that go far beyond any understanding achieved within most Western frames of reference.

If the world's literature holds any volume which might truly be designated as being complete, or, in the language of Kabbalah, as being "sealed with ten seals," that book is the *Zohar.* Since its completion some two thousand years ago, few works have exercised as much influence on humankind. The *Zohar* is the fundamental work of the Kabbalah and, thus, the premier textbook of Jewish mysticism, but because of the highly esoteric nature of its teachings, not to mention the difficulties presented by its original language, which was partly Aramaic and partly ancient Hebrew, the *Zohar*, which is an extension of the enigmatic *Book of Formation*, authored by the patriarch, Abraham, remained, for centuries, inaccessible to all but a few learned and carefully chosen initiates — a situation that might be aptly paralleled with the condition extant today relative to the "average" person's lack of knowledge concerning the secret rites of science.

The *Zohar* predicts that all inhabitants of planet Earth will one day come to grips with the profound mysteries of our cosmos. No longer will man be forced to bow to the wisdom of experts, scientists, and authorities who live in a rarified intellectual atmosphere, beyond the reach of the mainstream of humanity.

On that blessed day, in what has become known as the Age of Aquarius, the individual will again seize control of his sense of wonder and inquisitiveness, and, thus armed, will regain a thorough knowledge of the exact nature of the universe and each person's place in it.

This theme is woven into the rich fabric of the *Zohar*, but how was the average person to touch the quintessence of the Jewish mystical traditions if they were incarcerated in a work that only a learned Kabbalist, with knowledge of two ancient languages, could comprehend? The monumental task of drafting a complete modern Hebrew translation would require the efforts of an individual possessing sound judgment, keen perception, and, more importantly, Divine inspiration. Rabbi Yehuda Ashlag, of blessed memory, was such a man. Certain sections of Rabbi Ashlag's modern Hebrew edition of the *Zohar: Parashat Pinḥas* are herein presented in their first English language translation.

We are beginning to witness, and, indeed, some of us are already participating in, a people's revolution of enlightenment. This spiritual insurrection will be made possible as a result of the efforts of certain individuals who are dedicated to bringing about a Kabbalistic understanding of the cosmos and man's relationship and place within it. The prophet, Jeremiah, foresaw this abandonment of ignorance and its replacement by an overwhelming visceral comprehension of the very nature of existence.

"And they shall teach no more every man his neighbor, and every man his brother, saying, know the Lord: for they shall all know me, from the least of them unto the greatest of them." (Jeremiah 31:34).

The *Zohar*, *The Book of Splendor*, was for centuries widely revered as a sacred text of unquestionable value, and in certain communities it is still esteemed and studied to this day. When the state of Israel came into existence the Jews of Yemen, a remote and isolated principality in southern Arabia, were forced to abandon nearly all of their worldly possessions as they immigrated aboard airlines which they referred to as "magic carpets," but the one belonging that many of them refused to part with was their copy of the *Zohar.*

The Jews of Yemen, of course, represent the exception and not the rule. Today, for the most part, the mystical texts, with their intricate, introverted symbolism, are ignored and all but forgotten. Knowing nothing of its underlying paradigm — utterly alien to that of Descartes — those who pick up the *Zohar* today are apt to dismiss it as being nothing more than mere mystical poetry, of no value to the modern world. Thus, an immense body of esoteric knowledge remains sadly neglected. Once considered vital to the quest for personal understanding, the wisdom of the *Zohar* now lies buried so deeply beneath the heavy trappings of Newtonian science, technology, and the dubious "benefits" of Cartesian education that the vast majority of people know nothing of the ancient mystical traditions, and, hence, have no idea as to their sagacity and enduring vitality.

The *Zohar* is in the form of a commentary on the Bible. It is a record of the discourses of Rabbi Shimon bar Yoḥai, who lived in the second century of the common era. The *Tikunei Zohar* contains an account of how Rabbi Shimon and his son Rabbi Elazar, to escape the fury of Roman persecution, sought refuge in a cave and were forced to remain there for thirteen years. During this lengthy period of exile, the father and the son gave themselves over to discovering the reality of the universe.

When Rabbi Shimon emerged from the cave it is said that his body was covered with sores. His father-in-law, Rabbi Pinḥas

Ben Yair wept bitterly when he saw the state of Rabbi Shimon's body, exclaiming, "How bitter it is for me to see you in such a state!" Whereupon Rabbi Shimon replied, "I am happy that you see me like this — otherwise I would not be what I am." Clearly Rabbi Shimon regarded his wretched physical condition and discomfort as indispensable for his having reached the spiritual heights that he had attained.

Concerning the authorship of the *Zohar*, those who dismiss Rabbi Shimon as the author of the *Zohar* certainly do no credit to Jewish scholarship, when Kabbalists intimate with the *Zohar* have been unanimous in maintaining that its author was, indeed, the saintly rabbi of the Mishnaic period, Rabbi Shimon bar Yoai. Only those who are far removed from this branch of wisdom have expressed doubts as to this issue. On the basis of hearsay, invented by those who feared and thus opposed Kabbalah, some pedagogues have attributed the authorship of the *Zohar* to teachers of lesser rank than the Mishnaic authority, the holy, Shimon bar Yoai. Suffice to say that this author considers them, on this point, to be unequivocally in error.

The *Zohar* is a literature of immense variety and compass. It embraces so many diverse themes and such a wide range of topics — from physics to metaphysics, medicine, astronomy, astrology, psychiatry, the structure of the cosmos, and the nature of intelligence — that it may appear to espouse views and doctrines which are mutually exclusive and logically irreconcilable, but, as I pray will emerge for the reader, these seemingly disparate topics are like the miscellaneous parts of any viable macrocosm. While each may give the appearance of operating as a distinct and separate entity, each, in fact, depends for its existence on all of the other components. When carefully read and correctly perceived the *Zohar* serves only to add credence to the argument that the universe is a single, vital organism with all of its myriad fragments acting as interrelated elements in a unified design.

The *Zohar* contains several sections. The main section, which bears the general title of *Sefer HaZohar*, is generally connected and related to the weekly portion of the Torah. To this are attached the following: (1) *Idra Rabba* (Greater Assembly), which was written when Rabbi Shimon and his son Elazar emerged from the cave and selected eight disciples, who, together with himself and his son, formed the "Great Assembly," where, for the first time, the esoteric, internal teachings of the Torah were revealed. (2) *Sifra-di-Tzenuta*, (The Book of the Veiled Mystery), inserted before *Parashat T'zaveh*, deals with the structure of the creative process. (3) *Sitrei Torah*, (Secrets of the Torah), treats essentially the power of the Divine Names and how they are used to tap the immense power of the cosmos. (4) *Idra Zuta* (The Lesser Assembly) describes those teachings of Rabbi Shimon bar Yoai which were not revealed during the Greater Assembly, but on the day of Rabbi Shimon's death. (5) *Ra'ya Mehemna*, (Faithful Shepherd), the faithful shepherd being Moses, deals with those precepts and doctrines concerning the cosmos not covered in the discourses between Elijah, the Prophet and Rabbi Shimon bar Yoḥai. (6) *Midrash Ha'Ne'elam*,

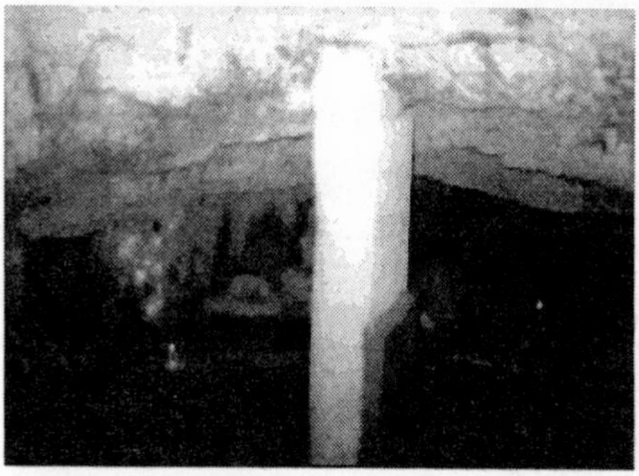

(Recondite Exposition), contains a vast collection of Scriptural exposition concerning the method of numerology, i.e. the permutations and combinations of the letters of the *Aleph Beth* and the Hebrew numerals. (7) *Zohar adash*, (The New *Zohar*) is an independent commentary along the same lines as the *Zohar*, but it embraces, in addition to the Torah, the Five *Megillot* (Scrolls): The Song of Songs, Ruth, Lamentations, Ecclesiastes, and Esther. (8) *Tikunei Zohar* (Emendations of the *Zohar*), addresses the same general subject matter as the *Zohar*, but also discourses upon teachings which are specifically directed to the Age of Aquarius. (9) *Tosefta* (Additions), adds some fragmentary supplements to the *Zohar* in which references to the *Sfirot* are made.

The *Zohar* is more than just a commentary on the Torah. In fact, in the *Zohar*'s own words a literal translation of the Bible is virtually worthless. It is most interesting to read the Zoharic words on a true veracity of Biblical exegesis, which stops just short of a complete repudiation of any literal translation or understanding of the Bible.

The *Zohar* declares, "Woe unto those who see in the Torah nothing but simple narratives and ordinary words." The truth of the matter is that every word of the Bible contains a sublime coded mystery which, when deciphered, reveals a wealth of elevated meaning. The narratives of the Torah are but outer garments in which the real meaning is clothed. And woe unto him who mistakes the outer garment for the Bible itself. This was precisely the idea to which King David addressed himself when he declared, "Open mine eyes that I might behold wondrous things from thy Torah."

Another passage from the *Zohar* states this same sentiment, when it queries, "If the Torah merely consisted of ordinary words and narratives like the stories of Esau, Hagar and Laban, or like the words spoken by the donkey of Balaam, or even by Balaam himself, why should the Torah have been referred to as *Torat Emet*, the Torah of Truth?"

Concealed within these statements hides what is perhaps the quintessence of Kabbalah. The Kabbalist simply cannot accept a diluted version of so important a document as that which came with the Revelations on Mount Sinai. He loathes the tedious, prosaic interpretations of the Scriptures that often pass for contemporary Judaism, for they create the mistaken impression that Judaism, as well as other religions established according to the principles of Mount Sinai, are nothing more than exercises in robotic legalism, completely divested of spirituality — formal, fossilized systems of "dos and don'ts" that deny completely the freedom of the individual.

Rabbi Ashlag had only to refer to Rabbi Shimon bar Yoḥai's discussion of ritual and precepts in the *Zohar* to remind us where he, himself, stood with regard to the viewpoint that "religious obligation" is a valid reason for performing empty religious rituals. "Prayer and ritual devoid of meaning and spirituality are similar to straw, the epitome of lifelessness." "Religion," cautioned Rabbi Ashlag, "does not permeate the structure of our society because of an inability on its part to fulfill the spiritual needs of the individual. If these needs are not met, then we may expect a totally despiritualized and demoralized society, the likes of which has never before been experienced in the history of mankind."

Unfortunately, there are those who pose as religious leaders who, for their own selfish reasons, spread false requisites for the study of the *Zohar* and discourage laypeople from "indulging" in its sublime treasures. Either these rabbis fear for their positions, because people tasting of Kabbalah might embarrass them with the incisiveness of their questions, or, perhaps, because their own upbringing deprived them of this great fountain of knowledge, they see no reason to allow others of "lower standing" to be given the opportunity of partaking of Kabbalah's spiritual elixir.

In one of the major works of the renowned Spanish Kabbalist, Rabbi Moses Cordovero (1522-1570), *Or Ne'erav,* he declares, "These Rabbis are the principal cause for all the world's suffering, the existing poverty and for the continuing lengthy exile with all its persecution and holocaust."

Quoting directly from the *Tikunei Zohar* Rabbi Cordovero substantiates his position on Rabbis who do not study the Kabbalah or, even worse, prevent others from taking up the study, when he cites the passage in which Rabbi Shimon bar Yoai goes even further in his condemnation of these Rabbis. "When the children below cry out with the proclamation of *Shema Yisrael* (Hear O' Israel) and there is no response from above," as stated in the Scriptures, "they shall call upon me, but I will not answer." (Proverbs,ch.:28). "This," the *Tikunei Zohar* continues, "is due to those who cause the removal of the Kabbalah and its Wisdom from the realm of the written and oral Torah and cause people not to become involved with its study. What do they say? There is nothing in Torah and Talmud but *P'shat* (the literal meaning). They cause the disappearance and drying up of the wells of the Lord's springs of relief. Woe unto these people! Better were it that they were never born, better were it that they never learnt *Torah Sh'Bi ktave* (the Written Torah), and *Torah Sh'bal Peh* (the Oral Torah), for they return the world to *Tohu Va'vohu* annihilation and nihility." (*Tikunei Zohar* 43).

These *Katot* (cults) of Rabbis have been, and are still in some quarters, blemishes and disfigurements on the face of Rabbinic Judaism. "The arid field of Rabbinism, the *P'shat* seekers are the fools and hate knowledge." (Tractate *Sanhedrin,* P.

99B). These Rabbis of ill-repute attempt to conceal from the layman the facts that the foremost Jewish legalists and talmudists were also famous Kabbalists, the Rabad, Abraham ben David of Posquieres (1125-1198), a distinguished authoritative scholar of the Talmud and the Ramban, Moses ben Nahman of Gerona, talmudic scholar and biblical exegete, (1195-1270) to mention only two. Fortunately, Mystic circles and the mystic schools, established at every important period throughout Jewish history, prevented the demise of Judaism and the Jew. It was and still is the Kabbalist who continues to keep Judaism well-watered and fresh by the living streams of spirituality.

The spiritual and esoteric study of the Torah and Talmud is the essence of Kabbalah. For those seeking to improve the quality of both their mental and physical well being, the *Zohar* provides each of us with an opportunity to become masters of our fate, captains of our destiny. Illustrations of the way in which the *Zohar* penetrates the external shell of Torah in order to extract the esoteric kernel, could, did space not forbid, be furnished on each and every verse and letter. I will only quote some examples of Zoharic exegesis on the *Parasha* to illustrate the point that the Bible is incomprehensible without the assistance and clarification of the *Zohar*.

And the Lord said unto Moses, "Go in unto Pharaoh, for I have hardened his heart." (Exodus 10:1). [To translate the Hebrew *Bo*, "Come", as it appears in the original text of the Bible as meaning "go" is a demeaning corruption of so valuable a document.] Rabbi Shimon wrote: It is now fitting to reveal mysteries connected with that which is above and that which is below. Why is it written here. "Come (*Bo*) unto Pharaoh"? Ought it not rather to have said,"go" (*Lekh*)? The Lord summoned and called Moses to "come" into the celestial realm, guiding Moses through a labyrinth right into the abode of the supernal mighty dragon (Egypt's celestial representative) from whom many lesser dragons emanate. (*Zohar* II, p.34a).

Another fine example of the *Zohar*'s penetrating insight to the cosmic code of the Bible concerns the almost impregnable fortress of mystery surrounding Genesis I.

Rabbi Shimon proceeded, taking as his text, "See now that I, I am he, and Elokim is not with me..." (Deuteronomy 32:39). He said: Friends, here are some profound mysteries which I desire to reveal to you now that permission has been given to utter them. Who is it that says, "See now that I, I am he"? This is the cause which is above all those on high. It is above those other causes, since none of those causes does anything till it obtains permission from that which is above it, as we pointed out above in respect to the expression, "Let us make man." (Genesis 1:26) "us" certainly refers to two, of which one said to the other above it, "let us make." [There are not two Lords.] The verse only refers to permission and direction of one to the other above it, since one above did nothing without consulting its colleague. However, that which has no superior or even equal, as stated, "To whom shall you liken me, that I shall be equal"? (Isaiah 40:25) This "cause" said, "See now that I, I am he and Elohim is not with me," from whom He should take the counsel, as in the other case of which it is written "And the Lord said, Let us make man."

The students of Rabbi Shimon, all rose and prostrated themselves before him, saying, "happy is the man whose Master agrees with him in the exposition of hidden mysteries of the Bible which have not been revealed to the Holy Angels." (*Zohar* I, p. 22b).

Again, in Psalms 145:18, King David declares, "The Lord is near unto all that call upon him, to all that call upon him in truth." Read the line 100 times. Meditate upon it, discuss it, carve it in granite. Without understanding what its key word really means, you still won't have the foggiest notion about the truth it is trying to convey. And if we can involve the word of the Lord in such mental short circuitry, what are we doing with our own prayers?

In the verse quoted above, the *Zohar* asks, "What, exactly, does the verse mean? Does it imply that one should not call upon the Lord in falsehood? Surely that is so obvious that it does not require stating. The significance of *emet* (truth) is simply that one should be aware of the truth, the real meaning of one's prayers." (*Zohar* III, p.183b).

There are many points which are of fundamental importance in the essential teachings of the *Zohar*. The declaration of the Lord's Unity in prayer does not merely mean the pronouncement of the word *Ead* of the *Shema Yisrael* (Hear O' Israel). It goes much deeper. It implies the conviction that all entities are to be regarded as manifestations of the Force of the Lord whose awesome power is never for an instant withdrawn from mankind. Prayer is our channel by which we can tap the astonishing power of the cosmos. To pray is thus, in the last resort, our connection to an experience of pure awareness and altered states of consciousness, which can lead to an improvement in the quality of physical and mental well being.

The *Zohar* reveals the dynamic interplay and interconnectedness of our universe and man's relationship to it. There is a constant conscious and unconscious interaction between the celestial kingdom of the Lord and our mundane realm below. The human body is a reflection of the vast cosmos. Human organs and limbs mirror the dynamics of the interstellar dance that is ever present within the universe.

The Creator, as portrayed by the *Zohar*, becomes manifest in the lower worlds by channels of bottled-up energies known as the Ten *Sfirot*: *Keter* (Crown), *Ḥokhmah* (Wisdom), *Binah* (Intelligence), *Ḥesed* (Mercy. *Gvurah* (Judgment), *Tiferet* (Beauty), *Netzaḥ* (Victory), *Hod* (Glory), *Yesod* (Foundation) and *Malkhut* (Kingdom). The method by which these ten energies assist mankind in tapping the cosmic energy-intelligence is an extremely complex subject, impossible to adequately explain within the limited context of this introduction. For those readers wishing to pursue this subject in depth, the ten *Sfirot* are given an exhaustive treatment in Rabbi Ashlag's monumental sixteen volume work dealing with Lurianic Kabbalah, *Ten Luminous Emanations*, and are also delved into in my *Kabbalah for the Layman* series.

The *Zohar* abounds with references to the dominant role played by mankind in achieving a mastery of his destiny and the improvement of his quality of life. It places religion in a context of spiritual experience, rather than rigid reactionary adherence to dogmatic doctrine for the sake of the Deity. Man, as portrayed by the

Zohar, is a spiritual entity whose fate is determined by the nature of his thoughts and actions. Thus, a verse like, "For dust thou art and unto dust shall you return," (Genesis 3:19) seems to conflict with the theme of the *Zohar* which states: "Whoever labors in the Torah upholds the world and enables each part to perform its function. For there is not a member in the human body that does not have its counterpart in the world as a whole. For as man's body consists of members and parts of various ranks, all acting and reacting upon each other so as to form one organism, so does the world at large consist of a hierarchy of created things, which when they properly act and react upon each other together form literally one organic body." (*Zohar* I, p.134b)

The preceding *Zohar* stresses the intimate connection between man and the cosmos. Compare this perspective with the Mishnaic declaration: "Know from where thou cometh: from a decadent drop; where are you going: to a place of dust, worms, and maggots. (*Avot*, 3:1) Man is seen by the *Zohar* in an infinitely more positive light. The *Zohar* maintains that man's corporeal body should not be treated as mere flesh and bones. Man's infinite aspect must also be taken into consideration, the eternal soul.

The Ari, Isaac Luria, stated the Kabbalistic view on this subject: "The blood of man provides the link between the soul of the upper realm and the corporeal body in the terrestrial realm." The flesh embodies the energy-intelligence of the desire to receive for oneself alone; the skin, which extends everywhere and covers everything, is a living symbol of the upper firmament; and the veins and arteries act as chariots to link the soul with the body. Blood contains both the energy-intelligence of sharing as well as the energy-intelligence that is found in all other parts of the body, the desire to receive for oneself alone.

The discovery that blood consists of red and white cells came as no surprise to the Kabbalist. Red had long been designated by Kabbalah as a color epitomizing desire to receive, while white had been defined as a symbol of desire to share. The blood, being the binding link between the soul and body, must, it was reasoned, contain within its molecular structure both aspects of desire. Blood unites all members of the corporeal family. When any member of the body suffers a contusion, the blood demonstrates its desire to impart by rushing to the scene of the accident. The red cells embrace the energy-intelligence of receiving, the white cells, the function of which it is to destroy infection, demonstrate the opposite energy-intelligence of sharing — small wonder, then, that mankind displays schizophrenic tendencies.

The idea of the soul's unquenchable yearning to be reunited with the Infinite, is a fibre woven throughout all sections of the *Zohar*. One of the key elements of the Zoharic world view, one could almost say the essence of it, is the idea of assisting mankind toward an awareness of the unity and mutual interconnectedness of all aspects and events, so as to achieve a state of consciousness in which everything is perceived as being inseparable from the single all-pervading cosmic unity. To consciously perceive and embrace the union of all of the universe's myriad manifestations is to experience the highest reality.

Explorations into the subatomic world in the twentieth century have helped to reveal the dynamic interplay within the cosmic unity. The components of an atom do not exist as isolated energy-intelligences, but rather as integral parts of an all-encompassing whole. Einstein's theories of General and Special Relativity, presaged by the author of the *Zohar*, also force us to abandon the rigid classical concepts of absolute time and space. From the Kabbalistic perspective, the fundamental importance of these new scientific findings is that they provide a framework for achieving altered states of consciousness through which all separate manifestations are experienced as nondelineated components in a vast intimate and integrated continuum. The *Zohar*, meanwhile, furnishes the mental and emotional apparatus by which an elevated awareness of the interconnectedness of past, present and future, space, time and motion, can be attained.

The *Zohar* declares that man was created on the sixth day of the Lord's creative process. Why was the creation of man saved for last? Because he is the culmination of all that preceded. Man, within himself, is an excellent draft and skeleton of the entire cosmos. In addition to being participators, more importantly, according to the *Zohar*, humanity was given the opportunity of becoming determiners of universal and galactic activity. The awareness of man's interpenetration of the universe is discussed at great length in the *Zohar*.

Rabbi Hiya commenced to discourse on the verse: "The blossoms appear on earth, the time of song has come, and the voice of the turtledove is heard in our land." (Song of Songs, ch. 2:12). He said, "When the Lord created the world, He endowed the earth with all the potential energy required for it, but it did not spring forth until man appeared. When, however, man was created, all the products that were latent in the earth surfaced above ground. Likewise, the heaven did not impart strength to the earth until man appeared. As it is written that all the plants were not yet on earth, the herbs of the field had not yet sprung up, the Lord had not caused it to rain upon the earth, "for there was no man to till the ground." (Genesis 2:5).

All the products of the earth were still hidden in its inner recesses and had not yet shown themselves, the heavens refrained from pouring rain upon the earth because man had not yet been created. When, however, man appeared, the flowers grew and all of the earth's latent powers were revealed, or, in other words, "the time of song had come."

The earth was then ripe to offer up praises to the Lord, which it could not do before man was created. The voice of the turtledove refers to the power, the energy-intelligence of the Lord, which was not active in the world until man was created. When man appeared everything appeared, and then, when man sinned, the earth was cursed and all good things departed. As it is written, "cursed is the earth for thy sake." (Genesis 3:17) This is reiterated in the verse, "When thou tillest the ground it shall not give its strength to you." (ibid., 4:12) And the same condemnation is echoed in the verse, "thorns and thistles it shall bring forth to you." (ibid., 3:18).

The relationship between the actions of man and cosmic events was again demonstrated when Noah sinned through drunkenness and the rest of the world also sinned before the Lord and the strength of the earth deserted it. This scourge continued until the patriarch, Abraham, appeared on the cosmic scene and once again, "the blossoms appeared in the earth," and all the powers of earth were restored. (Zohar I, p.97a).

The *Zohar* maintains that man's internal activities can determine external events. Man's thoughts influence, and are inseparable from, the external world. A similar view is expressed in the "participant observation" theory of quantum mechanics which also negates the idea of a clear-cut division between events, physical objects, and human consciousness, maintaining that the observer cannot possibly separate himself from that which he is observing.

The mysticism of the *Zohar*, stressing as it does the efficacy and importance of prayer, influenced considerably the Siddur or Hebrew prayer book. The Sephardic prayerbook embraces Zoharic angelology in its liturgy as do numerous other Jewish rituals and ceremonial observances. The *Zohar*'s mystical names and symbols permeate the gematrical (numerical) and astrological references found within the pages of the Sephardic prayer book, and many of these Zoharic references ultimately found their way into the prayer book of *ḥasidim*, the movement founded by Israel Bal Shem Tov in the eighteenth century. The fundamental purpose of ḥasidism, which borrowed from the example of the *Sephardim*, was to inject spirituality into the religion, as opposed to the thoughtless formalism prevailing within the liturgy and ceremonies of their fellow Jews in Lithuania, the *Mitnagdim*. For this reason the *ḥasidim* did not enjoy either credibility nor popularity among the *Mitnagdim* and eventually the enmity between them gave rise to an earnest attempt on the part of the *Mitnagdim* to halt the expansion of asidism.

The place that was assigned to the *Zohar* in the scheme of prayer and ritual by the *ḥasidim* was one of the basic points at issue between the two sects. Why the *Sefardim* of northern Europe did not also incur the wrath of the *Mitnagdim* remains a mystery. The struggle between the orthodoxy, based on external-body authority of the Talmud and the internal-mystically inclined Judaism founded upon the Zoharic interpretation of the Torah and Talmud, goes on to this day. It was and is essentially a contest between the formalism of dogmatic ritual, as practiced by Mitnagdim, wherein the participator has little if any say in his life's destiny, and the spiritually-directed practices of the *asidim* who believe, as their fellow Sephardic Jews did, that man's future rests within a frame of reference based upon his own behavior and activity.

The asid and the Sephardic Jew shared an intimacy with the cosmos. Both groups believed, based on Zoharic study and interpretation, that mankind could act as a determinator in our vast cosmos and shape the future of his existence. They also believed that suffering and pain could be alleviated and even eliminated from the Jewish existence, and also that it was within man's jurisdiction to bring an end to holocaust and catastrophe by applying the teachings of Kabbalah. Like the Sephardic Jew, the asid maintained that the quintessence of the Jewish religion lay in the internal-spiritual study of Talmud, combined with a determined belief in the efficacy of prayer. Thus, both groups opposed the robotic, despiritualized form of prayer observed within all three factions of Judaism. The *Mitnagdim*, contrarily, although they could not reject outright the validity of the teachings of the saintly *Tannah*, Rabbi Shimon bar Yoai and his *Zohar*, regarded Jewish life and religion as consisting of strict obedience to the law based upon the literal study of the Talmud and the precepts.

Rabbi Shimon's *Shaar Ma'amarei Rashbi* and *Hazal* inaugurated a new mystical system by which the Talmud was transformed from the spiritually impoverished obedience to dogmatic ritual of the past, into a Talmud, replete with vitality, spirituality, and an interesting study of Judaic lore and traditions. The Talmud, without the assistance of Rabbi Shimon bar Yoai's interpretation, is, to the Kabbalist's way of thinking, an exercise in lifeless, rigid ritualism, the result of which has been an abandonment of the study of Talmud, not only by most Jews, but even by the majority of Orthodox Jews.

Recently, the sect of *Mitnagdim* has declined dramatically, whereas Sephardic and asidic spirituality have enjoyed something of a renaissance. This spiritual blossoming, derived from the fertile soil of the *Zohar*, the trademark of true Sephardic tradition, fosters the conviction of an unbroken bond between the world of mankind, the cosmos, and the Lord.

The *Zohar* dates back to the early centuries after the destruction of the Second Temple. Shortly after the destruction of the Second Temple, Rabbi Shimon bar Yoai revealed the *Zohar*. It was also around this same time that the Talmud was being completed. The wisdom of the *Zohar* was transmitted orally from generation to generation. Not until the thirteenth century, some 1300 years after its revelation by Rabbi Shimon bar Yoai, did the actual text make its first known appearance.

Tradition attributes the mysterious journey of the *Zohar* from Israel to Spain to the famed Spanish Kabbalist, Rabbi Moses ben Naman, a.k.a. Namanides. Namanides played no small role in Kabbalah's development and was quite possibly the harbinger of the movement in Spanish Kabbalah which has come to be known as the Golden Age in Spain. It was, however, the famed Spanish Kabbalist, Moses de Leon, who revealed for the first time the existence of the actual writings of the *Zohar*.

In the year 1492, the Monarchy issued a decree of Jewish expulsion, and the Golden Age of Spain was forcibly terminated. Years later, following the destruction of the Sephardic community in Spain, the practical application of this esoteric wisdom would become an integral part of Jewish tradition and learning, but not until the great spiritual personalities of the time had returned to their source, their place of origin, the Land of Israel, Safed.

By the middle of the sixteenth century, the study of Kabbalah had been revived under the great Kabbalist luminaries, Moses Cordovero, Abraham Beruchim from Morocco, Shlomo Alkabetz of Salonica, Moses Alsheikh, who subsequently left for Damascus, and the "Ari," Isaac Luria, the founder of the Lurianic system of Kabbalah. Many of the leading Kabbalists of the eighteenth and nineteenth centuries contributed toward gaining acceptance for Kabbalah by providing an enlightened view of the mysterious universal truths. Prior to this period, however, devotees of the mystical perspective were generally considered to be half-crazed sorcerers, living according to the dictates of their demented imaginations.

Isaac Luria, the Ari, learned Kabbalah in Egypt and later taught it in Safed. The founder of Lurianic Kabbalah, on which Rabbi Ashlag's famous sixteen volume series, *Ten Luminous Emanations*, was based, the Ari attracted a host of disciples, but he, himself, wrote nothing. His highly complex teachings were taken down in writing by his most prominent disciple, Hayim Vital Calabreze, whose book *Etz Hayim* presents the essential ideas of the Lurianic system by which the, *Zohar* would become comprehensible.

Fundamental to the Kabbalistic world view is that the world we normally experience may not be what it seems. Kabbalists hold that irrefutable evidence pertaining to this perspective is to be found in the five books of Moses. The Torah is considered to be the means by which the hidden workings of creation became operative and recognizable. It is important to understand that the Torah referred to here is not merely the document given to the people of Israel on Mount Sinai. It is, rather, the root of all created things, the force that preceded and caused the whole observable universe. This force is the essential life-giving element from which emerges all manifestations, and it is to this supreme power which the Kabbalist is referring when the Torah is mentioned.

The Zohar and subsequent Kabbalistic writings provide a profound interpretation of the five books of Moses written on parchment. This conviction is expressed in the *Zohar*: "When the Holy One, Blessed Be He, wished to create the world, He reflected upon the Torah and created it." (Zohar I,134a). The *Zohar* compares this document to the body of man and Kabbalah to his soul — the reason being that while the body of the Law was given on Mount Sinai, outside the borders of biblical Israel, the soul of the Law was destined to be revealed only within the Land of Israel.

This idea finds expression in the initial prophesies of Isaiah when he says: "For out of Zion shall go forth the Law, and the word of the Lord from Jerusalem" (Isaiah 2:3). How can this idea be correct, it might well be asked, when there was no other law besides that given to Moses on Mount Sinai, which is outside the biblical territory of Israel? Does this mean that the Torah given to Moses is not eternally valid? It does not. The Torah revealed on Mount Sinai was for all generations. However, it contained truths which were to be revealed and elaborated upon at a later time. The author of the *Zohar*, Rabbi Shimon bar Yoai, in his wisdom, attributed the mystical aspect of the Torah, the Kabbalah, to the written Torah. However, the law given on Mount Sinai expresses only the surface meanings which are revealed for everyone, whereas the Kabbalah contains the deeper, more sublime meanings. Thus, we find two different aspects within the Torah, the revealed aspect being the outer shell, Kabbalah its inner essence.

The Torah of Mount Sinai, revealed to the people of Israel,

was written down in physical form outside the biblical borders of Israel. The Kabbalistic interpretation revealed at the time only to Moses remained in oral form. The Kabbalah, which un-veils the hidden essence of the universe, was to be revealed by Moses to Rabbi Shimon bar Yoai in the Land of Israel. He would give it the material form of the *Book of Splendor*. This is the meaning of the biblical verse, "For out of Zion shall go forth the Law."

Although Kabbalah often deals with profound matters, it does so in a way that can today be easily understood. This is indicated by one of its central teachings, namely, that the Divine word emanating from the infinite can be expressed in the language of finite man. This is not exclusively a Kabbalistic concept. It is found also in earlier written texts, particularly those of the *Mishnah* and the Bible which both contain not only imperative rules of conduct but also stories, songs, parables, and histories.

For the Kabbalist, the literal interpretation of the stories in the Torah are merely the outer garments beneath which are concealed exalted mysteries. In the view of the Zohar, the tales and parables of the Torah are symbolic reflections of the inner metaphysical realm through which the hidden, divine mysteries of the universe can be perceived. Rabbi Shimon berates those who presume that the simple tales of the Torah concern only commonplace incidents: "Woe unto the man who says the Torah merely presents narratives and mundane matters. For if such be the Torah, one dealing with mundane events, we in our day could compile a more superior one. And if the Torah comes to inform us of commonplace matters, then there are in the possession of the rulers of the world books of greater quality, and from these we could emulate and compile a Torah. However, the uniqueness of the Torah is that each word contains supernatural matters and profound secrets. See how precisely balanced are the upper and lower worlds. Israel here below is the equivalent of the angels above for whom is written: "Who maketh his angels into winds" (Psalms 104:4). When the angels descend they clothe themselves in earthly garments, without which they could not abide in this world, nor could it bear to co-exist with them. If this be so with angels, then how much more so must it be with the Torah that created the angels and all the worlds, the Torah through which we are all sustained. The world could not have continued to exist in the presence of the Torah had she not clothed herself in garments of this world."

When Rabbi Shimon says that without earthly clothes the angels could not stay in this world, he is speaking of the manner in which the unseen metaphysical truth is revealed. That which is of the spiritual realm — indicated in the *Zohar* by the term "angels" — cannot be revealed to man unless it is clothed in a corporeal garment. Only through some outward physical manifestation can the inner truth become known. Metaphysical concepts are, and must remain, clothed in material garments, and all actions perceivable by one or more of the five senses are merely the physical raiment of metaphysical influences — for each and every corporeal manifestation is the result of previous metaphysical activity. Thus, we discover that all physical manifestations are illusionary in the sense that they can be interpreted in different ways by different people. It is, in fact, almost impossible not to make errors, according to the Kabbalistic way of thinking, when we judge a thing only by its outward appearance.

Now to the second *Sod* (mystery) included in this passage of the *Zohar*, which is contained in the phrase, "nor could it bear to co-exist with them if they were not thus clothed." To explain this subtle but penetrating secret, let us consider the case of electricity. We know that the electric current must be contained within some sort of cable for it to be useful. In the case of a fallen power-line or a broken cable, there is the danger of electric shock or fire since the current is no longer enclosed. Within the metaphysical realm, the pattern is identical — for, in the words of an ancient Kabbalistic saying, "As above, so below." There is a great danger when an imbalance exists between the positive (imparting) and the negative (receiving) forces. The overloading of an electrical cable (short-circuiting an individual's mental capacities) signals trouble, since the receptacle or vessel simply lacks the proper insulation and safeguards to allow for the directed output of energy (the flow of normal thought processes). These analogies are relevant not only to the physical world, but to both the peripheral areas of spirituality and to its pure essence, and certainly they demonstrate the need for a suitable medium or garment in transmitting the sublime esoteric wisdom of metaphysics

The *Zohar*, which is interwoven with profound philosophic views, reveals that the biblical narratives are vehicles by which the Divine mysteries of our universe can be understood. The laws and commandments act as garments for true spirituality, the beauty of spiritual meditation is clothed in a garment of systemized prayer, as is the holiness of the Sabbath dressed in precepts which may seem mundane until their true metaphysical implications are fully understood.

The question of how we can be certain of the truth of the *Zohar*'s metaphysical interpretation of the Bible is carefully considered by its author: "And for those persons that do not know, yet have a desire to understand," declares the *Zohar*, "reflect upon that which is revealed and made manifest [in this world] and you shall know that which is concealed, inasmuch as everything, both above and below, is the same. For all that G-d has created in a corporeal way has been patterned after that which is above."

The knowledge of the essence of unseen elements revealed

by the Kabbalah is provided without recourse to the procedures of scientific research, obviating the necessity of going through the customary procedures of trial and error, action and reaction. The knowledge found in the Kabbalah is not based on experimental investigation of empirical data which are observed within the frameworks of time, space and motion. Kabbalah deals with realities which are beyond the limits of empirical observation and scientific method. Hence, Kabbalah is designated as being a form of mysticism in the sense that it reveals the unseen mysteries and operates independently of the fluctuations in the space-time continuum.

Traditional science and Kabbalah differ radically in several respects, one of the most notable being that Kabbalah posits the experiential existence of two basic levels of life, the spiritual and the material. It considers both proper subjects of investigation and analysis and also suggests that there are strong links between these two levels and that each depends on the other for its very existence. Science, on the other hand, insists on limiting the field of knowledge and observation to that which is subject to scientifically verifiable evidence, that is to say, it limits its investigation to the material level of life.

Both explicitly and by inference, the scientific method rejects the existence of a spiritual level of actuality. There are, however, scientists who do not deny absolutely the possible existence of a metaphysical plane of reality, but contend that as statements about spiritual matters can neither be proved nor disproved, therefore the study of metaphysics is not only invalid but totally futile. Religious scientists — quite a number are observant Jews — hold that science is not, as is popularly believed, in conflict with religion, and some even go so far as to admit that science is limited by its own methodology, but although they acknowledge the possibility of two sources of truth, physical and metaphysical, they still limit the range of scientific investigation only to that which is material.

Another basic difference between science and Kabbalah may be shown by considering the concept of "coincidence." An example would be a person who asks a perfect stranger for directions to a certain address and it turns out that the stranger lives at that address and is on his way there. People influenced by the so-called rational, scientific approach would insist that the two events are really unrelated and purely coincidental. Kabbalists maintain that such events are definitely related. That is, they are not only noticed by the Kabbalist, but they are noticed in a way that puts them together and some new significance is derived from their being together.

The difference between the scientific and the Kabbalistic views as they relate to so-called coincidence arises because science, however deeply it delves into the material world, is still only dealing with external elements, the outer surface. Science is limited to the observable world, but beneath the surface of the physical world, which is, for the most part, subject to scientific investigation, lies the essence, the real world, which scientists are now discovering, much to their consternation, is beyond the jurisdiction of empirical examination. For the Kabbalist, facts and data pertaining to the outward physical structure are of relatively minor importance. The Kabbalist is more concerned with aligning the two worlds, inner and outer, and with locating and strengthening the linkages between the world of illusionary appearances and the eternal essence of the world within.

A central theme of Kabbalistic teaching is that all things, events and manifestations that are perceivable by one or more of the five senses are components of a single ultimate reality. This theme is expressed by the *Zohar* when it discusses the nature and purpose of man. The *Zohar* holds that the universe cannot exist without the Torah and that man was created to study the Torah and to practice its teachings. "He who engages in Torah preserves the world and sustains each process of the universe so as to enable it to perform its function." (*Zohar* I, p.97a).

Kabbalists believe that the parts of man correspond to the order of the universe, and that man, as an integral part of the universe, can attune himself to the harmonious whole. This theme is expressed in the *Zohar* when it states that every part of the human body has its equivalent in the cosmos. "Just as the body of man is divided into infinite segments and varying parts, all acting and interacting upon one another and yet forming an organic being, likewise the universe is composed of an infinite number of created entities which act upon each other; and when these are made properly, they form a basic oneness." (*Zohar* I, p.134a).

Further expression of the interrelatedness of man and the cosmos is provided in the *Zohar* when it states that, "Man and the universe, are like the Torah, for the entire Torah consists of limbs and sections all acting upon each other, and when they are arranged and set properly there is the oneness and the totality of all things." (*Zohar* I, 134b)

This same view is elaborated upon by the *Zohar* when it points out that the body of the Torah consists of 248 positive precepts and 365 negative ones. The positive commandments correspond to the 248 joints of the human body while the negative commandments correspond to the 365 arteries and veins. The negative commandments are also related to the solar year which consists of approximately 365 days (*Zohar ḥadash*, p.77).

The Kabbalists of the Safed school held that there is a fundamental interaction between the creation of the world, its history, and the creation and development of man. They explored and developed this idea of interconnectedness and it assumed central importance in establishing a conceptual nexus between the creation of the world and its future perfection to be brought about by the efforts of man. (*Sha'ar Ma'amarei Rashbi*, p.7)

The concept of universal continuity, the awareness that all things are interdependent parts of the whole cosmos, is echoed by recent developments in quantum physics. The study of subatomic particles has led many physicists to suggest that the basic phenomena of matter are interrelated and form an essential unity. (D. Bohm & B, Hily Foundations of Physics, vol. 5, p.96) Kabbalists, however, hold that it is at the metaphysical level that the seemingly separate aspects of the universe can be observed as parts of a unified whole and that this can be achieved by understanding the layered esoteric meanings of the Torah.

The primary purpose of the Kabbalist is to obtain a direct mystical experience of reality. The multifaceted system of Kabbalah, the range of its methodology, encompasses not only mysticism and metaphysics but all the fields of contemporary science. However, the Kabbalist does not carry out the role of the detached, impersonal observer. Rather, he becomes involved in the world to the extent that he may influence or even determine the movement and state of that which he observes.

Kabbalists strongly believe in what is popularly called the power of mind over matter. This concept of self determination which is critical to the Kabbalistic world view, is given expression and defended when the Zohar discusses astrology. In an important passage in this discussion the *Zohar* says: "And Abraham, with the wisdom of astrology, gazed up at the stars and saw that he would not have children. And He [the Lord] took Abraham outside and said, "Look now toward heaven..." (Genesis 15:5)

Then the Holy One said to Abraham, "Do not gaze any longer into the wisdom of the stars for you shall have a son if you attach yourself to the upper realm and not to the stars." (*Zohar* I p. 90a,b)

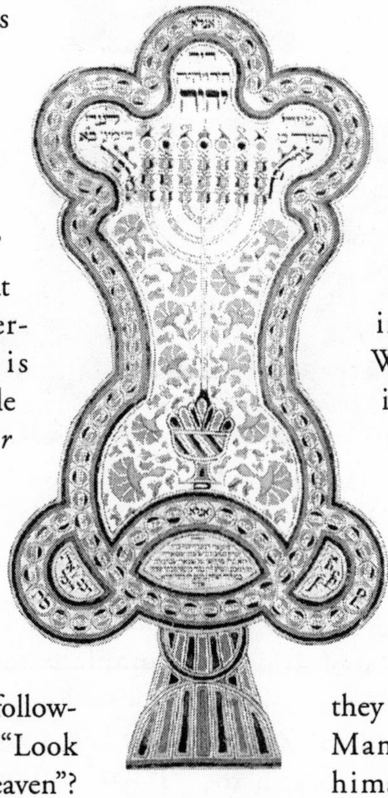

What apparently troubled the author of the *Zohar*, as well as other commentators on the Bible, were the words, "And he took him outside." Recognizing that a mystical interpretation is essential for Bible exegesis (*Zohar* II p.32b) the *Zohar* asks, why does the Torah give a naturalistic meaning to those words by following them with "Look now towards heaven"? The answer provided by the *Zohar* is that the dialogue goes far beyond the naturalistic meaning of the Lord literally leading Abram outside his physical home. It is explained that as an individual knowledgeable in the wisdom of astrology, Abram recognized the impelling nature of the influence of the stars and planets on man. Using his knowledge, he deduced that he was destined not to have a son. But the Lord revealed a paradox regarding man's existence in this world. While man is influenced by external forces he also has free choice. With regard to astrology this means that the stars impel but they do not compel. Man can remove himself from the impelling force of the celestial bodies. He has the ability to go outside the influence of all external forces, including those of the stars and planets. This is the esoteric meaning of the words, "And He took him outside."

Despite the growth and influence of Hassidism with its renewed interest in Kabbalah, and the changes brought about by modern physics which often show surprising parallels to Kabbalistic ideas, it would still be safe to say that the majorityof humankind remains as ignorant today as ever before of the sublime teachings of Kabbalah. However, with the publication of Rabbi Ashlag's new system for understanding the Kabbalah and the Zohar, this situation has begun to change. In his now famous work, the sixteen volume textbook, *Ten Luminous Emanations*, he devised a logical system through which the essence of the transcendent realm can be transmitted by means of a carefully chosen selection of symbols and illustrations. The intimate relationship between the physical and metaphysical realms is presented simply, together with a description of the process of evolution that culminated in the world as we know it today.

Rabbi Ashlag's other monumental work, the first complete modern Hebrew translation of the *Zohar* has also had a great influence on Judaic studies and marks a turning point in the attempt to render the Kabbalah comprehensible to contemporary students of Kabbalah. Realizing that a comprehensive translation would not be sufficient on its own, he composed a commentary on the most difficult passages within the *Zohar*. The beginning student,however, may find this commentary more difficult to comprehend than the original text. It is advised, therefore, that the reader might ignore these commentaries, inasmuch as they deal with another altered level of conscious comprehension, until, after becoming more familiar with Rabbi Ashlag's methodology, he or she may attempt to come to grips with the *Zohar*'s deeper inner meanings.

Just as the bizarre and stunning new ideas about mind and matter, which erupted among the scientific community over sixty years ago are only now beginning to gain the attention of the general public, so too are the Kabbalistic views of the universe, once reserved for a select few Kabbalists, now reaching a larger constituency.This translation is intended for the general reader with an interest in mysticism who may or may not have any knowledge of religion or science. However, between Zoharic reality and the rational, analytical thought processes with which we have been burdened since our earliest childhood, there is a wide chasm that may not easily be traversed. Still, with careful study, the reader's understanding of Jewish mysticism should steadily increase.

The Bible has long been viewed by many as nothing more than a collection of religious morality tales. Seen from a Zoharic perspective, the Bible is not primarily intended to merely improve the outward conduct of mankind, but to assist each individual in creating an intimate personal relationship with the universe. In ancient times, the most mundane events in everyday life and custom were associated with the grandeur of the cosmos. Even the treatment of jaundice with pigeons was identified with the deepest cosmological mysteries. Our ancestors were eager to understand the universe, but its secrets were revealed to only a select few.

This is not a book about religion. Rather, the *Zohar* is concerned with the relationships between the unseen forces of the cosmos and their impact on man. In essence, the Bible, upon which the *Zohar* is based, is a cosmic code which the *Zohar* deciphers and reveals. Rabbi Ashlag aimed at bringing back to the collective consciousness a breath of that mystic sentiment and feeling which are the aromatic life-essence for human satisfaction and world harmony. "Kabbalah," taught Rabbi Ashlag, "is essential and indispensible for the mental and physical well being of earth's inhabitants. It can lead to the Messianic dream of peace on earth and good will towards our fellow man."

The *Zohar* promises that with the ushering in of the Age of Aquarius, the cosmos will become readily accessible to human understanding. Already, for the perceptive observer, there are signs — such as the recent developments in quantum physics — that this revolution is already underway. It is becoming increasingly apparent that, in a very real and profound sense, man and the cosmos are inseparable.

Anyone who has delved even superficially into life's mysteries has been confronted with the paradox of uncertainty that surrounds physical existence. Indeed, for all but a fortunate few, those rare individuals who are seemingly "called" here for the purpose of accomplishing some specific task, life can sometimes seem to completely defy understanding. Life, for most of, us is a conundrum which we must attempt to resolve. Somehow, with scant evidence, we must reconcile hate with love, ecstasy with pain, evil with good, cruelty with kindness, melancholy with happiness, poverty with wealth, war with peace, life with death. We cannot, in good conscience, turn our backs on life's negative side. We cannot close our eyes to poverty and despair, genocide and hatred, and yet to dwell on those negative manifestations may seem, in light of our seeming powerlessness, to be useless and counterproductive.

How, then, can we possibly come to terms with such disparity and such barbarism in a world that many of us, despite much seeming evidence to the contrary, still consider to be a purposeful and ordered universe? Would a benign Creator allow such disorder and confusion to exist?

The *Or En Sof*, (Endless Light), must, as any serious student of Kabbalah knows, remain concealed. According to the Lurianic account of the origin of man and the universe, the world was created for the purpose of allowing the energy-intelligence, which would later manifest as the individuated souls of man, playing an active role in the process of existence. From that time forward it became the individual man and woman's prerogative to remove the illusion of darkness and thus unmask the Light.

The book which first and foremost provided the solutions to human conflicts and gave mankind an overpowering momentum to see the light of day was the *Zohar*. Through the *Zohar* one can raise his or her consciousness and transcend the crushing weight of earthly concerns. In the right hands it is a tool of immense power. It can, when correctly perceived, provide answers to man's most seemingly intransigent problems. It was and continues to be a people's book, striking a sympathetic chord in the hearts and minds of those who long for peace, truth, and relief from suffering. In the face of crises and catastrophe it has the ability to resolve agonizing human afflictions by restoring each individual's relationship with the Divine.

Thus, it is with hope, trust, and humility that we at the Research Centre of Kabbalah present to you the first English language translation of the following trilogy of Zoharic texts. We sincerely believe that any effort you exert in comprehending them will be repaid a hundredfold.

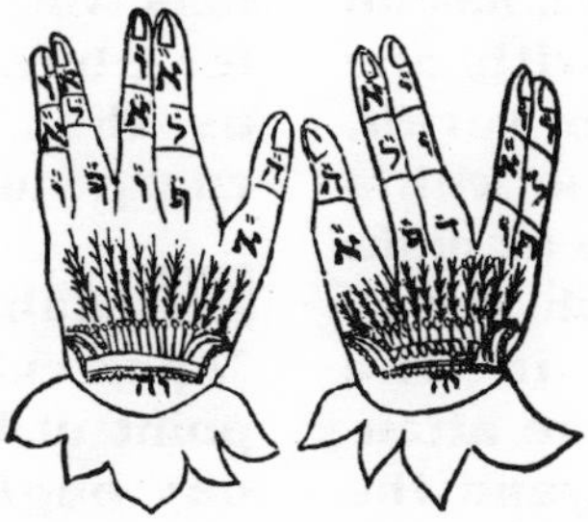

Parashat Pinḥas

HEAR, MY SON, THE INSTRUCTION OF YOUR FATHER

1 And the Lord spoke to Moses, saying, "Pinḥas, the son of Elazar..." (Numbers 25:10). Rabbi Elazar began, "Hear, my son, the instruction of your father, and do not forsake the teaching of your mother" (Proverbs 1:8). "Hear, my son, the instruction of your father..." This refers to the Holy One, blessed be He. "And do not forsake the teaching of your mother." This refers to the People of Israel. What is the instruction of your father? Instruction is the Torah which contains a number of rebukes, and punishments, as it is said: "My son, do not despise the instruction of the Lord, neither spurn His rebuke" (Proverbs 3:11).

2 And since everyone who engages in Torah in this world is worthy that a number of gates, a number of lights to the next world, be opened for him, when he departs from this world the Torah precedes him, going to all the gate keepers proclaiming, "Open the gates that the righteous nation may enter in. Prepare a seat for so-and-so the King's servant!"

(Isaiah 26:2). The Holy One, blessed be He, has no joy other than with one who engages in Torah. How much more so with a man who rises up at night to engage in Torah, for all the righteous in the Garden of Eden are attentive to his voice and the Holy One, blessed be He, is amongst them, as they put it: "The companions listen to the voice of she who dwells in the gardens. Cause me to hear it" (Song of Songs 8:13).

COMPANIONS LISTEN TO YOUR VOICE

3 Rabbi Shimon said: "This verse has in it the secret of wisdom. 'She who dwells in the gardens' refers to the People of Israel, i.e. Malkhut, which is with Israel in exile and accompanies them in their troubles. 'The companions listen to the voice...' refers to the camps of the heavenly angels, all of whom listen to your voice, the voice of your praises in exile. 'Cause me to hear it' is as it is said: 'Let me see your countenance, let me hear your voice' (Song of Songs 11:14). 'Let me hear your voice' refers to the voice of those companions who engage in Torah, for I have no praise such as that for those who engage in Torah."

4 Rabbi Shimon said: "Apparently at the turning point of the night, as the day begins to dawn, all those who are privileged to engage in Torah come with the Queen to welcome the King, and they grow stronger and take possession of the Shekhinah. Moreover, a cord of hangs over them, as the Sages have explained."

5 Come and See: Everyone who is privileged to be strengthened in the Shekhinah gains protection for himself from those matters that are considered to be opposed to the Shekhinah. Who is protected? He who does not tell falsehoods in the sign of the Holy Covenant or join a foreign god. And he who watches over himself to make sure he does right is, as it were, linked with the Mystical Unity of Israel which, in turn, protects him and greets him peacefully. And this is even more so if he has been

privileged to acquire the sign of the Holy Covenant.

6 Said Rabbi Shimon: "Israel at that time would have been extirpated from the world had not Pinḥas first done the deed of killing Zimri and Cozbi, and God's anger abated. This is what is said: 'Pinḥas, the son the Elazar, the son of Aaron the priest, has turned My anger away' (Numbers 25:10). Another explanation: 'Pinḥas, the son of Elazar, the son of....' The word ben, "the son of," occurs twice to complete the act. [See 11 below.]

7 Said Rabbi Shimon: "When the soul of a person transmigrates a second time without deserving to be changed for the better, it is as though he betrays the truth of the King and I apply to the verse, ... or has found that which was lost, and deals falsely therein, and swears to a lie...' (Leviticus 5:22). 'And deals falsely therein' means in the soul — it would have been better for him had he not been created, if he had not come into the world."

A COMPLETELY RIGHTEOUS AND AN INCOMPLETELY RIGHTEOUS PERSON

8 We have learned: A totally righteous person is not put off by an evil person and may challenge him (cf. Proverbs 28:4), but one who is not totally righteous is held back and is forbidden to challenge an evil person. Who is totally righteous? And who is incompletely righteous? And could it be that one who is not perfect in his deeds is nevertheless called righteous, that is, that you refer to him as incompletely righteous? (For who is lacking in his deeds, according to how they should be, ought to be called bad.) The answer to this is that a totally righteous person is one who has not undergone bad transmigrations and with his inheritance himself constructs buildings, puts up walls, digs wells and plants trees. That is to say, all the good deeds that he did are under his own control, and he has no need of correcting.

9 An incompletely righteous person is one who constructs buildings with someone else's inher-

itance, that is to say, whose soul is on its second migration because he was a wicked person the first time, and all his good deeds are needed to repair the soul from the first time that it came into the world, and so his buildings are built with someone else's inheritance. He digs wells with it and cultivates it, restores the foundation stones to the way they were, and labors there, but does not know whether it will remain his. For in terms of himself, that is, according to his deeds in this migration, he is good and is called a righteous person. But in terms of the legacy, that is, in terms of his deeds on the first occasion that he came into the world, he is not so. That is to say, he has not yet remedied the effects of the sins committed the first time.

10 He is like a person who constructs a beautiful and attractive building, but looks at the foundations and find them sunken and twisted in all directions. The building will not be perfect until he has demolished it and rebuilt it as it was, i.e., as it should be. Thus in terms of the superstructure of the building that he constructed, everything was good and wonderful [*213b] but in terms of the foundation it is bad twisted and for this reason is not referred to as a perfect deed, a perfect building. And so it is with the migrating soul. Although in terms of his deeds he is righteous, nevertheless, since he has not yet remedied the effects of the sins he committed the first time that he came into the world, he is called an incompletely righteous person and he is put off by a wicked person. And on this Scripture says, "When the wicked swallows up the man that is more righteous than he" (Habakkuk 1:13).

11 Come and see: One who is zealous for the Holy Name of the Holy One, blessed be He, even if he is not designated for greatness and is not worthy of it, he earns it and gains it. Pinḥas was not worthy of the priesthood at that time, but because he was zealous for the name of his Master, he earned everything and rose to the highest position, and everything was put right within him, and he was privileged to serve in the supreme priesthood. From then on he was referred to as Pinḥas ben [the son of] Elazar, ben [the son of] Aaron the priest, with the word 'ben' occurring twice since he completed two stages, that is, he made good for himself and also for the souls of Nadav and Avihu which had transmigrated into him, for they are the sons of Aaron and it is therefore written' ben Elazar, ben Aaron'. And this was because he was zealous for the name of his Master and put the wrong right, for he corrected himself also from the point of view of the souls of Nadav and Avihu that had transmigrated into him.

KEEP MY SOUL FOR I AM PIOUS

12 Rabbi Yehuda began: "'Keep my soul, for I am pious; Save your servant...' (Psalms 86:2). One has to look at the end of the verse, and then at the whole verse. At the end of the verse it says, 'Who trusts to You.' Should it not have said, 'Who trusts in You'? Apparently David promised not to be asleep when midnight passed, as it is written: 'At midnight I will rise to give thanks to You' (Psalms 119:62). He should have said, 'I arose', but the meaning is, 'I will arise and be bound to you for ever.'"

13 'Keep [shomrah] my soul'. He should have said 'shamor' [keep], but we have learnt that there is no letter in the Torah that does not have heavenly and precious secrets. He said 'shomrah', that is, the letters of shamor with the addition of the letter hei, for he was saying to the Holy One, blessed be He, 'shamor hei', i.e. 'Keep, O Lord' the hei, for it is that same part onto which the soul holds. When the soul leaves this world it enters the domain of the next world. If it so merits, a number of heavenly hosts come out to greet it, guard it, and bring it into its section in its rightful place. The letter hei, namely Malkhut, keeps it, to unite with it on new moons and Sabbaths.

14 But if it does not so merit, a number of angels of destruction are directed

against it, and push it outside. Woe to that soul that wanders in vain as a stone in the hollow of the sling. This is what was said: "He will sling out the soul of your enemies from the hollow of the slings" (First Samuel 25:29). And David made his request before the Holy One, blessed be He, and said, "Keep my soul that it be not rejected, and when they come out against it, may the portals be opened for it, and may it be accepted before You." "For I am pious...." Was David really called pious? Was he not a king, and was not kingship [malkhut] his characteristic? Said Rabbi Yehuda, "Yes, he was called pious, for it is written, `The sure pieties of David' (Isaiah 55:3). That is, since David was a trusted servant of the Holy One, he is called pious and this is the reason for `Keep my soul', i.e., do not abandon it to wander on the outside.

15 Rabbi Yitzḥak said: "Everyone who has a portion in righteousness, i.e. who keeps his covenant, inherits this land, that is Malkhut, as it is said: `Your people shall be all righteous; they shall inherit the land for ever' (Isaiah 60:21). And this righteous, which is Yesod, is called pious since he inspires piety. That is why David said, `Since I am holding onto that place, and am righteous therefore, `I am pious'; and because of this, `Keep my soul that it be bound up with You" (Psalms 86:2).

THE HEI ADDED TO THE NAME OF JOSEPH AND THE YUD TO PINḤAS

16 Rabbi Ḥiyya began: "He appointed it in Joseph [written with the addition of the letter hei Yehosef] for a testimony, when he went forth to the Land of Egypt. Pharaoh is quoted as saying, `the speech of one I knew not did I hear' (Psalms 81:6). We have learnt that the angel

taught Joseph 70 languages, as were known by Pharaoh, but in Hebrew he was greater than Pharaoh, for Pharaoh did not know the Holy Tongue (Talmud Sotah 36b). 'The speech of one that I knew not did I hear,' for he taught him languages that he had not known previously. But, if this is so, what is 'testimony' in the verse? Come and see: When Potiphar's wife took hold of him to seduce him, Joseph made himself as one who did not know her language, and so it was each day until the last one, as it is written: 'She caught him by his garment' (Genesis 38:12). What is the meaning of 'she caught him'? Until that time he had pretended that he did not know her language, but then she saw through him, that he did know her language, that he understood her intention. This is the meaning of 'she caught him': that she caught the trickery in him. 'By his garment' [beged], is another way of saying infidelity [begidah] and treachery. And the Holy Spirit, that is Malkhut, cried out to him, 'Keep you from the woman, from the alien woman who speaks flatteringly' (Proverbs 7:5). What is he trying to teach us here? He is teaching us that everyone who keeps himself from having an illicit affair as Joseph did is bound up with the Shekhinah and holds on to this testimony which is Malkhut. And this is the hei that was added to it, as it is written: 'He appointed it in Yehosef for a testimony.' Also in our section, a yud was added to the name of Pinḥas because he was zealous over the same matter, the affair of Zimri, for the yud hints at Malkhut [See below, 35d].

KEEPER OF THE COVENANT

17 Rabbi Yissa began: "'By the rivers of Babylon, there we sat down, yea, we wept, when we remembered Zion' (Psalms 137:1). Should it not have said 'Jerusalem' since it is written, 'If I forget you, O Jerusalem, let my right hand forget its cunning?' (Psalms 137:5). It is like a man who had a precious and beautiful palace and robbers came and burned it down. Whose is the anguish if not that of the

palace owner? Here also, whose anguish is it that the Shekhinah is in exile if not that of the righteous person, i.e., Yesod? And this fits in with what they taught, as it is written: 'The righteous perish' (Isaiah 57:1) — literally perish. For the whole purpose of Yesod is to give out emanations. But if the Shekhinah is in exile it has no one to whom they may be given and it is as if it were not present and had perished. Here also, 'When we remembered Zion' means when we remembered the anguish of Zion, which is Yesod, because of its lack of mating, for the anguish is Yesod's."

18 Rabbi Yissa said: "Whoever respects the name of his Master in this matter, and keeps the Covenant, is privileged to have his Master respect him over all. How do we know this? Because regarding Joseph, it is written, 'And he made him ride in the second chariot that he had' (Genesis 41:43); and also, 'And he set him over all the Land of Egypt' (ibid.). [*214a] Furthermore, when Israel crossed the sea, Joseph's coffin entered the water first and the water was unable to stay in its place. Therefore it is written, 'The sea saw and fled' (Psalms 114:3). What is the meaning of 'and fled'? The sea saw him about whom this is written, 'and fled'; that is, left its natural domain."

19 Come and see: He (Joseph) earned respect in his life and in his death. Why in his life? Because he did not want to cleave to Potiphar's wife, as it is written: "But he refused and said to his master's wife..." (Genesis 39:8). As it is written, "He did not listen to her, to lie by her or to be with her" (Genesis 39:10). For this reason he earned respect in this world. For it is written, "And she caught him by his garment," and also "And he fled and left his natural domain." Because Joseph fled he earned entry after his demise into the heavenly curtain that is in the Temple of the Holy of Holies. And so it was befitting that he received his due in this world and in the other world.

20 Pinḥas was privileged in this world and in the

next, and was enabled to live longer than all those who came out of Egypt. He was also enabled to serve as High Priest, both he and all his sons after him. There are those who say that he had earned the priesthood previously. However, this is incorrect. He earned it only through the slaying of Zimri and Cozbi. If he had earned it previously, how should we understand the words, "Because he was zealous for his God"? (Numbers 25:13), whose plain meaning is that he earned the priesthood because of this deed and had not gained it previously.

21 Come and see: Any priest who kills a person is considered forever unfit for the priesthood because he has marred his own status. Priesthood is the status of Ḥesed [loving kindness] and killing a person contradicts this. Since Pinḥas had killed Zimri and Cozbi, he was legally barred from remaining a priest. But because Pinḥas was zealous for the Holy One, blessed be He, He had to reinstate him, and also his seed after him for all time, into the priesthood. This is the meaning of the words, "Because he was zealous for his God." Said Rabbi Yitzḥak, "Come and see: Pinḥas' deeds were recorded in heaven and on earth." `In heaven' means before he came into the world. The reason his deeds were recorded on earth is that he was among those who came out of Egypt.

22 Rabbi Elazar, Rabbi Yossi, and Rabbi Ḥiyya were walking in the wilderness. Said Rabbi Yossi, "This that is written concerning Pinḥas, `Behold I give him My covenant of peace' (Numbers 25:12), refers to peace from the Angel of Death, the Angel who will never have control over him or have power to judge him. If you were to suggest that Pinḥas did not die, you would be mistaken. He did die but certainly not in the same way as others do and he lived longer than all the other members of his generation because he held on to that heavenly covenant. And when he did leave this world he departed from his fellow mortals with a longing for heaven and with wonderful devoutness."

23 Come and see: woe to those people who do not look out for their Master's honor and do not pay attention to the fact that He daily issues a proclamation about them. When a person observes the commandments of the Torah, defenders rise to recall his good points, but if a person transgresses the commandments his deeds accuse him before the Holy One, blessed be He. We have been told that Joshua was a high priest. And what is written about him? "...and Satan standing at his right hand to accuse him." If this is how it was for him, then how much more so for those ordinary mortals who do not respect the honor of their Master.

24 Look what is written: "Now Joshua was clothed in filthy garments..." (Zechariah 3:3). Were they really filthy garments? Surely they were the garments in which the spirit is attired in that world. Happy is the destiny of he whose garments are repaired and complete in that world! We have already learnt what raiment they clothe everyone with whom they want to sent to Gehenna. Here it is written, "Now Joshua was clothed in filthy garments, and he stood before the angel." Which angel? The Angel appointed to be in charge of Gehenna and who is also appointed to be in charge of everyone whom he sees in such clothes. And so it was with Joshua the high priest until a voice said, "Take the filthy garment off of him" (Zekhariah 3:4).

25 It follows from this that it is a person's bad deeds that make the filthy garments for him. "And he said to him, `Behold I cause your iniquity to pass from you, and I will clothe you with robes' (Zekhariah 3:4). For they clothed him in other garments, in which a person may observe the splendour of his Master's honor.

26 Come and see how it is with someone like Pinḥas, who did not leave this world until he had changed into other garments, which the spirit would enjoy in the next world. [*214b] In one hour he took off one set and put on the other, as it is written: "Behold, I give to him My covenant of peace" (Numbers 25:12). And they (the three rabbis) were continuing on their way and the sunlight was very strong, so they sat down in the shade of a rock in the wilderness. Said Rabbi Elazar, "Shade is without doubt the joy of the soul."

FROM ROSH HASHANAH UNTIL THE LAST DAY OF SUKKOTH

27 Rabbi Ḥiyya said to Rabbi Elazar, "I should like to discuss these days from Rosh haShanah until the last day of Sukkoth." Said Rabbi Elazar, "But we have already studied them, and the companions have made their comments about them." Said Rabbi Ḥiyya, "Of course, but I heard something about them from the great and holy luminary, i.e., Rabbi Shimon. Rabbi Elazar said to Rabbi Ḥiyya, "Tell us." To which Rabbi Ḥiyya replied, "It has slipped my mind and is not as clear as it should be." Said Rabbi Elazar, "Although the companions have already discussed this matter, and it is beautiful, the order of these days is the secret of Ḥokhmah [wisdom], as it is said: `amongst the harvesters in the field,' i.e., amongst those scholars who have already completed all the clarifications of Malkhut, which is termed `a field'."

28 Come and see: The order of unity is all in one. How is that? We have learnt, He began, "The Lord has made bare His holy arm" (Isaiah 52:10). This is one arm, which is the left column on which are dependent salvation, vengeance, and redemption. But why did the Lord make bare this holy arm of His? It was to raise up the People of Israel, i.e., Malkhut, from the dust and to welcome Malkhut with Zeir Anpin and unite them. When that arm is raised up against Israel because of their sinning, there is much fear in the world, until His anger is subdued and He rests that arm under her head to unite with her, as it is said: "His left hand under my head..." (Song of Songs 2:6). And then Judgment rests and He atones for sins.

29 Later the right column comes to embrace her. Then rejoicing engulfs the world, and all countenances shine. Subsequently, she, Malkhut, unites with the body, i.e., the central column, and then everything is called one without schism, for the central column incorporates the right and the left. Then everything is perfection and everything is joy and they, Zeir Anpin and Malkhut, certainly unite, which is not the case at other times.

30 The order of those days, from Rosh haShanah until the last day of Sukkoth, is like this. On Rosh haShanah, the left arm is awakened, i.e., the left column of Zeir Anpin, to welcome the Queen. The whole world is then in fear of Judgment, and the whole world has to be in complete repentance before the Holy One, blessed be He. Later, on the ninth of the month, the Queen comes (cf. Aharei Mot, 231) and the men of the temple, i.e., the children of Israel, make merry and immerse themselves in the river to purify themselves so as to be worthy of the mating of the Queen with Zeir Anpin on the next day, i.e., the tenth of the month, Yom haKippurim. For mating is accomplished by Zeir Anpin placing his left hand under her head, in accordance with the text, "His left hand under my head" (Song of Songs 2:6).

31 On the tenth day Israel fasts for their sins and makes atonement. For the Heavenly Mother, i.e., Binah, looks kindly on Malkhut in the mating, for on Yom haKippurim Malkhut rises and enwraps Binah, and makes atonement for all of the temple, i.e., Israel, since the left side of Zeir Anpin welcomes her on this day, for the head of Malkhut rests on the left.

32 On the first day of Sukkoth, the right column of Zeir Anpin begins to move towards Malkhut to embrace her. This is the hidden meaning of the verse, "And his right hand embraces me" (Song of Songs 2:6). Then everyone rejoices and all countenances shine. One of the ways of rejoicing is to pour pure water on the altar. People should be happy from rejoicing in many different ways. This joyfulness is caused by the right side of Zeir Anpin, for wherever the right side, i.e., Ḥasadim, rests there has to be joy for everyone. This is because she is happy to be embraced.

33 Later, on the day of Shemini Atzeret, which is Simat Torah, the mating of the body (i.e., the central column) takes place. This is the mating of all parts, for it includes the mating of the left side, of Rosh haShanah and Yom haKippurim as well as the mating of the right side, of the Festival of Sukkoth, since the central column incorporates the right and the left. Thus all is one and this is the perfection of all. And this day is definitely Israel's. It belongs to them alone, for no other people has a part in it. It is not like the festival of Sukkoth when 70 bulls are sacrificed for the 70 nations because the nations have no part in Shemini Atzeret. Happy is Israel in this world and in the world to come. About them it is written, "Because you are a holy people for the Lord your God..." (Deuteronomy 14:2). [cf. Parashat Tzav, 116]

THE RAINBOW

34 "Pinḥas, the son of Eleazar, the son of Aaron the priest, has turned My anger away from the children of Israel..." (Numbers 25:11). Rabbi Yehuda began: "Remember, I pray you, who ever perished, being innocent? Or where were the upright cut off? (Job 4:7). We learned there that whoever sees the rainbow in all its colors has to say the blessing: "Blessed is He who remembers the covenant", since this is the sign of a holy covenant that the Holy One, blessed be He, [*215a] placed in the world that the waters of the flood will not cover it again. This is because, when the numbers of wicked people increase in the world, the Holy One, blessed be He, wants to destroy them, but then he recalls for them that oath that He swore to the land, for it is twice written `not': "I shall not again curse...

and I shall not again smite..." (Genesis 8:21). And twice 'not' constitutes an oath, as it is said: "As I have sworn that the waters of Noah should no more go over the earth" (Isaiah 54:9).

35a Rabbi Yossi said: "A rainbow comes to protect the world. It is like a queen wearing royal apparel who appears before the king every time he is about to hit his son because he has done something wrong. The king sees her and his anger with his son leaves him and he rejoices with her, as it is written: 'And I shall see it and remember the everlasting covenant' (Genesis 9:16). And this is why a rainbow appears only in the royal apparel that Malkhut wears. These are the three colors: white, red and green, and they suggest the three columns. When there is a righteous person in the world, he personifies the covenant and thus protects the world. But if there is no righteous person, then there is a rainbow to indicate that the world is about to perish but survives because of it.

35b Rabbi Elazar said: "This rainbow, namely Malkhut, has never worn anything except the apparel of the patriarchs, i.e., Ḥesed, Gvurah, and Tiferet of Zeir Anpin, i.e. green, red, and white. The raiment of Abraham is green, and it was so colored when Ishmael issued from him. Red is Isaac, who acquired this color when Esau issued from him. This red stretches down to the planet Mars, whose literal meaning is 'the reddening star', which Esau is holding onto. White is the fine garment of Jacob, whose good countenance never changed, for his family was perfect and there was no blemish in him.

35c Rabbi Abba said: "That is good, but the holy luminary, i.e. Rabbi Shimon, said, 'White is Abraham, who was purified ('whitened') in the white-hot heat of the fire by Nimrod, who cast him into the fire ('Ur') of the Khashdim. Red is obviously Isaac, and green is Jacob, who is between the other two colors, for green includes white and red, which also represent the color of the sun. And about Jacob it is written, "Jacob shall not now be ashamed, neither shall his face now wax pale" (Isaiah 29:23) because the whole of the family was perfect. And the interpretation of this is: "Jacob shall not now be ashamed" because he shall not be seen in red like Isaac, who fathered Esau. "Neither shall his face wax pale." This means that he shall not be seen in white like Abraham, who fathered Ishmael. Instead he took white and red and enveloped himself in them. He incorporated within himself the two patriarchs Abraham and Isaac, who are white and red, and this is why his color is green, which includes white and red. (*215b) And the rainbow, i.e., Malkhut, puts on garments of white, red, and green when it appears before the king, Zeir Anpin."

35d Come and see: The secret of the holy covenant is the letter yud that adorns itself with a heavenly impression, i.e. the diadem of Yesod and is recorded forever in the everlasting covenant. And because Pinḥas was zealous for the covenant, that letter yud was written into his name. [The vowel 'i' in Hebrew is sometimes, as in Pinḥas' name, supplemented by a non-consonantal 'y' or yud.] The yud in the spelling of 'Pinḥas' is a small one, which is the secret of Malkhut, the secret of diadem of Yesod. This yud, which makes the spelling of 'Pinḥas' into 'Piynḥas', is definitely the covenant which emanated from the upper holy yud because Malkhut emanated from the yud of the Tetragrammaton [the unspoken four-letter name of God, yud hei vav hei]. And this is why Pinḥas has a perfect existence before the Holy King and shall never perish from the world. And because of this he was without sin for what he did at Peor [see Numbers 25:1-3]. For he was never lost from world's holiness. "Or where were the upright cut off?" (Job 4:7). This refers to Nadav and Avihu, who were not cut off from the world because their souls transmigrated into Pinḥas, who remedied the results of their previous sins [See Vaera, 87].

THE FAITHFUL SHEPHERD

36 The Faithful Shepherd said to him: "What you have said is good, but since Elijah is Pinḥas, who was zealous for the covenant, one must establish new and important interpretations about him. This is because this Parasha in the Torah is named Pinḥas after him, i.e. Elijah, who was the incarnation of Pinḥas, of whom it is said, 'Zealously have I been zealous.' (I Kings 19:10). This refers to two forms of zealousness, one for the heavenly name of God, Shaddai, Yesod of Zeir Anpin, and the other for the lower name of God, the Metatron Shaddai Almighty. [See below 39]. And this is why he made two oaths for the two of them and it is twice written, 'Not, not.'"

37 But Rabbi Yehuda said: "Whoever sees a rainbow in shining colors must recite the blessing, 'Blessed be He who remembers the covenant.' In exile the rainbow does not shine in its proper colors because in exile Malkhut does not receive the unification of the three columns, which are represented by the secret of the rainbow's three colors.

Furthermore, sometimes it hardly shines and at other times it doesn't shine at all. The rainbow's colors hint at the rights of the Priests, Levites, and Israelites. When the rainbow is radiant, it represents the union of the three columns.

38 Rise up now, Rabbi Yossi of Galilee, and say, for you said beautiful things in the previous discussion, that the rainbow only comes to protect the world. It is like the queen who, every time she is seen by the king, takes away his anger with his son, as it is written: "And I will look upon it and remember the everlasting covenant" (Genesis 9:16). Therefore the rainbow only appears in order to protect the world for it is part of the secret of Malkhut, as explained above. It appears only in royal apparel because of the secret of the three colors. But when there is a righteous person in the world, he is the covenant. This means he establishes the covenant, which means a union between Zeir Anpin and Malkhut, therefore there is no need to arouse Malkhut by the secret of the rainbow.

39 But how can the queen put on royal apparel in exile? For in exile the Holy One, blessed be He, draws away from the queen. The answer is that in exile she does not wear royal apparel, but is dressed in darkness, i.e. in blackness, and says: "Look not upon me, for I am swarthy" (Song of Songs 1:6). On the contrary, the rainbow that is viewed in the exile in none other than the angel Metatron, who is called Shaddai (Almighty), and he is the servant of Zeir Anpin, "the elder of his house who rules over all that he has" (Genesis 24:2), while his sons, i.e. those who merit the spirit, from the point of view of Metatron are called the servants of the Holy One, blessed be He. The queen's sons, i.e. those who merit the soul from Malkhut of Atziluth, are called sons. This is the reason why we pray "whether as sons or as servants."

ROSH HASHANAH MUSAF SERVICE

40 When the Temple was destroyed, so we are told, servants covered their heads in shame and men of action were weakened. This term "men of action" is derived from the name of Malkhut, about whom it is said: "Many daughters have done valiantly, but you have excelled them all" (Proverbs 31:29). That is, excelled regarding action, for Malkhut is called "action." If there is a righteous person whose merits and actions are such as to enlighten Malkhut and to strip the raiment of blackness from her, literally and not secretly, and adorn her with the garments of the shining colors of secrets of the Torah, what is written about him? — "And I will look upon it and remember the everlasting covenant" (Genesis 9:16). And I will look upon it — this refers to the shining secrets to the Torah, for light is called a secret (i.e. the numerical value of the letters of the Hebrew word for "Light" — Or — is the same as for the word "secret" — raz). Thus, light

signifies all the secrets of the Torah, as it is said: "For the commandment is a lamp, and the Torah is a light" (Proverbs 6:23).

41 When he looks at the rainbow, i.e. Malkhut, his anger at his son (Israel) leaves him, "and the king's wrath is abated" (Esther 6:10). And the king says to her, with the Amidah prayer before him, "Whatever your petition, it will be granted you, and whatever your request..." (Esther 5:6). Then she asks for her redemption and that of her sons, as it is said: "Let my life be given me at my petition, and my people at my request" (Esther 7:3). But a rainbow that appears in the world at a time of exile is of the servant, i.e. Metatron. That is to say, the enlightening of the heavenly mating clothes Metatron, and he is bearer of the three colors of the rainbow, which are the three columns. And sometimes she comes out completely, when her sons act correctly, while at other times she does not come out completely, when her sons do not act correctly.

42 [The beginning is omitted]

And those who make their acts agreeable to the King are zealous for His name, sanctifying it in public, as they sanctify it in heaven amongst the angels who are appointed over the other nations — each angel being known by the name of the nation. Israel, however, is known in heaven by the Tetragrammaton (the four-letter name of God), which is the life source of all the names.

43 And every name testifies to something about Him, about the Holy One, blessed be He. The name "El" [literally "God"] testifies that He can overcome every other god, as it is said: "But as for me, I would seek unto God" (Job 5:8). "El" is the master of every god. "Elohim" testifies that He is the God of gods. "Adonai" (literally "Lord") testifies that He is the Lord of lords. And so it is with each name. And each angel has a proper name and each group of angels is known by the name of its king. Israel, however, is known to Him by the Tetragrammaton.

44 And the secret of the matter is that, just as one man can have a number of horses, so it is that all of Israel are the sons of "Adam" (literally "man"); the numerical value of the letters of "Adam" is the same as that of the Tetragrammaton when the latter is spelled with the letter aleph [numerical value = 1], for the souls of Israel are the progeny of Zeir Anpin and Malkhut. And every son must be like a horse and beast of burden for his father, and be subject to him. This secret is expressed thus: "Man and beast You preserve, O Lord" (Psalms 36:7). For the people of Israel are the sons of Adam ["man"], which is the Tetragrammaton spelled with the letter aleph [the letters yud when spelled out equals twenty. Hei spelled with an aleph equals six. Vav spelled with an aleph equals thirteen. The final hei spelled with an aleph equals six. The sum of these letters is forty-five, which is the numerical value of the Hebrew letters used to spell "Adam".] And they make themselves as a beast of burden under him.

LEVIRATE MARRIAGE AND TRANSMIGRATION

45 And for this reason it is a commandment of the Holy One, blessed be He, that a man should marry his deceased brother's widow, to have a son for his brother that he be not lost to that world. And this is like the secret of the mixed kinds in the

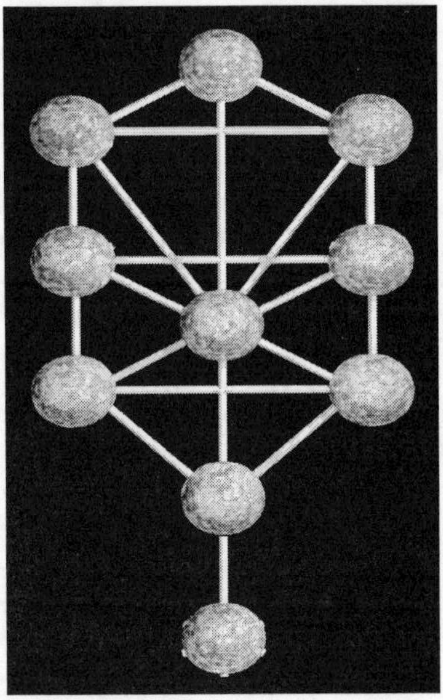

fringes (of a garment. cf. Numbers 15:38). For they have said: What I have forbidden to you in one place, I have permitted in another. I have forbidden mixed kinds in general, but permitted mixed kinds in the fringes. I have forbidden you to marry your brother's wife (Leviticus 18:16), but have permitted levirate marriage (Deuteronomy 25:5). Similarly, one may graft apples or dates, each on its own species, but it is forbidden to graft one species onto another. And on this it is said: "For man is the tree of the field" (Deuteronomy 20:19), for man is also forbidden to mate with one who is not of his species, namely the incestual relationships, but, for levirate marriage, one may mix two that do not go together so that the soul of the deceased shall not be lost and his name not be blotted out from Israel.

46 And this is the secret of transmigration. The wheel does not move without the flow of water through the conduit to turn it. So also, the conduit, the secret of the letter vav, is by which the wheel is turned. And the secret of the matter is that, just as the wheel will have no motion without the conduit, so also the wheel which is the letter yud will have no motion without the conduit which is the letter vav. A deceased brother's widow is hei, and we thus have the letters of Binah, that is (in a different order) Ben (the son of) Yah. For the son, who is Zeir Anpin, issues from the mating of Yah, that is Ḥokhmah and Binah, and his mother's name is implied in his name, Ben (the son of) Yah, i.e. the letters of Binah. With the letter yud, that is Ḥokhmah, He created the next world, which is a long world, i.e. the letter vav, and this is Zeir Anpin.

47 this reason, anyone who has no son, which is for Zeir Anpin, which is the secret of vav, which is the next world, will not be in the next world. For the sea, which is Binah, the secret of the next world, is parallel to it, to the vav, for the vav emerges from between the Yud-hei (Yah), where the yud is the secret of Ḥokhmah and the hei of Binah, which is called "sea". Therefore the vav is also likewise called the next world. And from the sea, which is Binah, a number of rivers separate, these being the Sfirot of the vav, which is Zeir Anpin, and they circumscribe the world, which is Malkhut, until they return to the sea, which is Binah, from which the rivers, which are Zeir Anpin, issued. This is why scripture said: "All the rivers run into the sea, yet the sea is not full; unto the place whither the rivers go, thither they go again" (Ecclesiastes 1:7). That is to say, they return from where they came: i.e. just as the rivers flow out of Binah, so do they return to Binah.

48 So also, regarding the soul of man it is written, "And the spirit returns to God who gave it." (*216a) [Ecclesiastes 12:7], i.e. it returns to Him in perfection, as He gave it. This is so if it returns in repentance, which is the heavenly Binah, that is called "Repentance", which is the letters of Ben-Yah. The letter hei in this word is multiplied by the letter yud in it, which means ten (numerical value of yud) times five (numerical value of hei) equals fifty, which, according to the numerical value of the letters, is yud and mem (ten and forty respectively), i.e. Yam (meaning sea). This is the secret of the letters yud-hei in Binah. The letters bet and nun of Binah form "ben" ["the son of"]. Ben is the river flowing from Binah (the sea). It is also Zeir Anpin, and it divides into six rivers like a tree spreading into a number of branches. And when a man repents, he clings to the river, which is Zeir Anpin and returns with its rivers to Binah, which is called Repentance, and is also called Sea. And this is the secret of the verse: "All the rivers run into the sea", as above.

49 And if the soul does not return perfect as it was when it was given, the verse "..thither they go again" is applied to it, and to all the other souls which are like it, i.e. not perfect. In other words, they return to this world in a transmigration. And so also if he is incomplete in not having a son, or if he has no daughter, which is necessary in this world (Malkhut) so that he can be perfected by her in this world, Malkhut, which was created with the letter hei, as it is written: "These are the generations of the heaven and the earth when

they were created" (Genesis 11:4). [The Hebrew word "b'hibaram", normally translated as "when they were created", can be divided into two words, "B'hei' b'ra'am", meaning "He created them with the letter hei — tr.] So a man who has no daughter has to transmigrate a second time because his soul is not perfect, and to him is the verse applied "...thither they go again".

50 Yud hei vav, three of the four letters of the Tetragrammaton, form the secret of Ḥesed, Gvurah, Tiferet. This is the secret of the verse: "Yea, all these things does God work, twice, even thrice, with a man" (Job 33:29). That is to say that the souls transmigrate in the secret of the letters yud, hei, vav, about which scripture says: "Yea, all these things..." Regarding the wicked, it is said: "And so I saw the wicked buried and they came" (Ecclesiastes 8:10). That is, despite being transmigrated they remained wicked, and it is they who worshipped false idols "These are your gods, O Israel" (Exodus 32:4 — said by the Children of Israel to the golden calf). [In other words, by associating the idol with "these" (eleh), the same word used in the verse from Job, "Yea, all these things..." — tr.], they do harm to "these", namely the secret of the yud, hei, vav, and about them it is said: "For three transgressions of Israel, yea, for four, I will not reverse it" (Amos 11:6). This means that, after they have corrupted themselves three times in their transmigrations, they have not merited "tikune" in yud, hei, vav, about which it is said: "In the place where the tree falls, there shall it be" (Ecclesiastes 11:3). [The Hebrew word here translated "shall it be" is spelt: yud, hei, vav — tr.] That is to say, the repair of the tree, which is man, is affected by yud, hei, vav. Then comes the second part of the above verse: for four I will not reverse it." This refers to the fourth and final letter of the Tetragrammaton, hei, and means "He will not send the soul back for a fourth transmigration, corresponding to the final letter, but it will be judged in Gehenna by the officials which are destruction, anger, and wrath.

51 And the garments of these three letters — yud, hei, vav — are known from the rainbow, namely white, red, and green. A person in his first transmigration is white, corresponding to the letter yud of the Tetragrammaton, which is Ḥesed; in the second he is red, corresponding to the hei of the Tetragrammaton, which is Gvurah; and in the third he is green, corresponding to the vav of the Tetragrammaton, which is Tiferet, called Jacob, the central column incorporating the other two, Ḥesed and Gvurah. And since the letters yud and hei (which are Ḥesed and Gvurah) are included in Jacob, the tree takes root, grows, and gives good fruits. About this is said: "Jacob shall not now be ashamed, neither shall his face now grow pale" (Isaiah 29:22); and that his chariot should not journey with the evil inclinations, which is the serpent, nor with all other types of evil beasts. And for this reason, it is written about him: "And he strove with an angel and prevailed" (Hosea 12:5). And because man is called a tree, he is, in this secret, similar to a tree planted in a place where it does not bear fruit. What can one do about it? One removes it and replants it elsewhere. This is why the scholars of the Mishnah (cf. Tractate Yevamot, 6,6) taught that a barren man who moves to the land of Israel will bear fruit, i.e. be able to make a woman conceive.

52 So also, a righteous man who wanders from place to place, from house to house, is like a person who goes through many transmigrations. And He shows mercy to the thousandth generation of those who love Him (cf. Exodus 20:6), until the righteous man achieves perfection in the world to come. But, a wicked person is not allowed more than three transmigrations. If he repents, however, his wandering is considered a transmigration and he achieves the perfection of a righteous man. For we

have learnt that "Exile atones for transgression" (Talmud Bavli, Berakhot 56a). This is why the sages of the Mishnah taught: "The righteous... do not return to their dust" (Talmud Bavli, Sanhedrin 82a), i.e. are not transmigrated.

53 But concerning the wicked, scripture says: "And he shall take other mortar and plaster the house" (Leviticus 14:42), i.e. that he shall take another body coming from the dust, in a transmigration, and amend his soul. "And man shall return to the dust" (Job 34:15) means that he will return to the earth as it was" (Ecclesiastes 12:7) intimates that he will return in a transmigration. And the dust shall return in a transmigration. This is because the wicked person is afflicted and is nothing but a bad woman — that is, the evil inclination, about which we have learnt: "A bad woman is as leprosy for her husband" (Talmud Bavli, Yevamot, 63a), for she is the body of the wicked. What remedy does the wicked person have? Let him divorce her and be healed. That is, he should get rid of his present body, transmigrate into another body, and so be healed. For she, the wicked woman that is the body, was the cause of exile: "And He drove out the man" (Genesis 3:24). "The man" refers to the soul; the particle "et" [the sign of a definite object in Hebrew] in the verse refers to the body, which is the spouse of man, who is the soul, as it says: "As a bird who wanders from her nest, so is man who wanders from his place" (Proverbs 27:8). In other words, because the man caused the bird, which is the soul, to wander from its nest (for it was driven out from its heavenly place because of his sins), so also does a man wander from his place in order that he should return in a transmigration.

54 And that is why: "Yea, the bird has found a house, and the swallow a nest for herself, where she may lay her young" (Psalms 84:4). "Yea, the bird" means the soul of the deceased brother who died without children. "Has found a house"

means that the soul has transmigrated and entered the widow's soul which has become its home. "And the swallow a nest for herself" refers to the redeemer who marries the deceased brother's widow and finds himself a nest in her. "Where she may lay her young" refers to a son and a daughter to whom she gives birth. Happy is he who makes a nest, that is, who marries the widow of his childless deceased brother. "And redeem what his brother has sold" (Leviticus 25:25), for the widow of his deceased brother is considered as though sold to him, for she is not his, but his brother's, and she is therefore called "what his brother has sold".

55 And this was why Moses said: "And the Lord was wroth (from the Hebrew root ayin bet resh) with me for your sakes" (Deuteronomy 3:26). And this is the secret of the conception (from the same Hebrew root ayin bet resh), for Malkhut conceived by the soul of Moses. The faithful shepherd saved sixty thousand souls in Israel a number of times, for he transmigrated in a number of generations and saved them. For this reason, the Holy One, blessed be He, ascribed to Moses the merit of all of them, and this is why the rabbis taught: "One woman in Egypt brought forth six hundred thousand at a birth" (Midrash Shir haShirim Rabba 1, 15, 3). [This was Yocheved, mother of Moses.] Moses was counted as equal to six hundred thousand of Israel. And although the rabbis expounded this verse with regard to other matters, there is no difficulty because "there are seventy interpretations in the Torah" (Midrash Be Midbar Rabba 13, 16).

56 This is the way in which Kabbalists offer a pearl [of truth] to their pupils, and if the pupils do not understand the hint, it is explained to them as a jest. For example, a man says that a single egg overthrew sixty villages, because the egg was dropped by a bird in the air onto the villages. The jest is that a man wrote on a piece of paper `sixty villages' and the egg dropped by the

bird erased these words. And heaven forbid that the sages of the Torah should say jocular and useless things of the Torah!

57 But they taught: The chicks are the students of the Mishna, and the eggs are the Bible scholars, or: The chicks are Zeir Anpin, onto which these students hold, whereas the eggs are Malkhut, onto which the scholars hold. He fell [Hebrew root: nun pe lamed] from the same young bird [Hebrew root: nun pe lamed]. This fallen bird is Zeir Anpin, who is called a young bird and fallen off, because the downfall is from Him, just as an egg drops from a bird. For an etrog, which, as it is the same size as an egg, may be likened to an egg, drops down from Him, which is to say that an egg and an etrog are Malkhut. That is why an etrog is egg-size, and it is said concerning an etrog: "On that day I will raise up the tabernacle of David that is fallen" (Amos 9:11), for the etrog has fallen into exile and has to be raised up again. And with it into exile fell sixty queens, who are Ḥesed, Gvurah and Tiferet, Netzaḥ, Hod and Yesod, each one of which includes ten, and they are called volumes [Hebrew root: kaf resh kaf] since they are entailed [Hebrew root: kaf resh kaf] in it. And this word "volumes" is used in the sense of "tie together", as in "How are the portions of the Shema tied together" (Talmud Bavli, Pesaḥim 30, 56a), i.e. joined together without interruption. And here also its meaning is that its six ends are tied together in it, and they are parallel to the sixty tractates, for the Oral Law, which is Malkhut, is divided into sixty tractates, which are parallel to the sixty queens referred to above. And young girls without number — these are: "The virgin's companions in her train" (Psalms 45:15), i.e. the palaces that are in creation, which are Halakhot [legal rulings] that have no reckoning, being in creation.

Commentary

And thus is the secret: a certain bird, i.e. *Zeir Anpin*, laid an egg that threw *Malkhut* into exile, and sixty volumes or villages were erased, for by this act of banishment, her *Ḥesed*, *Gvurah*, *Tiferet*, *Netzaḥ*, *Hod* and *Yesod*, which are called the sixty volumes or villages, were annulled.

58 And that fallen young bird is Ben Yah, i.e. Zeir Anpin, which is within the fifty gates of Binah, i.e. Yud Hei, where the yud (ten) is multiplied by the hei (five). The vav which is Zeir Anpin, is called fallen because it fell after him about whom it is said: "How are you fallen from Heaven, O day-star, son of the morning!" (Isaiah 14:12). This is Malkhut, which is so called because of its two states, for in one state it is black and in the other it is brightly lighted. (cf. above, Bo, 110-115), and Zeir Anpin followed after her when she was in exile, in order to raise her up. And that is why he is called "fallen off, or detached" and it is not written that he fell or falls. He is referred to rather as detached. That is to say, it is not he that falls but Malkhut who falls from heaven to earth. And he has in him yud and vav; i.e. Zeir Anpin includes the yud and vav of the Tetragrammaton, that are Ḥokhmah and Zeir Anpin and he descends through them in order to raise up the two letters hei of the Tetragrammaton, namely Binah and Malkhut, about whom it is said: "And the two of them went..." (Ruth 1:19). It is also written: "You shall surely let go" (Deuteronomy 22:7) [literally: "Letting go you shall let go"]. The first letting go refers to the first Temple, which was destroyed, and corresponds to the first hei. The second letting go refers to the second Temple which was also destroyed, and corresponds to the hei that is that last letter of the Tetragrammaton. The yud and the vav of the Tetragrammaton descend-

ed in order to raise up the two letters hei, as is written: (*216b) "Let the heavens be glad and let the earth rejoice" (Psalms 96:11). The initial letters of the four Hebrew words forming this verse are yud, hei, vav and hei, i.e. the Tetragrammaton, and so the yud and the vav are joined with the two letters hei.

59 Come and see: The sun is seen by day and hidden by night when it gives light to six hundred thousand stars. The Faithful Shepherd is similar. After his departure from the world, he returns in a transmigration and gives light to six hundred thousand souls in Israel, but only if the generation is fittingly adorned. This is the secret of transmigration, concerning which Ecclesiastes said: "One generation passes away and another generation comes, and the earth abides forever" (Ecclesiastes 1:4). One generation passes away and another generation comes — we have learned (Kohelet Rabba) that a generation is at least six hundred thousand. And the earth abides forever — this is the People of Israel, which is Malkhut, concerning which it is written: "And the earth is My footstool" (Isaiah 66:1), "and your seed shall be as the dust of the earth" (Genesis 28:14).

60 And the sages have taught us yet another secret. "One generation passes away and another generation comes." This means that the generation that passes away is the same generation that comes. A cripple goes and a cripple comes; a blind man goes and a blind man comes (cf. Sanhedrin 81a). And the sages further taught that Moses was destined to receive the Torah in the generation of the Flood, but did not receive it then because of the wicked people, as it is written: "for that he also is flesh" (Genesis 6:3). The numerical value of the word "b'shegam" ("for that he also") is the same (345) as that of "Moses". Why is Moses here (in Genesis) called "b'shegam"? In order to keep the matter secret. And Ecclesiastes even removed the "b" from "b'shegam" to conceal it even more, when he said: "I said that also ["shegam"] this is vanity (Ecclesiastes 8:14). "Shegam" here refers to Moses, and Ecclesiastes removed the "b" in order to conceal the matter.

61 And they taught about Jethro: Why is his name called Kenite? (cf. Judges 1:16). Because "he had severed himself from the Kenites" (Judges 3:11), which verse is here interpreted to mean that "Kenite is derived from the name Cain". [See 18 above and Zohar III, Naso] The great luminary, Rabbi Shimon, arose and said: "It is written about Cain, `I have gotten [Kaniti] a man with the help of the Lord' (Genesis 4:1), for she (Eve) saw Jethro through the holy spirit and that his sons would in the future sit in the Chamber of Hewn Stones (where the Sanhedrin used to meet)." This refers to Eve, who saw that Jethro would be a descendent of Cain; who would be amended through Jethro.

62 And so it was with Rabbi [Elazar ben] Pedat (Talmud Bavli, Ta'anit 25a), for whom time was pressured in distress and who had no more than a most meager diet from one Shabbat Eve to the next, like Rabbi Hanina (Talmud Bavli, Berakhot 17b). Why is this, since a heavenly voice had proclaimed: The whole world is fed only because of Hanina, my son, while for him a kab [2.2 liters] of carobs suffices from one Shabbat Eve to the next? (Berakhot 17b).

63 The answer is that he caused this in his first transmigration, when he destroyed, ("Destroy" in Hebrew has the same root as the word "carob") the link between the yud, which is Binah, and the letters kuf [Zeir Anpin] and bet [Malkhut] in "Yabak" [spelled yud bet kuf], and so he was left with only kab [spelled kuf and bet] of carobs (i.e. a meager diet). Yabak (yud bet kuf) are the initial letters of the words yihud [unity], berakhah (blessing) and kedusha (holiness). The letter yud stands for yihud (unity), which is the secret of the name "Ehyeh" ("I am") (Exodus 3:14). Ehyeh is Binah, from which the

emanation comes to the letter bet, standing for berakhah (blessing), which is the secret of the Tetragrammaton [yud, hei, vav and hei], which is Zeir Anpin, also known as kodesh (holiness) in which the letter "kuf", its Kedusha (holiness) is sanctified, i.e. the name Adonai, which is Malkhut.

And Rabbi Pedat caused, in his first transmigration, his kab (kuf bet) to be destroyed. This kab is holiness and blessing without the unity shining upon them. Thus he had only a kab of carobs. So, too, was it with Job, who was the son of a yebama (childless levirate widow), and he was punished because of what had happened to him in the first transmigration.

BEFORE THE GIVING OF THE TORAH THEY DEPENDED ON DESTINY

64 And those who do not know this secret say (in the words of Rava): "Children, life and sustenance is not a matter of one's merit, rather depends on destiny" (Talmud Bavli, Mo-ed Katan, 28a). Take the case of Abraham, who saw that he was not destined to have a son with Sarah, and the Holy One, blessed be He, took him outside, as it is said: "And He took him outside and said: Look..." (Genesis 15:5). And the rabbis taught: Abraham said before the Holy One, blessed be He: "Master of the World, I have looked at my constellations and I am not destined to have a son". And He said to him: "Leave your constellations (i.e. do not consult the stars), for Israel has no constellation [i.e. destiny]. (Talmud Bavli, Shabbat 156a). And He took him up above the stars and said to him: "Look now towards heaven and count the stars" (Genesis 15:5). So much for the words of the rabbis, but they have to be interpreted mystically!

65 Come and see: All creatures in the world, before the Torah was given, were dependent on destiny, even children, life and sustenance. But after the Torah was given to Israel, He removed Israel from the influences of the stars and constellations. This we have learned from Abraham, since his sons

were destined to receive hei from Abraham, that is, the five books of the Torah i.e. Malkhut. As it is said: "These are the generations of heaven and earth when they were created" (Genesis 2:4). B'hibaram [translated as 'when they were created'] can be read as two words: b'hei b'ra'am [meaning 'He created them with a hei]. He said to Abraham "Because of that hei that was added to your name [cf. Genesis 17:5], the heavens below you and all the stars and constellations will be subservient to your will because he raised above him. Moreover, it is said: "Lo [Hebrew hei], here is seed for you and you shall sow the land" (Genesis 47:23). That is, it shall be sown with hei. And from this we have learned that, only after "Abram" was changed to "Abraham", could he procreate Isaac, who was called "seed". "For in Isaac shall seed be called for you" (Genesis 21:12), which is the secret of the left column, from which Malkhut, the secret of hei, is drawn, and the sowing is thus in Malkhut.

66 For this reason, everyone who engages in the Torah is released from the influence of stars and constellations. By 'Torah' here is meant keeping its commandments. If it is not his intention to keep its commandments, then he is as one who does not engage in Torah, and the stars and constellations hold sway over him. This is even more true with respect to the common people, who are likened to animals, about which it has been taught: "Cursed be he who lies with any manner of beast" (Deuteronomy 27:21). The hold of the stars and constellations over them is certainly not annulled.

67 "As for man, his days are as grass: as a flower of the field so he flourishes" (Psalms 103:15). And about man it is said: "I was young and am now old" (Psalms 37:25). And later it is said: "He returns to the days of his youth" (Job 34:25). It is like a tree from which the old branches were cut off, but they grew again from its roots, as at the beginning. For old people die and return in a transmigration to this world as children. And this is the secret of the Holy

One, blessed be He, "renewing the creation every day continually" [Morning service, First introductory paragraph to the Shema]. For a thousand die each day and a thousand are renewed each day, returning in a transmigration to the world.

WINE MAKES GLAD THE HEART OF MAN — THE FIR TREES ARE HER HOUSE

68 "Wine makes glad the heart of man" (Psalms 104:15) This is the wine of the Torah, for the numerical value of the letters of the word yayin [wine] (10 + 10 + 50) is the same as the letters of sod [secret] (60 + 6 + 4). Just as wine has to be kept sealed so that it should not be used in a libation for idol worship, so also must the secret of the Torah be closed up and sealed, and none of its secrets be disclosed other than to those who fear Him. And it is not for nothing that a number of commandments are performed with wine; and blessings to the Holy One, blessed be He, are said. Wine comes in two [the letter bet = 2] colors: white and red, which are Judgement and Mercy. And this is why we have the added bet in b'yayin ["with wine"]. This bet hints at Judgement and Mercy. It is like the rose which has in it both white and red — white from the right side which is Ḥesed, and red from the left side which is Gvurah.

69 Why does it say [in the above mentioned verse] "levav [lamed bet bet] enosh"? ["the heart of man"] when "lev (lamed bet) enosh" [which means "the heart of man"] would be sufficed? The answer is that there is one heart (lev) hidden in another heart (lev), i.e. two hearts, whence the added bet [=2]. The first lev is the 32 (lamed bet, lev) Elohim in the works of creation, and this lev is the secret of Binah. The second lev is composed of the first letter of the Torah, B'reshith ["In the beginning"], and the last letter of the Torah, is lamed because the last letter of Israel is lamed, "in the eyes of all Israel" (Deuteronomy 34:12). And these two letters, the bet at the beginning of the Torah, and the lamed with which it ends come together to form the word lev [spelled lamed bet], i.e. the heart (lev) of Malkhut. This is why it is written levav. For the wine which is the illumination of Ḥokhmah is revealed and gladdens the heart (lev) of Binah and the heart (lev) of Malkhut, from where man receives it. The numerical value of the letters of lev lamed bet is 32, twice which is 64, which is eight less than 72; and 72 is the numerical value of the letters of the word vaykhulu "And [they] were finished" (Genesis 2:1). But shouldn't vaykhulu, which is the secret name of the illumination of Ḥokhmah, be the same as lev lev, whereas there is a difference of 8 between them? The answer is that the seven days of creation themselves, in which lev (lamed bet or 32 Elohims) of God shines, are to be joined to the number 64. But 64 and 7 is only 71, and we are still one short. This additional one comes from "This is the book of the generations of Adam" (Genesis 5:1), which is also considered to be a day of creation. Thus there are 8 days that, added to 64, make 72. And 72 is also the numerical value of the letters of b'yayin ["with wine"], which is the secret of the illumination of Ḥokhmah, as discussed above.

70 What is the meaning of the second part of the verse "Makes the face brighter with oil?" (Psalms 104:15). The faces, or countenances, are 12 in numbers: four of the lion, four of the bull, and four of the eagle: (*217a) There is Michael the lion, who is the secret of Ḥesed. His four faces are the four letters yud hei vav hei of the Tetragrammaton, where the yud and the vav are pointed with the vowel segol ["e"]. Gabriel is the bull, i.e. Gvurah. His four faces are the four letters of the Tetragrammaton, pointed with pataḥ ["a"]. The four faces of the eagle, which is Nuriel, are the four letters of the Tetragrammaton, when the yud is pointed with Ḥirik ("i"), and the vav with shwa [i.e. without a vowel]. They are appointed under the three Sfirot of Zeir Anpin: Ḥesed, Paḥad, Emet, which are Ḥesed, Gvurah, and Tiferet. These

are the steps of the three patriarchs, Abraham, Isaac, and Jacob. The sages have taught (in the words of Resh Lakish): "The patriarchs are God's heavenly chariot" (Midrash Bereshith Rabba 47, 6). The lights of the twelve countenances add up to yud bet kuf, which is the secret of the three names: Melekh (pointed as with Michael), Malakh (pointed as with Gabriel), Yimlokh (pointed as with Nuriel).

For the total numerical value of the letters in these three names — Yud Hei Vav Hei (the Tetragrammaton), Aleph Hei Yud Hei ("I am"), and Aleph Dalet Nun Yud ("The Lord") — is 112, which is the same as yud bet kuf.

C o m m e n t a r y

It is well-known that the unification of *Berakha* and *Kedusha*, which is the secret of *yud bet kuf*, forms the three names: *Aleph Hei Yud Hei* ("I am"), the Tetragrammaton, and *Aleph Dalet Nun Yud* ("the Lord") [as above, section 63]. This is the secret of "The Lord [*Yud Hei Vav Hei*] is king [*Melekh*], the Lord (*Yud Hei Vav Hei*) was king [*Malakh*], the Lord (*Yud Hei Vav Hei*) will be king [*Yimlokh*] for ever and ever." (cf. Morning Service for First Day of Rosh haShanah.)

The first *Yud Hei Vav Hei* has the same vowels as the word *melekh*, i.e. "e-e", and the secret is *ḥesed*, which is the four countenances of the lion, which is the Angel Michael who is appointed to a position below that of Abraham, who is *ḥesed*. As the text says: "There is Michael, the lion, who is the secret of *Ḥesed*. His four faces are *Yud Hei Vav Hei*, (the Tetragrammaton) where both the *yud* and the *vav* are pointed with a *segol* ["e"], i.e. as in the first *yud hei vav hei mem lamed kaf*. And this is the secret of *Berakha*, which is the secret of *Yud Hei Vav Hei*, which is *Zeir Anpin*.

The second *Yud Hei Vav Hei* has the same vowels as the word *malakh*, i.e. "a-a", and the secret is *Gvurah*, which is the four countenances of the bull, the Angel Gabriel who is appointed to a position below that of Isaac, who is *Gvurah*. As the text says: "Gabriel is the bull, i.e. *Gvurah*. His four faces are the four letters of the Tetragrammaton where the *yud* and the *vav* are both pointed with *pataḥ* ["a"]." That is, when they are pointed the same way as in the second *yud hei vav hei mem lamed kaf*. And this is the secret of the name *Aleph Hei Yud Hei* ("I am"), which is *Binah*, since the left column is drawn from the revelation of the left that is in *Binah*. The secret, therefore, is *Yihud* (Unity), for *Binah* unites *Zeir Anpin*, which is the secret of *Berakha* and *Malkhut*, which is the secret of *Kedushah* (See above, 63).

The third *Yud Hei Vav Hei* has the same vowels as *yimlokh*, i.e. "i" silent and "o", with the "i" under the *yud* and the silent vowel under the *vav*, for only the male letters (*yud* and *vav*) are pointed, not the female ones (*hei hei*). And the secret is *Tiferet*, which is the four countenances of the eagle, which is the Angel Nuriel, who is appointed to a position below that of Jacob. As the text says: "The four countenances of the eagle, which is Nuriel, are the four letters of the Tetragrammaton when the *yud* is pointed with a *ḥirik* ["i"] and the *vav* with *shwa* [i.e. it is without a vowel]. That is, the same way as in the *Yud Hei Vav Hei* having the same vowels a *yimlokh*. And this is the secret of *Kedushah*, which is the secret of *Aleph Dalet Nun Yud* (the Lord).

And when the text says: "the numerical value of the letters in those three names is 112, which is *yud beth kuf*", this refers to the secret of the three names: *Aleph Hei Yud Hei* ("I am"), *Yud Hei Vav Hei* (the Tetragrammaton), *Aleph Dalet Nun Yud* ("the Lord") [total value of letters = 112].

71 Rabbi Shimon was sitting and engaging in the study of this portion, when his son, Rabbi Elazar, came to him and asked: "How did it come about that Nadav and Avihu were able to transmigrate into Pinḥas? Had Pinḥas not been in the world when they died, and had only come into the world later, and they were transmigrated in him, and he had perfected their souls, it would have been fine. But Pinḥas was in the world at the time when Nadav and Avihu died, and his soul already existed in him, so how could they have transmigrated into him?""

72 He replied: My son, there is a divine secret here, namely: When Nadav and Avihu left the world, they did not take shelter under the wings of the Holy Rock (the Divine Presence), which is Malkhut. The reason for this is to be found in the verse: "And Nadav and Avihu... had no children" (Numbers 3:4). That is, they decreased the King's image, for they did not perform the mitzvah of being fruitful and multiplying, producing sons in the image of God. (cf. Genesis 1:28 and 27) For this reason they were not fitted to serve in the High Priesthood.

73 When Pinḥas was zealous for the Holy Covenant and went in amongst the crowds and held up the adulterers on sprear-point in the sight of all Israel, he saw the tribe of Shimon coming at him in large numbers, and Pinḥas' soul fled out of him in fear. Then the two souls that were naked, i.e. the souls of Nadav and Avihu, approached the soul of Pinḥas and were joined together with it,

and it then returned to him. His soul, together with the other two, then supported him, and he earned the right to priesthood in place of Nadav and Avihu, for which he had not previously been fit.

74 And about this it is written: "Remember, I pray you: Whoever perished, being innocent?" (Job 4:7). This was said about Pinḥas, who did not perish and did not lose his soul when it fled from him. The same verse continues: "Or where were the upright cut off?" This refers to the sons of Aaron, Nadav and Avihu, who returned to the world by transmigrating into Pinḥas and remedied what they had lost in their lifetime, i.e. the tikune of the covenant. This is why the word ben [the son of] is used twice regarding Pinḥas: "Pinḥas the son of Elazar, the son of Aaron" (Numbers 25:11), teaching us about the two souls that had transmigrated into him, i.e. the sons of Aaron. Thus ben Elazar [the son of Elazar] refers to Pinḥas, and ben Aaron [the son of Aaron] refers to Nadav and Avihu.

75 What does scripture say just before this chapter? — "And the Lord said to Moses: `Take all the chiefs of the people, and hang them up unto the Lord in the face of the sun: (Numbers 25:4). The question can be asked: What about when they are killed at night or on a cloudy day? Scripture warns that they must be killed in the face of the sun. Said Rabbi Yehuda: "In the face of the sun means that just as their sin was in public so must their death be in public."

76 Rabbi Shimon said: "This was not the reason why it said `in the face of the sun', but from this we learn that at whatever level a man sins before the Holy One, blessed be He, he must make amends in his soul at that same level. They sinned in the holy covenant, which is called sun, (which represents Zeir Anpin), and this is why their judgement and their tikune is in the face of the sun (which is the covenant) and not elsewhere. It follows that a man can not remedy the misdeeds he has committed other than in the place where he sinned, and that if he attempts to remedy them elsewhere he will never attain a proper tikune.

77 Rabbi Ḥiyya began: "`The trees of the Lord have their fill, the cedars of Lebanon which He has planted' (Psalms 104:16). And also: `Wine makes glad the heart of man, making the face brighter than oil' (Psalms 104:15). What is the connection between these two matters? We have learnt as follows: `Who causes the grass to spring up for the cattle, and herb for the service of man.' (Psalms 104:14). And did David really come with the holy spirit to speak the praises of cattle that has grass? Of course not! `Cause the grass to grow' refers to the sixty thousand myriads of angel messengers who were created on the second day of Creation. All of them are a burning fire. It is they who are meant by `grass.' Why are they grass? It is because they grow in the world as does grass: one day it is cut short, but then it returns and grows as previously."

78 And this is why the verse says: "Who causes the grass to spring up for the cattle." The secret is that Malkhut in the aspect of yud hei vav hei, filled with the letter hei, has the same numerical value, 52, as the word behemah [cattle].

yud, vav, dalet = 20, hei, hei = 10, vav, vav = 12, hei, hei = 10 = 52

As it is written: "A righteous man knows the soul of his beast" (Proverbs 12:10). `A righteous man' is Yesod; `beast' is Malkhut. And we have learned that a thousand mountains grow for Malkhut each day and each one of the mountains is sixty myriads of angels who are called grass (as above), and Malkhut devours them. (A commentary will be found above, Genesis 1, Hasulam 76.) (cf. Also: Midrash Vayikra Rabba 22, 10.)

79 "And herb for the service of man" (Psalms 104:14). These are the souls of the righteous, for that man, i.e. Zeir Anpin, who is riding on and controlling the beast, i.e.

Malkhut, devours them and takes them into himself. That is to say, the soul of the righteous rise up and are incorporated into Zeir Anpin in the secret of the water of Nukvah i.e. female waters (representing man's meritorious acts) in order to unite Zeir Anpin and Malkhut. Anoit is to their credit that the whole world is fed from that man, who is Zeir Anpin, for they cause his mating with Malkhut, and the food emanates to Malkhut, and Malkhut distributes it to the whole world. As is written: "And upon the likeness of the throne was a likeness as the appearance of a man upon it above: (Ezekiel 1:26). That is why it says "for the service of ha-adam", i.e. "the man", with the definite article — that is, not just any man, but the man, i.e. Zeir Anpin. And this is in order to "bring forth bread from the earth" [blessing before a meal], i.e. to bring forth provisions for the world from the holy earth, which is Malkhut.

80 And "wine" [in the verse] is old wine drawn from above, i.e. the illumination of Ḥokhmah, which is drawn from Binah. "Makes glad the heart of man". "Man" here refers to the secret of that youth (*217b) who attained old age, and later returnes to be a youth as formerly, and he is Metratron, Prince of the World, who says: "I have been young and now am old" (Psalms 37:25), which is in the secret of "hither and thither". When he is in the secret of "hither", to receive wisdom, he is old, and when he is in the secret of "thither", he is young. Scripture therefore says about him: "As for man, his days are as grass" (Psalms 103:15), for he is like grass which is cut and grows again. When he returns to youth, his first three upper Sfirot are cut, but later he returns and reaches old age, i.e. grows again.

81 "Making the face brighter than oil" These are the faces that are called large countenances and small countenances. The completed first three of Zeir Anpin and Nukvah are the large countenances, and the first three of the six ends of Ze'ir and Nukvah are the small countenances. Than oil — i.e.

than the drawing down of the next world, i.e. of Binah, from whom the oil derives, as well as greatness of the divine holy one. "And bread that stays man's heart" (Psalms 104:15), that is that bread upon which the heavens, which is the secret of Netzaḥ and Hod, bestow a blessing. The heavens mill the manna for the food of the righteous in general, which is the secret of Yesod and Malkhut, who are called righteous and righteousness, and who accept the M'N that Netzaḥ and Hod grind for them. Then it is drawn out to a number of hosts who are called "levav enosh" ["the heart of man"]. And everything comes from the divine emanation, from Binah.

82 "The trees of the Lord have their fill" (Psalms 104:15). These are the internal divine trees, i.e. Zeir Anpin and Malkhut, "The cedars of Lebanon which He has planted;" They are Zeir Anpin and Malkhut, who are uprooted. The Holy One, blessed be He, who is the emanating source, planted them in place of Binah.

What is the connection between `the trees of the Lord' and `the cedars of Lebanon'? The `trees of the Lord' refers to the Tree of Life, which is Zeir Anpin, and the tree of knowledge of good and evil (cf. Genesis 2:17), which is Malkhut. `The cedars of Lebanon' are the fifty gates of Binah which He planted in Zeir Anpin and Nukvah, which are called five hundred years, for they are the secret of Binah, Ḥesed, Gvurah, Tiferet, Netzaḥ and Hod in which Ze'ir Anpin and Nukvah rise up and encloth. In terms of Zeir Anpin, whose Sfirot are in tens, they are fifty, while in terms of Binah, whose Sfirot are counted in hundreds, they are five hundred.

83 "Which He has planted, wherein the birds make their nests" (Psalms 104:16-17). In the shadow of Zeir Anpin and Malkhut the souls of the righteous make their nests, and all the hosts of the holy are fed from there. "As for the stork, the fir trees are her house" (Psalms 104:17). The stork [Ḥasidah] is Malkhut, which is the daughter of the patriarch

Abraham, who is called pious [Ḥasid], and who performed deeds of loving-kindness [Ḥesed] for all men. This is why Malkhut is called a stork [Ḥasidah]. "The fir trees are her house." This means that she sits between the arms of the world, which are Ḥesed and Gvurah of Zeir Anpin. These become for her Ḥokhmah and Binah, which are heads [rashim], which is why he says: her house is in the fir trees [b'roshim], that is to say: her house is at the top (b'rashim).

FOR THE WIND PASSES OVER IT AND IT IS NOT (PSALMS 103:16)

84 Rabbi Yossi and Rabbi Abba rose at midnight to engage in Torah. They were still sitting and engaging in Torah, when Rabbi Yossi said: Rabbi Ḥiyya's comment on the verse "As for man, his days are as grass" (Psalms 103:15) is beautiful [see above, 80], but what is taught about the end of the verse: "For the wind passes over it and it is not, and its place knows it no more?" (Psalms 103:16). He replied: It is certainly as follows: "As for man, his days are as grass" is as explained by Rabbi Ḥiyya. "As a flower of the field" — this is the known field, i.e. Malkhut. "So he flourishes" means that he is renewed and returns as formerly (as above, 80).

85 "For the wind passes over it and it is not" This is the heavenly concealed and holy wind [or spirit] which is hidden from all, i.e. the spirit of Binah, which engulfs Metatron and then "is not". And this is the secret of Enokh, about whom Scripture says: "...and he was not, for God took him" (Genesis 5:24). The reference here is to the higher aspect God, i.e. Binah, who is an upper spirit, hidden and concealed. "And its place knows it no more" This is the small spirit of Metatron that is engulfed by the upper spirit of Binah. And what is written further on? [Psalms 103:17]: "But the loving-kindness [Ḥesed] of the Lord is from everlasting to everlasting" That is, the high priest, who is Ḥesed, introduces him into the Holy of Holies and takes him and has him

born as before: "and renews his youth like the eagle" (Psalms 103:5) and he becomes young again.

Commentary

The angels are parts of *Malkhut*, and as *Malkhut* has two states, one in which it receives from *Binah* and in the other from *Zeir Anpin* [see above, *Bo*, 110-115], so also does Metatron have the same two states. In the first state he receives from *Binah*, and then the spirit of understanding [*Binah*] descends upon him, and he is engulfed by it as is a candle flame by a torch "and is not". Subsequently he attains the second state and is reborn from *Malkhut*. During the first state, when he receives from *Binah*, he is considered as old, this being the secret of the first three. In the second state, when he receives from *Zeir Anpin* and *Malkhut*, he is called young, this being the secret of the six lower *Sfirot*. These states are repeated and he is sometimes in the first state and at others in the second. With respect to the statement, "For the wind passes over it and it is not": This is the heavenly spirit, and the meaning is that in the first state he receives from *Binah* and subsequently "is not", and "its place knows it no more" This is because the small spirit is engulfed by the upper spirit, for the small spirit of Metatron is lost in the larger quantity of the upper spirit of *Binah*, as a candle flame in the light of a torch. The question "What is written further on?" refers to his second state, in which a high priest, which is *Ḥesed* of *Zeir Anpin*, introduces him into the *Yesod* [foundation] of *Malkhut*, and he is re-built anew from the aspect of the six lower *Sfirot*. And where he says: "The high priest, who is *Ḥesed* of *Zeir Anpin*, introduces him into the Holy of Holies, into the *Yesod* of *Malkhut*", the meaning is that he is reconstructed as he was prior to his entering the first state. "And he becomes young again" means that he again comes in the aspect of the six lower *Sfirot*.

THE FAITHFUL SHEPHERD

86 Said the Faithful Shepherd: Holy luminary, the commentary [above] of Rabbis Abba, Ḥiyya, and Yossi on the verse "As for man, his days are as grass" is very nice, but what about "The wind passes over it and it is not"? Here matters have to be developed. What "passes [ayin bet resh hei] over it"? It refers to "wrath [ayin bet resh hei] and indignation and trouble" (Psalms 78:49), where it is one of these evil angels, the one called "wrath", and this is the meaning of the verse "The wind passes over it", which should therefore be rendered "The spirit of wrath is on him". And the verse is to be applied to one who dies childless, who transmigrates.

87 In order that the monitors of sins should not recognize him, the childless deceased, it is necessary to perform for him a change of place, a change of name, and a change of action. This is how it was with Abraham, as Scripture tells us. "Get out of your country and from your kin" (Genesis 12:1) is the change of place. "Neither shall your name anymore be called Abram, but your name shall be Abraham" (Ibid, 17:5) is the change of name. And there is also the change of action, for he changed from doing bad deeds, as he had at first, to doing good deeds. A similar thing happens to the spirit of the man who dies childless, for the Holy One, blessed be He, banishes him from that world because he died childless (i.e. change of place), and brings him to this world in a transmigration into the son that is born out of his wife's levirate marriage (i.e. change of name), and this has already been discussed above (49).

88 "Change his countenance and send him away" (Job 14:20). Because He changes His countenance when He banishes him from the heavenly world, it is said: "The wind passes (ayin bet resh hei) over it", which is to be understood as referring to one of the evil angels whose name is "wrath" (ayin bet resh hei). And when He sees that he has altered, when He

meets him, andthe other demons of destruction ask about Him: "Is this your sinner?", He answers them and says: "he is not", for he does not recognize him, and this is the secret of the verse "change his countenance".

89 What is the secret of the verse "and send him away"? When he is banished from his place and implanted elsewhere, i.e. after he has already entered a body in this world, it is said about him: "And its place knows it no more", for "he will take other mortar and plaster the house" (Leviticus 14:42), i.e. he took another body of different dust, for body is termed house. And this is the secret, "And he shall break down the house, its stones and its timbers" (Leviticus 14:45), i.e. those bones, flesh, and sinews that he had previously, returned to the dust. What is written about him? "Dust is the food of the serpent" (Isaiah 65:25), for the dust that is made up of the deceased's body is like a serpent, since it was afflicted by his having used it. And later "he will take other mortar and plaster the house", i.e. build for himself bones and sinews and be renewed, as an old house that is made new, that is which is renovated.

90 What about (*218a) "and its place knows it no more"? This is said about his spirit, for his small spirit is engulfed in the divine spirit.

C o m m e n t a r y

For his small spirit that was faulted because he had no children is now incorporated, by means of transmigration, in the whole spirit of the child born as the result of the levirate marriage of his widow who is fitted to have children. This matter can be likened to a fruit-tree that does not bear fruit. One takes its branches and grafts them onto the branches of another, heavenly, tree that does bear fruit, and the two merge together and both produce fruit. At that point it is said about him "Its place knows it no more", for the one, faulted spirit disappears to the extent that even its place is no longer recognizable.

91 And so it is with a man who lives in a city where bad people dwell, and he is unable to keep the mitzvot [commandments] of the Torah and is not successful with the Torah. He should change his place of residence and move from there, and settle somewhere with good people, sages of the Torah, who keep the mitzvot. This is because the Torah is called a tree, as it is written: "It is a tree of life to those that take hold of it" (Proverbs 3:18). Man, too, is a tree, as it is written: "For the man is the tree of the field" (Deuteronomy 20:19), and the mitzvot of the Torah are like fruits. And what is written about it? "You may destroy and cut down only the trees which you know are not fruit bearing trees" (Deuteronomy 20:20) That is to say, you may destroy it from this world and cut it down from the next world. This is why he has to move from the place where there are evil people and where he can not succeed with the Torah and mitzvot, and implant himself elsewhere, amongst the righteous, where he can succeed with the Torah and mitzvot.

92 As the childless man is called impotent and his wife barren, so also is the Torah when unaccompanied by mitzvot considered barren. On this we have learned: "Not the expounding of the Torah is the chief thing but the doing of it" (Rabban Shimon ben Gamliel in Pirke Avot 1, 18). The companions came and spread themselves out in front of him and said: We have certainly learned something new here — how one spirit can be incorporated in another. We were as someone whose vision was blurred and then became clear. Originally we had only a tradition about these mat-

ters, but now they have been clearly explained.

93 Moreover, we learnt in the First Part that Satan prefers control over the righteous more than anything else, because he can then afford not to consider the rest of the world. While they were still discussing this, a shade came upon them, and asked: How do we know that the devil prefers control over the righteous to control over the whole world? We know this from Job. For the Holy One, blessed be He, saw that generation was deserving of annihilation, and when Satan came to denounce [them], the Holy One, blessed be He, then said to him: "Have you considered My servant, Job, that there is none like him in the whole earth, a wholehearted and upright man...?" (Job 1:8). By drawing Satan's attention to Job, He saved the whole generation. The matter can be likened to a shepherd when a wolf comes to devour his flock and destroy them. Being wise, what does the shepherd do? He gives the wolf a lamb that is stronger, fatter, and larger than the others, the leader of the flock, and the wolf, out of his desire to have control over the lamb, forgets about the rest of the flock. What does the shepherd do next? While the wolf is preoccupied with that lamb, (*218b) he flees with the flock and brings them to safety. Later, he returns to the lamb and saves it from the wolf.

94 This is exactly what the Holy One, blessed be He, did with the generation. He offered the righteous man for indictment in order to save the generation on his account. And if, like Jacob, the righteous man is strong, the verse "And a man wrestled with him" (Genesis 32:25) is also applied to him. This is even more the case when he overcomes the accuser until he says: "Let me go" (Genesis 32:27). Holy Luminary said: O Shade, O Shade, that is just how it is. Happy is the portion of that righteous man who is strong in suffering afflictions, and how much more so the one who, by means of his afflictions, manages to overcome his accuser who has spread his control over the whole generation,

and it is accounted to him as though he (the righteous man) had saved them, and the Holy One, blessed be He, appoints him as shepherd over them in the place of the accuser.

This was how the Faithful Shepherd came to be the shepherd over Israel, and not only that, but he will control them in the next world. And this was because he saved them that they should not be lost to the next world, for he guided them in the Torah and good deeds.

95 While they were yet talking, the Faithful Shepherd himself came and said to them: And why was the right arm afflicted, when the way of all doctors is to let blood initially from the right arm? Since the left arm is the one that is nearer the heart, why is blood not let from it? Or, to put the question in other words: Why is it that one righteous man is afflicted and another is not? He answered: Because the Holy One, blessed be He, does not want overly to strike, and one righteous man suffices. But if the illness is serious and spreads throughout the parts of the body, blood is let from the left arm also, i.e. other righteous men are also afflicted.

96 He said to him: If the two of them were not afflicted at the same time, that would be fine, but what about the case of the two righteous men, one of whom suffers from diseases and troubles, while the other is treated with kindness? Why is it that if the disease, i.e. the sins of the generation, spread, blood is not let from both of them, i.e. both the righteous persons, who are the two arms, so that healing may be given to all parts of the body, i.e. the whole of the generation. And in the case where the illness does not become more serious, and does not spread throughout the parts of the body, why is more blood let from the right arm than from the left? Why is one righteous man made to suffer and not the other? He said to him: Why don't you give the answer?

97 He said to him: Certainly the body and the two arms stand for the three patriarchs and the head for Adam haRishon [the Biblical Adam]. The right arm is Abraham, the left Isaac, while the body represents Jacob. Within the body, the liver is on the right, the spleen to the left, these being the two Klippot of Esau and Ismael. The heart is Jacob, between them. The lungs and kidneys represent Abraham and Isaac, the lung being water, hinting at Ḥesed, for it draws in all sorts of potion, while the kidneys are fire, which cooks the seed that descends from the brain.

Commentary

Every generation has in it the full stature of Man, paralleling the spiritual stature on high, and he considers the leaders of the generation as being a continuation from *Adam haRishon*, the secret of whom is the three first *Sfirot.* Other righteous men are a continuation from the patriarchs. Some are from Abraham, who is *Ḥesed*, termed the right arm, and, within the body, the secret of the lung. Others are from Isaac, which is the secret of *Gvurah*, termed the left arm, and, within the body, the secret of the kidneys. Yet others are from Jacob, which is the secret of the body including the two arms, and, within the body, the secret of the heart. Esau is the secret of the liver which is all blood, and the spleen stands for Ishmael, for they are the heads of the nations on the right and on the left. An explanation follows as to the change of order and why Esau is on the right and Ishmael on the left.

98 And since Abraham is water, i.e. Ḥesed, if, therefore, his offspring impairs Ḥesed, he places his off-

spring in the exile of Edom, which is the waste matter of Gvurah from the left, and there they receive their punishment: because of them being the opposite of their nature. This is why the liver, and the gall that is in the liver, are to the right of Abraham, i.e. to the right of the body, his sword, i.e. the Malkhut of the klippah of Esau being the gall. (*219a) About this it is said: "But her end is bitter [= marah, which is also means `gall'] as wormwood" (Proverbs 5:4). And if the sins become greater in number amongst the sons of Abraham, i.e. amongst those who extend from the side of Ḥesed, who are in the exile of Edom, and the disease spreads over them from the side of the liver, they have to be smitten and blood has to be let from the right arm, i.e. from those righteous who come from the side of Ḥesed, and not from those of the side of Gvurah, for the fault is in those of the side of Ḥesed; and "whoever has his money taken is as though his blood were spilled" (cf. Midrash Leviticus Rabba 22, 6), for he remains poor, and a poor man is considered as dead. (cf. Talmud Bavli, Nedarim 64b: "Four are considered as dead: the poor man, the leper, the blind man and the childless man").

99 But if the sins become greater in number amongst the sons of Isaac, i.e. those who descend from him impair the degree of Gvurah, which is the secret of Isaac, they are then put into exile amongst Ishmael, which is the klippah of the right, which is the opposite of the nature of the children of Isaac, in order to increase their punishment. The disease spreads from the side of the spleen, which is to the left of the body and controls the children of Isaac who impaired the nature of the left, and blood has therefore to be let from the left arm, that is to say, from those righteous who come from the side of Gvurah, and not from any others. This is because the impaired here are those who come not from Abraham, the right arm, but from Isaac, the left arm.

100 And if sins become

greater in number amongst the children of Jacob, i.e. those who descend from him impair his nature, which includes both sides, Ḥesed and Gvurah, who are scattered in exile amongst the children of Esau and Ishmael, i.e. in the klippot of the right and of the left, then the disease spreads over the body, which is the aspect of Jacob, and blood has to be let from both arms. But if all three of them, i.e. those from Jacob, from Isaac, and from Abraham, are diseased together, i.e. all of them have discredited their own roots, the disease then rises to the head, and blood has to be let from the veins that are in the head. And these three types of righteous, those descended from Abraham, Isaac, and Jacob, become a chariot for Adam haRishon and the patriarchs, and acquire from them strength to suffer torments and protect the generation throughout the world.

101 Woe to that generation that causes the patriarchs and Adam haRishon to be struck, for this includes also the righteous men amongst them (in that generation), for there is no difference between Adam haRishon and the righteous of a generation and the patriarchs. This is because the righteous are the souls of the patriarchs and of Adam haRishon, and their distress, pain, and anguish reach to the patriarchs and Adam haRishon. It is like the sea: when a number of rivers flow out of it and return to it, impure and dirty, and the sea extracts their impurity and dirt. And because of the sea's strength, for it is strong, it does not suffer from their dirt, but throws it out, and the rivers remain clear and pure, without dirt.

102 It can also be likened to a mother who cleans the dirt from her small children. In such a manner the patriarchs cleanse the sins and the dirt from their children, Israel, when there are amongst them people of righteous deeds who are strong enough to suffer torments for the sake of the generation. At that time there is no difference between them, i.e. between the patriarchs, for they cleanse the sins of the generation like fathers. They all came and greeted him (the Faithful Shepherd), and said to him: Sinai, Sinai, through whose mouth the Holy One, blessed be He, and his Divine Presence speak, who is able to confront him in any matter? Happy is our portion that we have merited hearing new matters in this First Part through you, so that the Shekhinah may give light in the exile.

103 He said to them: Rabbis of every generation, those who have been or will be, and how much more so the Holy Luminary, that is, Rabbi Shimon, whose wisdom will shine in all the generations that come after him: do not give the Holy One, blessed be He, quiet in the Torah, until the Holy Spirit is poured out on us. (There appears to be an omission in the text here). For none but you may use Metatron Sar Hapanim since your name is intimated in the initials of his, for the initial letters of the words Metatron Sar Hapanim are Mem shin hei, which spell Mosheh (Moses).

THE PATIENT'S PULSE IN THE EXILE OF EDOM

104 And now there is need of a doctor to know by how much the pulse of the patient, Israel, has increased in the exile of Edom, for it is said about him "that I am love-sick" (Song of Songs 5:8). For a number of doctors gathered over him to consider the pulse rate in order to know when his illness would come to an end, but not one of them could understand them, for no doctor is competent to read the pulse beats of this particular patient, for there are beats of kuf shin resh kuf, kuf shin kuf, kuf resh kuf, as the prophet said about them: "Like as a woman with child, whose time of delivery draws near, is in pain and cries out in her pangs" (Isaiah 26:17).

105 And all the ten shofar calls, which are kuf shin resh kuf, kuf shin kuf, kuf resh kuf [where kuf = teki'ah, shin = shevarim, resh = teru'ah, these being the different sounds made on the shofar in the Rosh haShanah Mussaf Service, in three groupings in the order given here — tr.], are included in the three, for which there is a mnemonic, namely kuf shin resh, which are teki'ah, shevarim, teru'ah, for these are the only three sounds that there are. The teki'ah [one long continuous note — tr.] stands for the length of the exile. The shevarim [three medium length notes — tr.] teaches about the proximity of the exile, and the teru'ah [series of nine staccato notes — tr.] about the coming redemption, for the sounds of the teru'ah teach about duress after duress with no respite between them. And clearly, since the other nations make Israel's exile more difficult, it is the duress that they exert that brings the redemption closer. And so it is, too, in our case of the patient's pulse beat: as the beats come faster, one on the other,

with no space between them, the man's soul leaves him.

106 kuf shin resh kuf, kuf shin kuf, kuf resh kuf, which are the secret of the exile's beats, as above, make the mnemonic kuf shin resh, that is teki'ah, shevarim, teru'ah, by which falsehood [Hebrew: sheker, shin kuf resh, i.e. the same three letters as in the mnemonic] is removed from the world. Concerning this was the oath: (*219b) "The Lord will have war with Amalek from generation to generation" (Exodus 17:16), for the redemption will come by the beats hinted at in kuf shin resh kuf, kuf shin kuf, kuf resh kuf. And then a simple, double, triple and quadruple song will arise in the world, where the letters of the Tetragrammaton will ascend and join together. First will come yud, then yud hei, then yud hei vav and then yud hei vav and hei, where yud is the simple song, yud hei double, yud hei vav is triple and yud hei vav and hei is quadruple, and their numerical value together totals 72. At the time of the redemption this '72' name will awaken. At that time the prayer will be answered: "And therefore the righteous shall see and be glad, the upright exult and the pious rejoice in song" (Addition to the third blessing of the Amidah on Rosh haShanah and Yom Kippur). The word here translated "therefore" is in Hebrew Uvkhen, the numerical value of whose letters is 78, i.e. 72 with the addition of 6, which is the value of the letter vav. This added vav refers to the sixth thousand [of years since the Creation — tr.]. The Second Temple was destroyed 172 years before the previous thousand, in the year 3829 [As is stated in Talmud Bavli, Avodah Zara 9a].

107 While they were still sitting, they saw a shade standing over them that came and went, hither and thither in the house. They were astonished. Said Rabbi Abba: Yossi, my son, I shall tell you what happened with me when I was with the Holy Luminary, that is Rabbi Shimon, one day when we were walking in the Valley

of Ono, and engaging in Torah the whole of that day, and because of the intensity of the sun's heat, we sat in a niche under a rock.

108 I asked him to explain to me why it is that, whenever the number of wicked in the world increases and Judgement rests on the world, the righteous amongst them are smitten on their account? For this is what we have learnt about the sins of the generations: that is the holy and righteous who are caught. [cf. Talmud Bavli, Shabbat Shabbat 33b]. Why should this be so?!? Could it be because they (the righteous) do not admonish the world (i.e. the wicked) about their deeds? For there are many who do admonish, however they (the wicked) will not accept it from them (the righteous) and the latter give in to the former because they do not listen to them. Is this why they are caught for the sin of the generation? Or maybe it is because the world has no protector and the righteous are caught and die so that the wicked can exist on their (the righteous') merit? And I asked him: Were the righteous not to die and not to be caught for the sins of the wicked, but if the wicked were to perish, then would not this be a cause of joy for the righteous that the wicked should perish? [cf. "And when the wicked perish, there is joy" (Proverbs 11:10).]

109 He said to me: The righteous are certainly caught for the sins of the generation, and we have already discussed these matters. But when the righteous are caught with diseases and pestilences, it is in order to atone for the sins of the world, for then atonement is effected for the sins of the generation, since the side of Kedushah is thereby uplifted and the devil surrenders. How do we know about this? — We learn it from all the parts of the body, for when all parts of the body are in trouble and a serious illness prevails in them, one limb has to be whipped so that all of them should be healthy. And which is the limb that is to be flogged? It is of course the arm, from which blood is let, and

then all parts of the body regain health.

110 And so it is that all mortals are parts of the one body. When the Holy One, blessed be He, wishes to grant healing to the world, He inflicts diseases and pestilences on one righteous man from amongst them, and, for his sake, gives healing to everyone. Where do we learn this from? From the verse: "And he was wounded because of our transgressions; he was crushed because of our iniquities; (the chastisement of our welfare was upon him); and with his stripes we were healed" (Isaiah 53:5). "And with his stripes": this refers to the letting of blood, as one who lets blood from the arm, for in that stripe (the puncturing of the skin for the letting) "we are healed", that is to say, we, the parts of the whole body, find healing.

111 And He never smites the righteous man unless it is in order to grant healing to the generation and to make atonement for their sins, for the devil prefers more than anything else that Judgement should have control over the righteous, for he does not then consider the rest of the world important and he doesn't watch over them because of his great joy that he has control over the righteous; and the righteous person who suffers because of the generation merits heavenly rule, in this world and in the next world. And where there is a righteous man and things go well for him, the explanation is that the Holy One, blessed be He, is not concerned to make atonement for the world.

112 I said to him: But what is the situation when there are two righteous men, where one of them is righteous and things do not go well for him, while the other is righteous and things go well for him? If they do not live at the same time, then what you have said makes sense that is, that: the righteous man for whom things go well lives at a time when the Holy One, blessed be He, is not concerned to make atonement for the world, while the righteous man for whom things do not go well lives at a time when the Holy One, blessed be He, is concerned to make atonement for the world. But what about the case where there are two righteous men, both living at the same time, and the one suffers from diseases and pestilences while the other enjoys all the good things of the world? He said to me: One, or possibly two, righteous are sufficient for the atonement of the generation, for the Holy One, blessed be He, does not need to smite all of them, just as it is unnecessary to smite and draw blood from more than one arm in order to grant health to all parts of the body. Similarly, one righteous man suffices.

113 But if the illness strikes all parts of the body, it is then necessary to let blood from both of the arms. So also in our case. If the number of serious sins in the world increases, then all the righteous have to be smitten in order to grant healing to the whole generation. But when they (the sins) are not so many, then only one righteous man is smitten, and the other righteous live in peace, for the world is not such that all of them need to be smitten. And if the people is healed, the righteous are also healed, but it sometimes happens that the righteous are inflicted with diseases throughout their lives in order to protect the generation, at a time when the sins are more serious. When the righteous die, then everything is healed, and atonement is made.

NONE OF THE NATIONS SWAY EXCEPT ISRAEL

114 We got up and continued on our way. The intensity of the sun's heat was very great and made it difficult for us to continue. Then we saw some trees in the wilderness with water under them. We sat down in the shade of one of the trees in the wilderness, and I asked him, Rabbi Shimon: Can you explain to me why it is that of all the nations of the world the only one that goes in for swaying is Israel, for when Jews engage in Torah they sway back and forth? And this is not something that they learnt from anyone else, but they just can not stand still.

115 He said to me: You have reminded me of a heavenly matter, and people do not know and do not pay attention. He sat down for a while and cried. Then he said: Woe to people who go around like the beasts of the field, without understanding. In this matter alone are the holy souls of Israel distinguished from the souls of the other peoples, worshippers of idols. The souls of Israel are derived from the holy burning light, which is Malkhut, as it is written: "The spirit of man is the lamp of the Lord" (Proverbs 20:27). And when this lamp is kindled from the divine Torah, which is Zeir Anpin, its light does not repose for even a moment, and this is the secret of the verse: "O God, keep not silent" (Psalms 83:2), which is written about Malkhut. And something similar is written about the souls: "Those who make mention of the Lord, keep you not silent" (Isaiah 62:6), i.e. you have no respite. Once the light of the lamp has taken hold of the wick, the light will never rest.

116 This is how it is with Israel, too, for the souls of the Jewish people are of the light of the lamp which is Malkhut. Once he has raised one Torah subject, the light begins to burn, and they are unable to obtain respite. This is why they sway hither and thither and from side to side, just as the flame of the lamp flickers, for it is written: "The spirit of man is the lamp of the Lord" (Proverbs 20:27).

117 And it is written: "You are men" (Ezekiel 34:31). This means that you, and not the nations of the world, are called men. The souls of the idol worshipping peoples are of extinguished straw, with no light resting on them. This is why they are reposed and do not sway, for they have no Torah by which to be enflamed and no light rests on them. This is why they stand like trees in a blaze, burning without a light resting on them, and so they are reposed without any light at all. Said Rabbi Yossi: So this is the explanation of the matter. Happy is my lot that I have merited hearing this matter.

ISRAEL REJOICES IN THEIR MAKER

118 Arise Rabbi Abba to expound new matters in the Torah, as you said in the First Part. Rabbi Abba began: "Sing unto the Lord a new song, and his praise from the end of the earth" (Isaiah 42:10). How beloved are Israel before the Holy One, blessed be He, for their rejoicing and their praises are only in Him! For so we have learnt that any rejoicing of Israel in which they do not involve the Holy One, blessed be He, is no rejoicing. And in the future Samael and all his band will denounce that rejoicing, and Israel will be left with sorrow and weeping, and the Holy One, blessed be He, will not be a party in that sorrow.

119 But whoever involves the Holy One, blessed be He, and his Divine Presence in his rejoicing, if the accuser should come to denounce that rejoicing, the Holy One, blessed be He, and His Divine Presence participate in the sorrow that results. For does not Scripture say: "In all their affliction, He was afflicted" (Isaiah 63:9)? And how is this? It is as the verse says: "I will be with him in trouble." (Psalms 91:15).

120 And how do we know that Israel has to involve the Holy One, blessed be He, and His Divine Presence, in their rejoicing? It is as is written: "Let Israel rejoice in their Maker" (Psalms 149:2), the meaning of which is that Israel has no rejoicing that is not in their Maker. There is a question to be asked here. Why is the Hebrew text [here translated `Maker'] "Osav" [literally: "Makers"] when it should be "Oso" [literally: "Maker"]? The answer is that this refers to the Holy One, blessed be He, and His Divine Presence, and a person's father and his mother, for, even if the latter (the father and mother) be dead, the Holy One, blessed be He, uproots them from the Garden of Eden and brings them with Him to that rejoicing, so that they can participate in the rejoicing with the Holy One, blessed be He and His Divine Presence. And the meaning of "Osav" here is as in the verse: "He only that made him can make His sword to

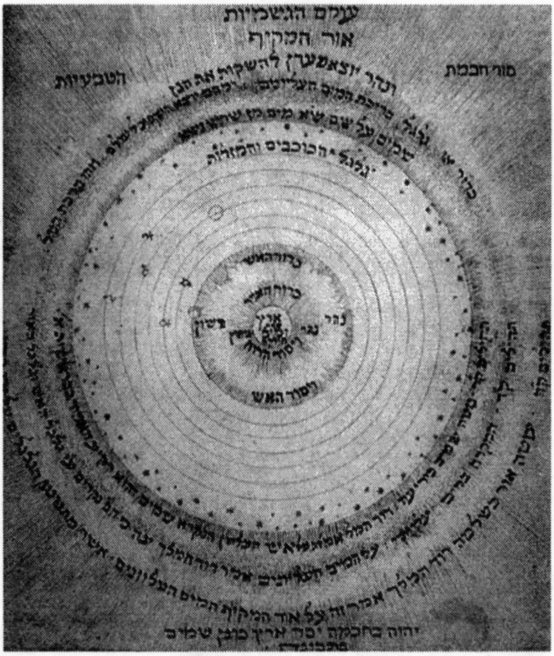

approach unto him" (Job 40:19).

THREE CRAFTSMEN: HEAVEN AND EARTH AND water

121 An alternative explanation of "Makers" [in the plural] is that it refers to the Holy One, blessed be He, the person's father and his mother, since man is made in partnership between man, his wife, and the Holy One, blessed be He [cf. Talmud Bavli, Kiddushin 30b]. And in this secret it is written: "Let us make man" (Genesis 1:26), "us", being in the plural, implying a partnership with his father and his mother. For we have learnt that the Holy One, blessed be He, made three craftsmen with whom to produce the world, namely: the heaven, the earth and the water, and each one of them served for one day, and then later each served for a second day, as previously.

122 On the first day the heaven produced its craft, as it is written: "And God said: Let there be light, and there was light" (Genesis 1:3). On the second day the waters gave of their craft, as it is written: "And God said: Let there be a firmament in the midst of the waters, and let it divide the waters from the waters" (Genesis 1:6), where half the waters ascended on high and half remained below; and had the waters not divided there would have been no world. On the third say the earth did as it was commanded, as it is written: "Let the earth put forth grass, etc." (Genesis 1:11). And the next verse says that indeed "the earth brought forth grass" (Genesis 1:12).

123 So far each of the three craftsman had produced of its craft and they had done what they had been commanded to do. Three other acts remained in the Act of Creation. On the fourth day, the first craftsman, the heaven, was commanded to do its craft, as it is written: "And God said: Let there be lights in the firmament of the heaven..." (Genesis 1:14), an so we have the skies. On the fifth day it was again the turn of the second craftsman, the waters, as it is written: "And God said: Let the waters swarm..." (Genesis 1:20). On the sixth day the earth again produced its craft, as it is written: "And God said: Let the earth bring forth a living creature..." (Genesis 1:24).

124 These three craftsmen having finished their tasks, the Holy One, blessed be He, said to them: I have one more creation to make, namely Man. Join yourselves together and let us, I with you, make Man. The body shall be made by you, but I will be a partner with you by giving the soul, and we shall make Man. And just as formerly the three craftsmen worked in a partnership in the Act of Creation, so also was it subsequently with the creation of Man.

There is the father, with whom He made the works of the heavens and the works of the waters, from whom comes the whiteness that is in man; and the mother, who is the third craftsman, like the earth, from whom comes the redness in a newlyborn child. And then there is the Holy One, blessed be He, who participated with them, from whom comes the soul. And in respect of this secret, the text has Osav ("Makers") rather than Oso ("Maker") [see above 121] in reference to the Holy One, blessed be He, a person's father and his mother.

125 And even though his father and his mother might have departed from this world, a man rejoices with all the three partners in his making, as we have learned: When a man involves the Holy One, blessed be He, in his rejoicing, the Holy One, blessed be He, comes to the Garden of Eden, and takes his father and mother from there, for they are partners with Him, and brings them with Him to that rejoicing, and all of them are there together but mortal men do not know it. When, on the other hand, a man is in trouble, the Holy One,blessed be He, is there with him alone, and He does not inform his father and mother, as it is written: "In my distress I called upon the Lord, and cried unto my God" (Psalms 18:7).

THE FAITHFUL SHEPHERD

THREE PARTNERS: THE HOLY ONE, BLESSED BE HE, A MAN'S FATHER AND HIS MOTHER

126 Said the Holy One, blessed be He: I and My Divine Presence are the partners in the soul, a person's father and mother are the partners in the body, for his father injects the whiteness in the newlyborn child, i.e. the white of the eyes, bones, sinews, and brain, and the woman supplies the black of the eyes, hair, flesh, and skin. The heavens, the earth, and all their host also participate in man's creation. The angels, too, take part, for from them come the good inclination and the evil inclination, that man should be portrayed in both of them. The part of the sun and the moon is to give him light by day and by night, and even the beasts, cattle, birds, and fish participate in man, for he makes a living from them, and the same is the case with the trees and the seed of the earth.

127 What does the Holy One, blessed be He, do? He uproots Israel's father and mother from the Garden of Eden and brings them with Him so that they should be (*220a) with Him at the rejoicing of their children. And so it is at the time of the Redemption, for there is no rejoicing like that of the Redemption, about which it is written: "Let the heavens be glad and let the earth rejoice, and let them say among the nations: The Lord reigns... Then shall the trees of the

wood sing for joy before the Lord, for He is come to judge the earth" (First Chronicles 16:31, 33), for then the Holy One, blessed be He, brings the fathers and mothers of Israel to be at their rejoicing.

BEHOLD I GIVE TO HIM MY COVENANT OF PEACE

128 The same shade returned as previously [see above, 107] and walked around the house in the likeness of a man. Rabbi Abba fell on his face. Said Rabbi Yossi: I recall that in this spot I saw Rabbi Pinḥas Ben Yair. One day he was standing on this spot and asked as follows: In the verse "Pinḥas the son of Elazar the son of Aaron the priest" (Numbers 25:11), why is "Pinḥas" written "Piynhas" with the addition of the small letter yud. [See above 35d, for a fuller explanation.]

129 The answer is because there are two sets of recorded alphabets, one alphabet of larger letters and one of small. And this is to be clarified further as follows: the large letters belong to the next world and are in the aspect of Binah, which is called the next world, while the small letters belong to this world and are in the aspect of Malkhut, which is called this world. Here lies the reason for the small letter yud, which is a letter of the holy covenant, i.e. Malkhut. Since Pinḥas was zealous for this covenant, a small yud was added to him, which is the secret of this covenant, i.e. Malkhut.

130 At the same time, the Holy One, blessed be He, said: What can I do with Moses, for this covenant came from Moses, and the bride, who is Malkhut, is his. It is not nice to give her, Malkhut, to another, unless Moses knows about it and desires it. It just is not nice. The Holy One, blessed be He, started by saying to Moses: Moses, "Pinḥas the son of Elazar the son of Aaron the priest..." Moses interrupted Him and asked: Master of the Universe, what is all this about? The Holy One, blessed be He, answered him: You are the one who has given his soul for Israel a number of times so that they should not disappear from the world,

while he, Pinḥas, "has turned My wrath away from the Children of Israel" (Numbers 25:11). Said Moses: What do You want of me? Is not everything Yours? And if You want to cause Malkhut to rest on him (Pinḥas), who can tell You what You should do?

131 Said the Holy One, blessed be He, to Moses: Since it is all yours, you tell Pinḥas that My Divine Presence will rest within him. Said Moses: In all sincerity, let Malkhut be with him. Said the Holy One, blessed be He, to Moses: You tell him yourself, and in a loud voice, that you are handing the Shekhinah over to him, willingly and sincerely. Thus the verse (Numbers 25:12): "Wherefore say" — you say it willingly — "Behold I give to him My covenant of peace." Moses started to say: "Behold I give..." as though he were talking just to the Holy One, blessed be He. What should have been said was: "Wherefore say to him, behold I give him My covenant of peace", but not this is written but "Wherefore say" without "to him", the meaning being that Moses was commanded to say it. Should you suggest that the Shekhinah was taken away from Moses and given to Pinḥas, you would be wrong, for it is like a candle that is used to light something else. The one gains the benefit of the light, while the other is no poorer.

132 The same shade came, sat down, and kissed him. They heard a certain voice saying: Make room, make room for Rabbi Pinḥas ben Yair, for he is amongst you. As we have learned: in every place where a righteous man made a new interpretation of a matter in the Torah while he was in this world, he comes (from the next world) and visits that place. And this is even more likely when there are other righteous men in that place, deriving new interpretations and speaking about the Torah. And so it was that Rabbi Pinḥas ben Yair came to visit his place and found there a number of righteous men revealing new interpretations of the Torah, and that matter was renewed as previously before Rabbi Pinḥas ben

Yair. In other words, that same Torah matter that Rabbi Pinḥas had spoken of [above, 131] was re-established when you mentioned it in his name.

133 Rabbi Abba said: This interpretation of Rabbi Pinḥas ben Yair is very nice, for it is indeed not written: "Wherefore I give", but "Wherefore say: Behold I give to him", meaning that Moses was commanded to say to him, as noted above. And just to think that this matter was hidden with you from that pious man, and you said nothing until now. Happy is our portion that we were privileged to be here with the help of the holy shade.

WHATEVER YOUR HAND IS ABLE TO DO WITH YOUR OWN STRENGTH, THAT DO (ECCLESIASTES 9:10)

134 Then he began and said in the name of Rabbi Pinḥas: "Whatever your hand is able to do with your own strength, that do" (Ecclesiastes 9:10). How good it is for a man to try to fulfill the will of his master while the flame is yet burning and resting on his head. For the light of that flame is koaḥ (power) resting upon him, and so is it written: "And now, I pray, let the power [koaḥ] of the Lord be great" (Numbers 14:17). The power of the Lord — this is the power [koaḥ] that rests on the head of the righteous and of all those who willingly undertake the will of their master, which is the Shekhinah. And about this we have already learned: "Whoever responds with all his power: 'Amen. May His great name be blessed...' [Response in the Kaddish prayer — tr.] — his judgement of 70 years is torn up" (above, Vayikra, 337, and cf. Talmud Bavli, Shabbat 119b).

135 He surely has to awaken all his parts with great power [koaḥ] in the worship of the Holy One, blessed be He, for by means of this powerful awakening that he summons up, he also awakens that holy and divine power [koaḥ] which is Malkhut, and he is uplifted in holiness and shatters the power and hold of the devil, and about this it is written: "Whatever your hand is able to do with your own strength, that do" (Ecclesiastes 9:10), for it is with your own strength (*220b) that you have to perform the will of your master.

136 "For there is not deed, nor device, nor knowledge, nor wisdom in the grave [Sheol] to which you are going" (Ecclesiastes 9:10). For it is in this power [koaḥ], that there is deed; i.e. the effort to engage in Torah in this world is called 'deed', i.e. the world of action, to complement the end of the thought. 'Device' refers to the world that depends on speech, i.e. Malkhut, which is called speech, for device depends on speech, and this is why all the numerology and the solstices and equinoxes of the world are in the moon, which is Malkhut. 'Nor Knowledge' refers to the secret of the six ends, which is Zeir Anpin, which are dependent on thought, and are called to the world of that thought which is Binah. 'Nor Wisdom' refers to Ḥokhmah, on which everything is dependent, as it is said: "In wisdom [Ḥokhmah] have You made them all" (Psalms 104:24).

137 And all of them, the deed, device, knowledge, and wisdom, are included in that same power [koaḥ] which is the Shekhinah that rests on the head of the righteous. This is not the case on the side of Sheol, which is a step of Gehenna. For the end of everyone who does not try with this koaḥ to enter with it into deed, device, knowledge, and wisdom in this world will be in the grave [Sheol], where there is no deed, nor device, nor knowledge, nor wisdom, for the devil is the way to Sheol, as it is written: "Her house is the way to the netherworld" [Sheol] (Proverbs 7:27). Whoever becomes listless in that holy koaḥ is attacked by the devil, whose house is Sheol.

138 which you are going". Do, indeed, all men go there? The answer to this is in the affirmative, but the righteous rise up again immediately, as it is written: "He brings down to the grave and brings up" (I Samuel 2:6). This verse, however, is not to be applied to the wicked who never for a moment considered repentance, for

they go down to Sheol and do not ascend again. Even the completely righteous go down there. Why should this be? It is because they take from there a number of wicked and bring them up from there. Who are the ones that they bring up? They who considered repentance in this world, but were unable for they left the world (i.e. died). And it is for these wicked people that the righteous go down to Sheol and take them and bring them up from there.

YOUR EYES ARE AS THE POOLS IN ḤESHBON (SONG OF SONGS 7:5)

139 Said Rabbi Yossi: It is written: "Adding one thing to another to find out the account" (Ecclesiastes 7:27), and he asked: the account of the numerical values of letters is in the moon, which is Malkhut, but in which of her levels (is it located)? He did not answer, but said: I have heard this matter, but do not remember it. The same shade arose and kicked Rabbi Abba in the eyes. He fell on his face out of fear, and while he was still lying there, a verse came to him, as it is written: "Your eyes are as the pools in Ḥeshbon [a place name, meaning 'account'] by the gate of Bath-rabbim" [literally: "daughter of the many"] (Song of Songs 7:5).

The eyes refers to Malkhut, i.e. its Ḥokhmah which is called eyes, and they are appetizers, i.e. delicacies to the divine Ḥokhmah which is drawn from above, from Binah, and her eyes are filled by Ḥeshbon and solstices and equinoxes and become pools flowing out from the right in all directions until they are counted in every account and intercalation of the moon from the outside, i.e. of the external spheres — Malkhut, the stars and the constellations — in order to make an account. And this is "by the gate of Bath-rabbim", which is the moon, which is Malkhut, from the outside.

C o m m e n t a r y

Ḥokhmah (wisdom) is termed Ḥeshbon (account), meaning numerological calculations, [see above, *Pikudei*, 28], and Rabbi

Yossi's question is: At what level of *Malkhut* does the account become visible? As the text says, the account of the numerical value of the letters is in the moon, but in which of her levels or steps? It is known that *Malkhut* has two states. In the one she receives from the left of *Binah*, without the right, and she has *Ḥokhmah* without *Ḥasadim*. In these circumstances, *Ḥokhmah* can not illuminate at all, since it is without *Ḥasadim*, and for this reason returns the intercalation of the moon to *Binah*, to the secret of father and mother, and then "And the Lord God made the rib, which He had taken from the man, into a woman, and brought her to the man" (Genesis 2:22). She is then built from the aspect of the right, which is the secret of *Ḥasadim*, but she is then again not fitted to receive *Ḥokhmah* from the left (See above *Bereshit Aleph*, 110-115). However, since she still has the implements of the first stage, the secret being the implements of her rear and external spheres, *Ḥokhmah* can be revealed in those rear and external implements [see above *Vayakhel* 53] in such a way that the internal aspect of *Malkhut*, that is the construction of the second stage which it received by intercalation, they are the building of *Ḥasadim*. However, since the first state was not able to exist previously because of the lack of *Ḥasadim*, now, since *Malkhut* has received a multiplicity of *Ḥasadim* in the second state, *Ḥokhmah*, which was in the implements of the first state, awakes and puts on those *Ḥasadim*, and they illuminate through her.

Regarding the statement in the text: "And these are her eyes that flutter in the direction of the divine *Ḥokhmah*": the eyes of *Nukvah* were restored in the second state to be delicacies for the divine *Ḥokhmah*. (By the cycles and accounts, which is the secret of *Ḥokhmah* which is drawn to *Malkhut* in the first state.) And intercalations: this is the secret of the construction of *Ḥasadim* and the inner implements that are drawn to her by intercalation in father and mother in the secret of the verse: "And the Lord God made the rib, which He had taken from the man, into a woman" (Genesis 2:22).

"Are filled and become pools flowing out from the right": The eyes filled up and became pools of the lights of *Ḥasadim* that flow out from the right of *Binah* and *Zeir Anpin*. And from these eyes comes forth the emanation in all directions, i.e. both to *Ḥokhmah* and to *Ḥasadim*.

"Until they are counted in every account and intercalation of the moon from the outside": until the emanation is revealed in the implements of the external *Malkhut*, which is the secret of the implements of the first state, and there are received *Ḥokhmah* from the side of Ḥeshbon, and *Ḥasadim* from the side of the intercalations, for there is the place where the eyes, which are the secret of *Ḥokhmah*, are revealed.

And what the verse "Your eyes are as the pools in Ḥeshbon" has to teach us is: The emanation of your eyes, of *Malkhut*, are full of *Ḥasadim*, which are called pools. And also of *Ḥokhmah*, which is called Ḥeshbon, in order to illuminate them.

"By the gate of Bath-rabbim", i.e. the external sphere of *Malkhut*, the implements of the first state.

"By the gate of Bath-rabbim", this is the moon from the outside. This is where the eyes of *Malkhut* are revealed. And not in the eyes in their place, which is where the inner implements are, for in their place is the secret of "pools which flow out from the right in all directions", as above.

IN THE EVENING SHE CAME AND IN THE MORNING SHE RETURNED (ESTHER 2:14)

140 Rabbi Abba said to Rabbi Yossi: That holy pearl that was in your possession with the help of the holy pious one who visited us, i.e. the instruction of Rabbi Pinḥas ben Yair [see above, 128], with the help that came to us [see above, 132] — it is so beautiful that I must go

over it again. For it is certainly unnecessary to remove a woman to another place unless her husband so commands and gives her permission to go. Accordingly, one first of all informs her husband and placates him so that he should command her and give her permission to go to that place. So the Holy One, blessed be He, placated Moses until he gave his permission. Then He said to him: "You say it — Behold I give him My covenant of peace, that it should abide within Pinḥas", and so long as he (Moses) had not given her (the Shekhinah) permission to go, she did not go.

141 How do we know this? From the righteous one of the world, which is the Yesod of Zeir Anpin, who gave Malkhut permission to abide amongst the righteous in this world, and she dwells amongst them as a bride in all her jewelry, and the righteous of the world sees it, and is happy. But she lies in the arm of her husband, which is the secret of the right column and the left column, which are Ḥesed and Gvurah of Zeir Anpin, and returns from there to be with the righteous, subsequently returning to her husband, as it is written: "In the evening she comes and in the morning she returns" (Esther 2:14). In the evening she comes to her husband, i.e. at midnight, for then is the mating of the left; and in the morning, when she is full of Ḥasadim from the mating of the right, she returns to the righteous of the world, everything being done with the permission of her husband, Zeir Anpin.

142 What Moses said was: Behold I give him My Covenant, which is the secret of Malkhut. Just as the Righteous One on high gives, so also do I give a present — on condition that the present be returned, i.e. just as the Righteous One on high gives on condition that it be returned. As "in the evening she comes and in the morning she returns", as expounded above, so also with Moses. And because of this covenant, he earned the high priesthood, which is the secret of Ḥesed, and if he had not had Malkhut with him, Pinḥas could not have arisen to the level of the high priesthood, for the covenant is an aspect of Malkhut, when she is always cleaving to the upper right, which is Ḥesed of Zeir Anpin. And this upper right will, in the future, construct the Temple, which is the covenant, i.e. Malkhut.

A THIRD TEMPLE IS NOT MENTIONED IN THE TORAH

143 Rabbi Abba said: I have remembered a certain matter I heard from the Holy Luminary, Rabbi Shimon, who heard it in the name of Rabbi Eliezer. One day a clever gentile came and said to him: Old man, old man, I have three questions that I want to put to you. (*221a) The first is: You say that another Temple will be built for you, but the Temple is not to be built more than twice. The First Temple and the Second Temple are mentioned, but you will not find a Third Temple in the Torah, and that which you had to build has already been built, and there will never be another one, for Scripture has referred to the two houses of Israel, and about the Second Temple it is written: "The glory of this latter house shall be greater than that of the former" (Ḥaggai 2:9).

144 The second question is: You say that you are closer to the divine King than all other peoples. Whoever is close to the King is forever rejoicing, without pain, without fear, without troubles. But you are perpetually in pain, troubles, and agony, more than anyone else. Take us — no pain, trouble nor agony approaches us at all, whence it follows that we are close to the divine King and you are far from Him, and this is why you have pain and trouble and sorrow and agony, which we do not have.

145 My third question is: You do not eat of an animal found dead nor ritually slaughtered so that you will be healthy and your body healthy. We eat anything we want and we are physically strong and healthy and all our limbs are fit. You do not eat everything and are sick with bad illnesses and depressed more than all other peoples. You are a people whom God hates above all. Old man, old man, do not say anything to me because I shall not listen to you, nor accept it from you. Rabbi Eliezer lifted up his eyes, looked at him, and turned him into a heap of bones.

146 When his anger had subsided, he looked back, cried, and said: "O Lord, our Lord, how glorious is Your name in all the earth!" (Psalms 8:1). How strong is the power of the holy and mighty name in all the earth, and how beloved are the words of the Torah, for nothing is so minor that it will not be found in the Torah, and even the smallest thing in the Torah issued from the mouth of the Holy One, blessed be He. Those matters that that wicked one asked, I too, once asked of Elijah, and he replied that in the heavenly academy these matters were laid out before the Holy One, blessed be He, as follows:

147 When Israel came out of Egypt, the Holy One, blessed be He, wanted to establish them in the country as are the holy angels on high, and He wanted to build a Temple for them, bring it down from the upper heavens, and plant Israel in the land as a holy planting, after the pattern of the heavenly form, as it is written: "You bring them in and plant them in the mountain of Your inheritance" (Exodus 15:17). And where would that be? "The place, O Lord, which You have made for You to dwell in" (Exodus 15:17). In that place which You, O Lord, have made, and in no other. "The place, O Lord, which You have made for You to dwell in" refers to the First Temple, and the continuation of the verse, "The sanctuary, O Lord, which Your hands have established", refers to the Second Temple. Both of them are the work of the Holy One, blessed be He.

148 But when they angered Him in the wilderness, they died, and He brought their sons into the land, and the Temple was constructed by man, which is why it did not last. For the building has to be the work of the Holy One, blessed be He. King Solomon knew that the Temple that he built was

built by man and would not therefore last, which is why it is written: "Except the Lord build the house, they labour in vain that built it" (Psalms — attributed in the heading to Solomon.) And indeed it no longer exists. In the days of Ezra, because of the sin, they had to rebuild the Temple, which is why it had no lasting existence. And up until now the first building of the Holy One, blessed be He, has not been placed in the world, but concerning the future it is written: "The Lord is the builder of Jerusalem" (Psalms 147:2), that is, He, the Lord, will build and no other. It is for this building that we are waiting, and not for a structure of man which has no permanence.

149 The Holy One, blessed be He, will bring down the First Temple and the Second Temple from on high simultanously. The First Temple, which is equivalent to Binah, will be covered, and the Second Temple, which is parallel to Malkhut, will be in the open. That house that is called the Second Temple will be in the open so that the art of the Holy One, blessed be He, will be visible to the whole world. And then there will be perfect rejoicing, and the desire of the heart will be fulfilled throughout its existence.

150 The First Temple that will be covered or concealed, ascends on high over the Second Temple that is revealed, and the whole world will see the clouds of glory that surround the Temple that is revealed, and within those clouds will be the First Temple in a hidden action, rising to the height of the glory of the heavens, which is Binah, and this is the building for which we are waiting.

151 So far this has not happened in the world, for even the City of Jerusalem will not be the result of man's skills, for it is written: "For I, says the Lord, will be for her a wall of fire round about, and I will be the glory in the midst of her" (Zekhariah 2:5). If this is what is written about the City, how much more so will this be the case for the Temple, which is His dwelling place. And this action of the Holy One, blessed be He, should have been apparent at the beginning, when Israel came out of Egypt, but it was delayed for the End of Days, for the (*221b) Final Redemption.

WHY ISRAEL HAS MORE TROUBLES THAN OTHER PEOPLES

152 This is the core of the second question asked by that gentile, for there can be no doubt that we are closer to the divine King than any of the other peoples. This must be so for the Holy One, blessed be He, made Israel the heart of the whole world, and the relationship of Israel to the other nations is as that of the heart to other parts of the body. And just as the other parts of the body have no existence, even for a moment, without the heart, so it is that none of the other peoples can exist in the world without Israel. Jerusalem, too, has the same relationship with the other countries, being as the heart to the parts of the body, which is why it is in the center of the whole world just as the heart is in the center of the limbs.

153 And Israel's situation amongst the other nations is as that of the heart amongst the limbs. The heart is soft and weak, but gives existence to all the limbs and they, the limbs, do not know pain, trouble, and agony at all, but only the heart does — for in it is existence and intelligence. Pain and anguish come nowhere near the other limbs, for they have no (independent) existence and know nothing. None of the other limbs comes near to the King, who is wisdom and intelligence that reside in the brain, except the heart. And the other limbs are far from Him and know nothing about Him. Thus it is that Israel is near to the Holy King while the other peoples are far from Him.

WHY ISRAEL, WHO DOES NOT PARTAKE OF ANIMALS FOUND DEAD OR NOT RITUALLY SLAUGHTERED, IS WEAK

154 The third question posed by that gentile was that Israel, does not partake of animals found dead or those not ritually slaughtered, nor of the

filth and dirt of reptiles and insects as do the other peoples, but is nevertheless weaker than they are. This is how it is. For the heart, which is soft and weak and is the king and the existence of the other limbs, does not take from man's food for its nourishment other than from the clearest and purest of all the blood that is made from the foodstuffs, and its food is clean and clear and is softer and weaker than all the rest. And it (the heart) leaves the remaining waste matters for the other limbs, and the other limbs are not concerned as to the cleanliness of their food, but take all the waste matters, even the worst, and they are strong as befits them.

155 This is why all the other limbs have skin eruptions and scabs and leprous boils, and the heart has none of them, for it is clean and clear, and has no blemish whatsoever. Thus took the Holy One, blessed be He, Israel, who is clean, clear, and without blemish, for Himself, as Scripture says: "You are all fair, my love, and there is no blemish in you." (Song of Songs 4:7). Rabbi Yossi came, kissed his hands, and said: If I had come into the world just to hear this, it would have been sufficient.

NOW THE NAME OF THE MAN OF ISRAEL THAT WAS SLAIN (NUMBERS 25:14)

156 "Now the name of the man of Israel that was slain" (Numbers 25:14). Said Rabbi Isaac: This verse should have been written: Now the name of the man of Israel whom Pinḥas slew, and not `that was slain', without mentioning the one who did the slaying as though he was unimportant.

157 The answer to this is as put by Rabbi Eliezer. Since

the Holy One, blessed be He, had raised Pinḥas to the level of high priest, He did not want to mention Pinḥas in the context of a man slaying, for this is hardly fitting for a high priest. Before he elevated him to the high priesthood, He did mention him, and said: "And Pinḥas saw... and took a spear... and thrust both of them through..." (Numbers 25:7-8). But once he was elevated to the high priesthood, his name is not mentioned in the context of killing, for this is unbefitting, and the honor of the Holy One, blessed be He, had compassion with him because it is not right for a high priest to be mentioned in the context of a killing. "And the name of the woman that was slain" (Numbers 25:15) is also given without stating who the slayer was, for the same reason.

WHAT IS NOW FIRST WILL BE LAST AT THE RESURRECTION

158 Rabbi Shimon was traveling from Cappadocia to Lod, and Rabbi Yehuda was going with him. While they were en route, they were met by Rabbi Pinḥas ben Yair and two donkey drivers following him. Rabbi Pinḥas' donkey stopped. He prodded him with a spur that he should continue, but he did not do so. Said Rabbi Pinḥas to the donkey drivers: Leave him be, for he can discern the smell of new countenances approaching us, or a miracle will happen to us. While they were still there, Rabbi Shimon appeared from behind one of the rocks, and the donkey continued to move. Said Rabbi Pinḥas: Did I not tell you that he discerned the smell of new countenances?

159 Rabbi Pinḥas dismounted from his donkey, embraced Rabbi Shimon, and cried. He said to him: I saw in my dream that the Shekhinah had come to me, and given me large presents, and I had rejoiced with her. And now what I saw has come to pass. Rabbi Shimon said: I knew that it was you from the sound of your donkey's footsteps. Now the rejoicing is complete. Rabbi Pinḥas said: Let us sit down somewhere, as a Torah discussion has to be lucid. They found a well of water and a tree and sat down.

160 Rabbi Pinḥas said: I

used to view matters such that the resurrection of the dead would be performed on us by the Holy One, blessed be He, in one way, and that what is now first to leave will be the last at the resurrection. How do we know this from those bones, the ones into which the Holy One, blessed be He, breathed life at the hands of Ezekiel. At the beginning it is written: "And the bones came together, bone to its bone" (Ezekiel 37:7), and later it is written: (*222a) "And I beheld, and, lo, there were sinews upon them, and flesh came up" (Ezekiel 37:8). And the same verse continues: "And skin covered them above; but there was no breath in them." From here, too, we can learn that what a person takes off first will be the last to be put on again. Initially, man is stripped of spirit, and then his skin rots, followed by the flesh, then the sinews, and finally the bones. At the resurrection it will be the other way around: initially the bones, then the sinews, followed by the flesh, and lastly the skin.

THE RESURRECTION OF THE DEAD

161 Rabbi Shimon said: The earlier teachers had difficulties with this passage, but the truth is that the Holy One, blessed be He, performed strange miracles and signs with these bones into which he breathed life. Come and see: "Remember, I beseech You, that You have fashioned me as clay, and You will bring me into dust again" (Job 10:9). And then, in the next verse: "Have You not poured me out as milk, and curdled me like cheese? Have You not clothed me with skin and flesh, and knit me together with bones and sinews?" When a person has rotted in the dust, and the time of the resurrection of the dead has arrived, the Holy One, blessed be He, will re-make him from the remaining bone that has not rotted away. (See above Vayera, 127). Make it like leaven in dough and as cheese from milk and as flowing as a stream of pure milk. For the Creator will form from this kneading process the renewed human form, churned as cheese and kneaded like dough. After this structure is done he will create anew the skin, veins and bone.

162 In the above quoted verse (Job 10:9-10) all the

verbs are in fact in the future form. Not `Have You not poured me out', but `Will You not pour me out'. Not `Have You not clothed me with skin and flesh', but `Will You not clothe me with skin and flesh'. This is because the reference throughout is to a future time, that of the resurrection.

163 And what is written afterwards? "You have granted me life and favor" (Job 10:12). This is the spirit of life. And if you ask: But it is written `have granted' in the past tense and not `will grant' in the future. I should answer that Job's intention was to say: "You have granted me life and favor", for in that world You have given me the spirit of life. But — the verse continues — "And Your Providence", i.e. that of the King's matron, Malkhut, "has preserved my spirit", i.e. guards my spirit in that world. And why does he refer to Malkhut, as `Your Providence' [from the Hebrew root pey kuf dalet]? Because you will in the future come across [same Hebrew root pey kuf dalet] first.

164 And the secret of this matter is that all the souls of the righteous are hidden and concealed under the King's throne, which is Malkhut (which is called a throne), and she protects them so that they can be returned to their place. As it is written: "And Your Providence guards my spirit". What is `Your Providence' [Hebrew root pey kuf dalet]? It is as in the verse: "Let another take his charge" [Hebrew root pey kuf dalet] (Psalms 109:8). `Your Providence' refers to the King's matron, i.e. Malkhut, for all the spirits are pledges [Hebrew root pey kuf dalet] in her hands, as it is written: "Into Your hand I commit my spirit" (Psalms 31:5), and she protects them. Thus is it written "has preserved my spirit", for she preserves it.

165 David said something similar: "Keep my soul for I am pious" (Psalms 86:2). [Note: the form of the imperative here used for `keep' can also be read as feminine singular past tense of the same verb — tr.] `Keep' refers to the King's matron, for she has

kept my soul because I am pious. And as a general rule, whenever Scripture does not explicitly state 'God', the reference is to the matron who is Malkhut. As for example, in the verse: "And He called to Moses" (Exodus 24:16), where God is not mentioned by name, or "And He said: If you will diligently hearken to the voice of the Lord your God" (Exodus 25:26), where the speaker again is not named and the reference is to Malkhut.

166 Rabbi Pinḥas cried and said: And did I not tell you that in my dream the Shekhinah had given me great gifts? The meaning was these sayings of Rabbi Shimon. Happy is my portion that I have merited seeing you and hearing this. He said to him: What you have said concerning the time of the resurrection is correct regarding the one bone that does not rot, but what happens to the other bones that are there? He said to him: They will all be included in the totality of that one bone and will be incorporated with it and they will all be made into one dough, out of which man will be formed. As they said in the verse: "The Lord will guide you continually, and satisfy your soul in drought, and make strong your bones, and you shall be like a watered garden, and like a spring of water whose waters fail not" (Isaiah 58:11). What is the meaning of 'make strong' (Hebrew root: het lamed tzadik)? It is as in the verse: "He has withdrawn (Hebrew root: het lamed tzadik) Himself from them" (Hosea 5:6). In other words, they will all be transferred from their place and incorporated in this bone, making one dough, and then "you shall be like a watered garden, and like a spring of water."

THE FAITHFUL SHEPHERD

167 The Faithful Shepherd said: Woe to those whose hearts are blocked off and whose eyes are closed, for they do not know that when the night comes the gates of Gehenna are opened, for it is called bitter or gall, and the odors that spread from it

rise up to the brain. And a number of forces of the evil inclination spread throughout the parts of the body. And the gates of the Garden of Eden which are the eyes of the heart, are blocked off and not opened, for all the lights that are in the eyes issue forth from the heart.

INTO YOUR HAND I COMMIT MY SPIRIT (PSALMS 31:6)

168 And the gates of the heart, which are the eyes, are blocked off, so that they should not view the evil spirits, that is Lilith. And thus they do not control the lights of the heart, which are angels, that spread throughout all the limbs, as the branches of a tree in every direction. At that time the lights are shut off in the heart, and they gather to it, as doves into their dove-cotes, as Noah and his wife and all the species who entered with him into the ark.

169 And the evil spirits that overcome all the parts of the body are like the waters of the flood which prevailed over them fifteen cubits [cf. Genesis 7:20]. This is because he had sinned in the matter of Yah, and Yah had left the body. [The letters of Yah, yud hei, have the numerical value 10 + 5 = 15 — tr.] That is to say, Yah had left Elokim [i.e. the letters of Yah, yud hei, left the letters of Elokim, which are aleph lamed hei yud mem, leaving behind the letters aleph lamed mem — tr.], and He remained a mute [Hebrew: Ilem, aleph lamed mem.], without sight, hearing, smell or speech. And the secret of the matter is to be found in the verse: "I was dumb [from the Hebrew root: aleph lamed mem] with silence" (Psalms 39:10). The word here used for 'with silence' is spelled dalet vav mem yud hei, which can be read as two words: dalet vav mem and yud hei, dom Yah, which means: 'Yah was silent'. In other words, at the time of the Flood, the evil spirits prevailed for fifteen (= Yah) cubits over the body, and they encompassed the body, as a furrow surrounds the ditch and the flower-bed.

C o m m e n t a r y

The gall in the body stands for Gehenna and the evil inclination, and the heart for the holy Garden of Eden.

When the night comes, the gates of Gehenna are opened, for it is called bitter or gall, and its odors rise up to the brain. These odors are the forces of Judgement, and thus the brains leave a man and he sleeps.

And its odors spread out — they are like the odor of Gehenna, and the brains leave. And then the gates of the Garden of Eden, which is the secret of the eyes, are blocked off, as he says "And the gates of the Garden of Eden, which are the eyes of the heart, are blocked off." And why are the eyes called the gates of the heart? Because all the light that is in the eyes comes from the heart. Thus, the heart is the Garden of Eden, and the lights that are in it are the secret of the angels who spread forth, that is, the secret of *Elokim,* into all the parts of the body and gain control over them. But at night, when they do not control the lights of the heart, which are the angels that spread out throughout all the limbs, etc., the lights are all shut off in the heart and gather to it. That is, all the lights that spread throughout the body return and collect together at their source, at the heart, which is the secret of the Garden of Eden. This is like Noah's Ark, for when judgement, i.e. the waters of the Flood, prevailed, they all collected together in the ark, as he says: Like Noah and his wife, etc.

In connection with the Flood, it is written: "Fifteen cubits upward did the waters prevail" (Genesis 7:20), where the fifteen cubits hint at the name [*Yah* i.e. 10 + 5 = 15], formed of two of the letters in the name *Elokim.* The waters, that prevail refers to the shells [*klippot*] that became strong enough to push the name *Yah* out of the world. And in our case also the forces of the *klip-*

pot grow strong and force the name *Yah* out of *Elokim*, that is to say from the lights of the heart, which is the secret of *Elokim* (as noted above), which spread throughout all parts of the body.

"Because he had sinned in the matter of *Yah* and *Yah* had left the body". What he is saying here is that the letters of *Yah* had left *Elokim*, who spreads through the body, and then He was left mute — that is, only the three letters of the word `mute' remained of *Elokim* after the letters of *Yah* were removed, and this teaches us that the body, per se, is without sight, hearing, smell or speech.

This, therefore, is the secret of the verse: "I was dumb with silence" (Psalms 39:10), where the letters of `with silence' can be re-arranged to read `*Yah* was silent', i.e. that *Elokim* remained mute. Thus: "I was dumb".

170 (*222b) Just as Noah sent the dove out on his mission, so also does the soul of man send out his spirit on its mission, and for this reason a man must commit his spirit with the Matron, who is Malkhut, as it says: "In Your hand I commit my spirit" (Psalms 31:6). But if it is imprisoned by the powers of the evil inclination in sins of the body, what does Scripture have to say? "Into Your hand I commit my spirit; You have redeemed me, O Lord, the God of truth." For the Holy One, blessed be He, redeems him from their hand.

171 And during the time that the soul is guilty, what is said about his spirit? "My hand upon it! The evil man shall not go unpunished." (Proverbs 40:21), for he goes from hand to hand in the camps of the evil inclination, which rest upon him in his sins and cast him out from place to place. It is this that is happening when a man

sees himself in his dream in another country or another kingdom, and sometimes in the refuse — all depending on his sins. But if he is righteous, then all of the camps of the good inclination, about whom it is said "And their faces and their wings were stretched upwards" (Ezekiel 1:11), accept his spirit and they raise it upward to the place of the beasts, the bearers of the throne, which is Malkhut, and there he sees a number of visions, likenesses and prophetical revelations. And this is why the sages taught "The dream is one-sixtieth of prophecy" (cf. Berakhot 57b).

172 Furthermore: "Keep my soul, for I am pious" (Psalms 86:2). But what the sages taught was: "An ignorant man can not be pious." (Pirke Avot 2,6) For the Torah was given from the right side of the Holy One, blessed be He, which is Ḥesed. For this reason, one who engages in Torah is called pious, and therefore I say to the Holy One, blessed be He: Keep my soul, and do not judge it according to the deeds of these ignoramuses, about whom it is said: "An ignorant man can not be pious." And should you ask about the many ignorant people who act with loving kindness [Ḥesed], I would refer you to the teaching: "Who is a pious man? He who behaves piously with his Maker." Like David, how was an author [the Hebrew root of `author' means `join together']. And what did he join together? He joined together the heavenly Torah, which is Zeir Anpin, with the Holy One, blessed be He, who is Malkhut, and this is what is meant by `behaving piously with his maker': that he united the Holy One, blessed be He, and His Shekhinah. This, therefore, is the reason for "Keep my soul, for I am pious."

TWO VISIONS

173 When a man dies, what is written about his soul? "When you walk, it will lead you; when you lie down it will watch over you; and when you awake" at the resurrection of the dead, "it will talk with you" (Proverbs 6:22). This is fine as far as the resurrection of the dead is concerned — that it should awaken the body of man at the resurrection of the dead — but what will be the reward of the soul in the next world?

174 The answer to this is that the Holy One, blessed be He, dresses the soul as formerly in clouds of glory, and as formerly it enters into a vision. In the same sort of way that the body has 248 parts, it will also be in a vision included in 248 lights that spread forth from that vision, for the numerical value of the letters of "b'mar'ah" [in a vision] is 248. And it is said about it: "If there be a prophet among you, I, the Lord, make Myself known to him b'mar'ah, in a vision" (Numbers 12:6) and with the apparel of clouds of glory about which it is said: "And I shall look upon it and remember the everlasting covenant" (Genesis 9:16). This is the vision that enlightens. "I speak with him in a dream" (Numbers 12:6): this is the vision that does not enlighten, being made up of 365 lights, corresponding to the numerical value of yeshenah (sleep), as in the verse: "I sleep" (Song of Songs 5:2). One vision, therefore, is for the soul in this world, and the other vision is for the soul in the world to come, and they give light to the work of the hands of the Holy One, blessed be He, namely, the souls.

175 And their secret is to be found in the verse: "This is My name forever" (Exodus 3:15). The numerical value of Yah [yud hei] is 15, and that of `My name' [sh'miy = shin mem yud] is 350, which, together, comes to 365. "And this is My memorial [zikhriy] unto all generations" (Exodus 3:15). The numerical value of zikhriy [zayin kaf resh yud] is 237, which, together with vav and hei (6 + 5) comes to 248. And heralds descend and ascend before Him, proclaiming: "Give honor to the likeness of the King", i.e. to the soul.

176 And this is the meaning of the verse: "And God created man in His own image: in the image of God created He him" (Genesis 1:27). In other words, He created him in two forms:

one, in His own image; and the other, in the image of God, i.e. with two countenances. The first one is as it is said: "But you saw no form: (Deuteronomy 4:12), and regarding the other forbidden forms it is written, "a graven image, even the form of any figure" (Deuteronomy 4:16). In respect to the second, it is said: "And he beholds the form of the Lord" (Numbers 12:8). And 613 angels raise up the soul in these forms, all of them with "their faces and their wings stretched upwards" (Ezekiel 1:11), to establish the verse that is said about them: "I bore you on eagles' wings and brought you unto Myself" (Exodus 19:4).

177 Just as the Children of Israel came out of Egypt and went with clouds of glory and all that honor, so, too, is the exit of the soul from the body — that "putrid drop" (Pirke Avot 3,1): the soul goes to the two gardens, the Upper Garden of Eden and the Lower Garden of Eden, whose heavens and earth were created with the Tetragrammaton [the four-letter name of God: yud hei vav and hei], for whom it was said; "Let the heavens be glad and the earth rejoice" (Psalms 96:11). At that time the verse: "Your Teacher shall not any more hide [Hebrew root: kaf nun pey] Himself" from you (Isaiah 30:20) will be fulfilled in man. And although it is written: "Each had six wings [Hebrew root: kaf nun pey]; with two he covered his face..." (Isaiah 6:2), nevertheless "Your eyes shall see your Teacher" (Isaiah 30:20). And Moses our Master, may Peace be upon him — the master of the prophet and sages — merited these two visions.

The Holy Luminary, that is Rabbi Shimon, said to the Faithful Shepherd: You are the one who merited in your lifetime what the righteous will merit after their lives. Happy is your portion!

Commentary

Malkhut is called *mar'ah* (vision), because it is the place where *Ḥokhmah*, which is called *r'iyah* (vision = sight), is revealed. And

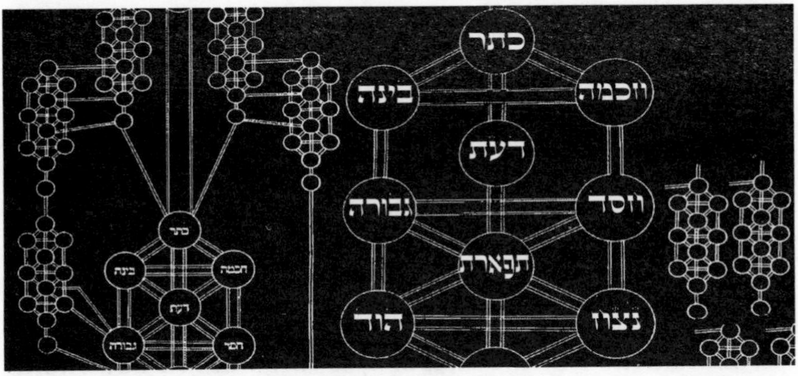

there are two aspects to the mar'ah:

a) When it is mating with *Zeir Anpin*, and the *Ḥasadim* have control over *Malkhut* as over *Zeir Anpin*, the illumination of *Ḥokhmah* is also included in these *Ḥasadim* that are in *Malkhut* and which are in any event drawn down from above, since they are mainly *Ḥasadim* and not *Ḥokhmah*. This vision (mar'ah) is therefore termed the illuminating vision, for it gives light from above downwards. And being with *Zeir Anpin* in a mating and included in Him, it is an aspect of Him. And this vision (mar'ah) is examined in the aspect of *vav hei* of the Tetragrammaton, for *Ḥasadim* are *vav kuf*, which is the secret of *vav hei*.

b) The second aspect is when *Ḥokhmah*, which is the secret of *yud hei*, is revealed in *Malkhut*. And although here also it is mating with *Zeir Anpin*, in this case, the *Ḥokhmah* of *Malkhut* is in control and not the *Ḥasadim* of *Zeir Anpin*. It is known that *Ḥokhmah* is not drawn down from above, and it is therefore in the aspect of the vision (*mar'ah*) that does not illuminate below. It is then written about it: "This is My name forever" (Exodus 3:15). [The Hebrew word for 'forever' is l'olam, spelled either: *lamed* ayin *vav lamed mem* or *lamed* ayin *lamed mem*.] In this verse, the shorter spelling is utilized, i.e. with *vav* omitted, which means something is concealed. For it has to be concealed that it is not drawn downwards, for this is the root of all the 365 'Do not's' in the Torah. And this is why there is a hint about it. The numerical value of '*shmiy*' ('My name'), together with *yud hei*, is 365, for *yud hei* is the secret of *Ḥokhmah* and the First Three, which is the inner meaning of the verse "This is My name forever" that has to be concealed.

But the aspect of the illuminating vision, which is the secret of the illumination of the *Ḥasadim*, is to be drawn downwards from above, this being a mitzvah (commandment). And this is the root of all the 248 positive commandments, therefore it is written about it: "And this is My memorial unto all generations" (Exodus 3:15). Intimation of this is to be found in the fact that the numerical value of zikhriy ('My memorial'), together with *vav hei*, comes to 248. For the lights of *Ḥasadim* are the secret of *vav hei*, and there are 248 such lights, paralleling the 248 positive commandments that stretch down from these 248 lights. And the soul of the righteous man who performed these 248 positive commandments is attired, after its departure from the world, in these 248 lights.

"The Holy One, blessed be He, dresses the soul as formerly in clouds of glory" [174, above]. This refers to the secret of the seven clouds which are *Ḥasadim*, paralleling the secret of *Ḥesed, Gvurah, Tiferet, Netzaḥ, Hod, Yesod, Malkhut.* By means of these clothes, it enters into a vision, in the same sort of way that the body has 248 parts [174 above]. This means that it puts on the 248 lights of the illuminating vision. And it is said about it: "And I make Myself known to him in a vision" (Numbers 12:6), where the numerical value of *b'mar'ah* ('in a vision') is 248. And it is said about it: "And I shall look upon it and remember the everlasting covenant" (Genesis 9:16) — this being the illuminating vision [174, above] because sight and light belong to it inasmuch as it is drawn downwards from above. Although it is mainly *Ḥasadim*, it is nevertheless called sight, since the *Ḥasadim* are included of the illumination of *Ḥokhmah*. "I speak with him in a dream" (Numbers 12:6) refers to thevision that does not illuminate [174, above]. That is to say, the secret of *yud hei*, about which it is written, "This is My name forever" (Exodus 3:15), which is the secret of the control of the *Ḥokhmah* that is in *Malkhut*, as discussed above: it has to be concealed that it should only illuminate upwards from below. And the time when it is in control by itself without *Ḥasadim* is the secret of "darkness and no light" (as above, Gen. I, page 47e *Napik*).

"Being made up of 365 lights, as the numerical value of *yeshenah* (sleep) in the verse 'I sleep'" (Song of Songs 5:2) [174, above]. For it is then in the aspect of closing of the eyes, which is the secret of darkness and sleep, and about this Scripture says: "I sleep". One vision, therefore, is for the soul in this world [174, above]. One vision is in force in this world, which is the secret of *Malkhut*, which is the vision that does not illuminate.

"And the other vision is for the soul in the world to come" [174, above]. And it is really one vision, for here *Malkhut* is at the secret of *Binah*, which emits *Ḥasadim*, and it is then the illuminating vision.

"And they are the work of the hands of the Holy One, blessed be He" [174, above]. Both of the visions give light in the souls that are the work of the hands of the Holy One, blessed be He. And their secret is to be found in the verse: "This is My name forever" (Exodus 3:15). The numerical value of *Yah* [*yud hei*] is 15, and that of 'My name' [*Sh'miy = shin mem yud*] is 350, which, together, come to 365 (175 above)]. For the aspect of *Ḥokhmah*, which is the secret of *yud hei*, has to be concealed and that is why 'forever' [*l'olam*] is written in the abbreviated form [*lamed ayin lamed mem* and not *lamed ayin vav lamed mem*], for this is the root of the 365 negative precepts of the Torah, as explained above. Thus 'My name is *Yah*' [*shin mem yud yud hei*] has the numerical value of 365, while *vav hei* with 'My memorial' [*Zikhriy* — *zayin kaf resh yud*] comes to 248, since the *Ḥasadim* that are included in *Ḥokhmah* are drawn down from above, which is the secret of *vav hei*, i.e. *vav kuf*, since they are mainly *Ḥasadim* and it is a *mitzvah* to draw them down, and this is the root of all the 248 positive precepts in the Torah, as above, and this is intimated by the fact that '*zikhriy vav hei* has the numerical value of 248.

And these two visions are the secret of the two images, for the image of *Zeir Anpin* is the illuminating vision, and the image of *Malkhut* is the secret of the vision that does not illuminate. And this is the meaning of the verse: "And God created man in His own image; in the image of God *Elokim* created He him" (Genesis 1:27). In other words, He created Him in two forms, i.e. with two countenances [176, above]. 'His image' refers to the form of the illuminating vision, and 'the image of God' *Elokim*, refers to the vision that does not illuminate for *Malkhut* is called *Elokim*. It is said: "But you saw no form" (Deuteronomy 4:12). And concerning those "who do not take good heed of themselves", it is said: "Lest you deal corruptly and make a graven image, even the form of any figure" (Deuteronomy 4:16). And regarding the other forbidden forms [176, above]. This refers to the deeds of the wicked who desire to continue here by way of forms, as it is written: "The form of any figure"; but regarding the illuminating vision, it is said: "And he beholds the form of the Lord" (Numbers 12:8). Thus: from the illuminating vision, which is the secret of the 248 positive precepts, are drawn 248 angels who raise the soul up. And from the vision that does not illuminate, which is the secret of the 365 negative precepts, are drawn 365 angels who raise the soul up.

These, together, make 613, as the text [176, above] says: And 613 angels raise up the soul. And the secret of the 365 negative precepts is drawn from the concealment of the name in the secret of the verse: "This is My name forever," where l, olam is written without a vov, as discussed above.

All of them with "their faces and their wings stretched upwards" (Ezekiel 1:11). That is, that they have no mating and drawing down from *yud hei,* which is the secret of enclothment, but their illumination upwards from below is concealed.

"To establish the verse that is said about them: `I bore you on eagles' wings and brought you unto Myself" (Exodus 19:4) [176, above]. "Eagle" is the secret of the central column, from which comes the correction that *Ḥokhmah* should illuminate only upwards from below [as above, Gen. I, 60e, *Mahloket*], and this correction is therefore called "eagles' wings", and for concealment is called wings, the middle column is called "eagles".

"To go to the two gardens" [177, above]. That is, two *Malkhuts*, for *Malkhut* is called a garden whose heavens and earth were created with the Tetragrammaton. For *Malkhut* in the aspect of the illuminating vision is the secret of *vav hei,* and *Malkhut* is the aspect of the vision that does not illuminate is the secret of *yud hei,* the two of them together making *yud hei vav* and *hei,* the complete Tetragrammaton.

"Whose heavens and earth" means the mating of *Zeir Anpin* and *Malkhut* is called earth. In both of the aspects there is a mating of *Zeir Anpin* and *Malkhut*: In the illuminating vision, *Zeir Anpin* is in control, that is His attribute of *Ḥasadim,* while in the vision that does not illuminate, *Malkhut* is in control, that is its attribute of *Ḥokhmah.* And in the future, the mating of *yud hei* will be disclosed and the above-mentioned eagles' wings will pass, as the text says: At that time the verse, "Your Teacher shall not any more hide Himself" (Isaiah 30:20) will be fulfilled in man, where the word here rendered "hide" comes from the same Hebrew root as the word for "wing", i.e. the wings will be no more.

ANI AND HU

178 Another interpretation of the verse "Keep my soul for I am pious" (Psalms 86:2) is as follows: Why should He keep my soul? So that I should behave piously with Ani (literally: I), i.e. that I should unite with and bring the Ḥesed from the Tetragrammaton which is Zeir Anpin to Ani which is Malkhut, for it has been said about it: Ani and Hu, where Ani is Malkhut and Hu is Zeir Anpin. Woe to anyone who separates (*223a) Ani from Hu, i.e. to anyone who causes a separation between Zeir Anpin and Malkhut, as it is said: "It is He (Hu) that has made us, and not we ourselves" (Psalms 100:3), where Hu stands for Zeir Anpin. This is because everything is one, i.e. Ani and Hu are one, without distinction.

This is what is said: "See now that I, even I (Ani) am He (Hu)... I kill and I make alive, I have wounded, and I heal, and there is none that can deliver out of My hand" (Deuteronomy 32:29). I (Ani), the Tetragrammaton, am He (Hu), and no other. And this 'Ani' is derived from the Hebrew for 'The Lord' (aleph dalet nun yud), i.e. the letters of 'Ani' (aleph nun yud) are found in the word for 'The Lord'. The Tetragrammaton is the central column, i.e. Zeir Anpin.

179 And because the Tetragrammaton, which is Zeir Anpin, is on the right, i.e. Ḥesed, He said: "Keep my soul, for I am pious" (Ḥasid), meaning that I shall behave piously towards you and with Ani (myself), which is The Lord, which is Gvurah. That is to say, I shall unite the Tetragrammaton, which is Ḥesed, with The Lord, which is Gvurah, and the Ḥasadim will be drawn down from the

Tetragrammaton to The Lord, and she, too, will be Ḥesed. And both the names, the Tetragrammaton and The Lord, combine together in Tiferet, which is the central column, and come together thus; yud aleph hei dalet vav nun hei yud, for it is the central column that combines Ḥesed, which is the secret of the Tetragrammaton, with Gvurah, which is the secret of The Lord. And the inner meaning of the matter is with Ḥesed and Gvurah, which are the right and left columns, about which it is said: "And their faces and their wings are stretched upwards" (Ezekiel 1:11), since 'their faces' is the secret of Ḥokhmah, Binah, and Da'at, and the two columns to the right and the left, which are Ḥokhmah and Binah, are stretched upwards. And so with the two wings, the secret of the right and left columns, which are different from each other, and are therefore stretched upwards. And in Tiferet, which is the central column, that is called: "The Lord [the Tetragrammaton' is the man [Ish] of war" (Exodus 15:3), because He fights with the left column, and makes it smaller in order to bring it together in unity with the right (see above Lekh Lekha 13e). And the verse continues: "two [wings] of every one [ish] were joined one to another" (Ezekiel 1:11), for the two names, the Tetragrammaton and The Lord were joined together in it, and thus "and two covered their bodies" (Ezekiel 1:11), for the wings joined the body and became as one. And Tiferet is called body, this being the inner meaning of the verse: "his body was like beryl" (Daniel 10:6). And so it is with the two columns, right and left of the upper Sfirot which are Ḥokhmah and Binah, that are the two names, the Tetragrammaton and the aleph, hei, yud, hei, about which it is said "their faces and their wings stretched upwards", also join together and combine by the central column, which is the secret of Da'at. And they come together thus: yud aleph hei hei vav yud hei hei.

THREE TIMES WAS DAVID CALLED A SERVANT

180 It is written: "Save Your servant, You, My God... Rejoice the soul of Your servant... Give Your strength to Your servant" (Psalms 86:2,4,16). David is thrice referred to as a servant in this psalm wich parallels the three times that a man has to be as a servant in the prayers, as taught by the sages of the Mishnah: "In the first (three) blessings, a man should be as a servant arranging praises before his master; in the intermediate blessings, as a servant asking for a favor of his master; and in the last (three) blessings, a man should be as a servant thanking his master for a favor received, and going" (Quoted in Talmud Bavli, Berakhot 34a, in the name of Rabbi Hanina).

181 And these are the three occasions that a man has to make himself as though a servant in terms of worship. And the sages of the Mishnah taught: There is no worship but prayer (Quoted in Talmud Bavli, Ta'anit 2a). And the three patriarchs are called servants next to her, i.e. in the name of the Shekhinah, which is the worship of the Lord. And so also is Moses referred to as the servant of the Lord, which is why "And to Me the Children of Israel are servants" (Leviticus 25:55). But in terms of their other qualities, all Israel are called the children of kings from the point of view of the Malkhut in them. And why should Malkhut be termed worship? It can be likened to the way of a woman who serves her husband, or children who serve their father.

DAVID BECAME POOR, PIOUS AND A SERVANT

182 And David became poor, pious and a servant, as it is written: "A prayer of David. Incline Your ear, O Lord, and answer me, for I am poor and needy. Keep my soul, for I am pious. Save Your servant, You, my God" (Psalms 86:1-2). He became poor at the gate of the king, which is Malkhut, about which it is said: "O Lord, open my lips" (Psalms 51:15). 'Lord' is the Palace, and he became poor to the gate of the king's palace, which is 'Lord', i.e. Malkhut. And what does it say? "Incline Your ear, O Lord, and answer me". And this is the lower Shekhinah, which is Malkhut, which is an ear to receive and listen to prayers, as it is written: "For He has not despised nor abhorred the lowliness of the poor; neither has He hid His face from him, but when he cried to Him, He heard" (Psalms 22:25).

183 For he became "poor and needy" in respect of the letter `dalet' of the word `Eḥad' [aleph ḥet dalet] (= one), which is the secret of Malkhut in the first state, when it is receiving from the left column, for it is then weak, for the letter `dalet' teaches us of its weakness [dalah]. And Malkhut requests help from the other two letters of Eḥad (One), i.e. from aleph ḥet. And this is the secret of Zeir Anpin which, in this state is Malkhut, is called brother (aleph ḥet), and Malkhut sister, being then at one stage evolving from Binah, as a brother and sister, which is the central column, i.e. Zeir Anpin, to fulfil the verse: "I was brought low [same root as the word `poor'] and He saved me" (Psalms 96:6), so that the Messiah son of Ephraim should not die, for the Messiah son of Ephraim is drawn from Malkhut when the latter is feeding from the left, and is full of judgement. And David further requested of Him at this gate on behalf of Israel, who is poor, that the verse "And the poor people do You save" (11 Samuel 22:28) be established for them, and this is why he made himself poor, which is the secret of the left column.

184 And afterwards he requested for the priests, which is the secret of the right column, Ḥesed, that the worship be returned to its place, and he made himself as a servant. And later He gave the Torah from the side of Ḥesed, to make a benefit [gemul] with the letter `dalet', from the Torah. In other words, the Torah, which is the secret of Zeir Anpin, the central column, unites the Ḥesed of the right-hand column with the Gvurah of left, and then he makes a benefit with the dalet, which is the secret of Malkhut receiving Ḥasadim and becoming rich, in the secret of the two letters `gimel' and `dalet' that follow each other in the order of the alphabet.And this is why he became pious.

What this means is that he thereby corrected the secret of the three columns, Ḥesed, Gvurah, Tiferet. He made himself poor to correct the left-hand column. He made himself a servant to correct the worship of the priests which are the right-hand column, and he made himself pious to correct the central column, so that Ḥesed should emanate to Malkhut. Subsequently he corrected the three columns Ḥesed, Gvurah, Tiferet, and when he reached the three upper Sfirot — Ḥokhmah, Binah, Da'at — he began to say: "Lord, my heart is not haughty, nor my eyes lofty, neither do I exercise myself in things too great, or in things too wonderful for me" (Psalms 131:1), i.e. he did not touch them.

185 Solomon said: Since Binah (understanding) belongs to Moses, I shall ask for upper Ḥokhmah (wisdom), which is above the level of Moses. It is written: "I said: I will get wisdom, but it was far from me" (Ecclesiastes 7:23), for upper wisdom was not given to him. But what about the verse: "And the Lord gave wisdom to Solomon" (I Kings 5:9)? Is there not a contradiction here? The answer is that this refers to lower wisdom, which is Malkhut. And he wanted to ascend upwards from below, i.e. from lower Ḥokhmah he wanted to attain upper Ḥokhmah, but it drew away from him. This is because there is no man in the world, apart from Moses, who can ascend to Binah, and how much truer is this for upper Ḥokhmah which is above Binah. In terms of upper Ḥokhmah, "a wise man is preferable to a prophet" (cf. Talmud Bavli, Baba Batra 12a). And even though the verse "I said: I will get wisdom, but it was far from me" was applied homiletically to a red heifer, whose reason he could not understand (Midrash BeMidar Rabba, Hukkat, 19, 3), "there are seventy possible interpretations of Torah", this, too, being a term in the secret of Scripture.

THE SECRETS OF ELAZAR, YOSSI, YEHUDA, YUDAI, ABBA AND RABBI SHIMON AND HIS COMRADES

186 Said the Faithful Shepherd; Rabbi Elazar,

Rise up and say some new interpretations before the Divine Presence, so that you may be of assistance [ezer] to your father, as your name requires, for the letters of 'Elazar' make up the two words 'ezer' and 'El', i.e. 'el' from the right, which is the secret of Ḥesed, and Ezer from the left, which is the secret of Gvurah. This is what is written: "I will make him a helpmeet (ezer) for him" (Genesis 2:18), for Malkhut, which is built up from the left, is referred to as a helpmeet for him. In what way does it become a helpmeet for him? With good seed [zera'], the word for 'seed' being spelled zayin resh ayin, which are the letters of 'ezer' [ayin zayin resh] in a different order.

C o m m e n t a r y

'*Ezer*' is the left-hand column, and so long as it is not united with the right, it has no seed [*zera*] and no emanations, but when it unites with the right it is the opposite, for all the seed comes from it.

The name '*Elazar*' contains the right and the left in unity, for its first two letters spell '*el*', which is the right column, and its remaining three letters spell '*ezer*', which is the left. Thus, '*ezer*' ('helpmeet') becomes '*zera*' ('seed'), for there is no seed other than that which comes from it.

187 And let Rabbi Yossi rise up with you, for he is a perfect throne for his Master, for the numerical value of Yossi [yud vav samekh yud, i.e. 10 + 6 + 60 + 10 = 86] is the same as that of 'the throne' [haKissei, hei, kaf samekh aleph, i.e. 5 + 20 + 60 + 1 = 86] and that of 'God' [Elohim, aleph lamed hei yud mem, i.e. 1 + 30 + 5 + 10 + 40 = 86], i.e. Malkhut.

And let Rabbi Yehuda rise

up with him, for the letters of `Yehuda' [yud hei vav dalet hei] make up the two words Hod [hei vav dalet] and Yah, the latter of which instructs us about the first stage of Malkhut, which is then the first three. The letters of the name `Yehuda' can also be re-arranged to spell the Tetragrammaton [yud hei vav and hei] plus dalet. That means that it instructs us about Zeir Anpin, called the Tetragrammaton, and Malkhut, called dalet, prior to its being joined in a mating with the Tetragrammaton. This dalet is the secret of the four beasts. (The numerical value of dalet is 4.) And about them it is said: "And their faces and their wings were stretched upwards" (Ezekiel 1:11).

This pertains to alof them, for they do not yet have the unity of right and left and are ready to receive the central column that will unite them. Therefore, they are the four beasts, for after the unification of right and left, they are considered as three beasts, which is the secret of the three columns, each one of which has four countenances. And from him, from Yehuda, came David, who gave thanks to the Holy One, blessed be He, at the level of thanks-givings [hoda-ot], which is from the side of Hod.

And let Rabbi Ela-i rise up with him, for the numerical value of the letters of Ela-i [aleph lamed ayin aleph yud, i.e. 1 + 30 + 70 + 1 + 10 = 112] is the same as

that of Yabbak [yud bet kuf, i.e. 10 + 2 + 100 = 112], which, in a different order, spell baki (= erudite), for he is erudite in the Halakhah.

188 And let Rabbi Yuda-i rise up with him, for the numerical value of the letters of Yuda-i [yud vav dalet aleph yud, i.e. 10 + 6 + 4 + 1 + 10 = 31] is the same as that of El [aleph lamed, i.e. 1 + 30 = 31], meaning `God', and he is like the angels, Michael and the others, who have the letters of `El' in their names. It is as in the expression: "It is in the power of my hand" (Genesis 31:29), where the word rendered `power' is `el'. And the secret of `el' [aleph lamed] is as follows: the aleph is the likeness of a man, for the letter has the form of a body with two arms (see above, Balak, 159), and the lamed is the secret of the three beasts, each one of which is with four countenances, and the three beasts are intimated in the three yuds that ascend to lamed, which are at the beginning of the three Havayas which are "The Lord reigns, the Lord reigned, the Lord will reign forever", where `the Lord' in each case is the Tetragrammaton. In other words: the three yuds at the head of each Tetragrammaton [yud hei vav and hei] hint at the three beasts, each of which has four countenances, for in each name are the four letters of the Tetragrammaton. And this is the secret of the letter lamed of `El'. And let Rabbi Abba rise up with them, for the numerical value of the name Abba [aleph bet aleph, i.e. 1 + 2 + 1 = 4] is four, i.e. the four beasts.

Commentary

For they are in the aspect of *Ḥesed* and *Gvurah*, right and left, for Rabbi Yuda-i, whose name has the numerical value of the letters of the word `*El*', is the secret of *Ḥesed*, which is the secret of the three beasts, each of which has four countenances, i.e. that are united in the central column, as above. And Rabbi Abba is

Gvurah and the left column, and is therefore intimated in the number '4', which is the secret of the four beasts, which teaches that the central column has not yet united them. See above, the adjoining paragraph.

189 (*223b) Rabbi Shimon is like a tree, and Rabbi Elazar his son and his comrades, the five that we have just mentioned, are like large branches coming out of the tree, similar to arms and legs, where arms are Ḥesed and Gvurah, and legs are Netzaḥ and Hod.

Commentary

Rabbi Shimon and his son Rabbi Elazar are the secret of the central column, *Da'at*, *Tiferet*, *Yesod*, which are the trunk of the tree. Rabbi Yuda-i is *Ḥesed*, and Rabbi Abba *Gvurah*, as explained above. Rabbi Ela-i is *Netzaḥ*, and Rabbi Yehuda *Hod*. Omitted here are Rabbi Yitzḥak and Rabbi Ḥiyya. It would appear that this was prior to the *Idra* (a section of the Zohar), and subsequently the orders were changed. There were ten pupils in the *Idra Rabba*, whose names are given there, but later only seven remained, as at the end of the *Idra*.

FOR THE LEADER (PSALMS 60:1) GIVE THANKS (I CHRONICLES 16:8). REJOICE O RIGHTEOUS (PSALMS 31: 1): GIVE PRAISE, MELODY, TUNE, SONG, BLESSING, ETC.

190 Rise, Rabbi Shimon, and let us hear new matters from you on this verse: "For the Leader, upon Shushan Eduth, Mikhtam of David, to teach." (Psalms 60:1). (Said Rabbi Shimon:) The first word 'For the Leader' [Lamnatzeaḥ, lamed mem nun tzadik ḥet] contains the letters of Netzaḥ [nun tzadik ḥet], the meaning of which is nigun tzaḥ ('pure

melody'), and with it is called "The Lord (Tetragrammaton) is a man of war" (Exodus 15:3) for the nations of the world, but mercy and justice are on Israel. And the secret of the matter is contained in: "And when the wicked perish, there is joy" (Proverbs 11:10). Thus, when God is victorious [menatzeaḥ = leader, also] over the wicked, there is a pure melody.

The letters `mem and `lamed' of the word Lamnatzeaḥ (`For the Leader') have the numerical values of 40 and 30 respectively (= 70), and are the secret of the seventy names that He has. Together with Netzaḥ and Hod, they come to 72, which is the numerical equivalent of Ḥesed [het samekh dalet, i.e. 8 + 60 + 4 = 72]. And the secret of the matter is in the verse: "In Your right hand bliss for evermore [Netzaḥ]" (Psalms 16:11), for Netzaḥ is to the right, which is Ḥesed.

191 Having clarified that `For the Leader' is the secret of the Sfirah Netzaḥ, he continues: next Hod, about which it is said: "Give thanks to the Lord" (I Chronicles 16:8). Then righteous', which is Yesod, about which it is written: "Rejoice O righteous in the Lord" (Psalms 31:1), and also: "Sing with gladness for Jacob" (Jeremiah 31:7), which teaches about the unity, Tiferet, Yesod, Malkhut. For `sing' is Yesod, in which there is rejoicing. Jacob is Tiferet and rejoicing Malkhut. Tiferet, about which it is said: "Praise God" (Psalms 150:1), "Praise the Lord", "Praise Yah" and with the Tetragrammaton, which is a name for Tiferet. With melody and tune: this is Ḥesed and Gvurah, melody being Ḥesed, and tune Gvurah. With song and blessing is Ḥokhmah and Binah, song being Ḥokhmah, and blessing Binah. Happy is Keter and praise is Malkhut.

192 Mizmor [mem zayin mem vav resh] (`psalm'), which is Gvurah, has in it the letters resh zayin and the letters mem vav mem, from the side of the tune of Torah and the tune of prayer. For the left column, when it has control by itself, light becomes resh zayin, (secret) which is the reverse side of light. And therefore it has in it mem vav mem, (flaw) containing a hold for the external ones, and all of this is from the side of holiness.

The Psalm that is sung by the evil forces in mem vav mem zayin resh, i.e. mum zar (rather than mizmor), meaning a foreign blemish, and this is why they said "Melody in the house, destruction in the house" (cf. Talmud Bavli, Sota 48a), and it is from the aspect of a menstruating woman, bond-woman, daughter of idol worshippers, prostitute. And these are the letters of Mizmor, i.e. resh zayin, mem vav mem,

Melody (Niggun, nun gimel vav nun) is Ḥesed, containing the letters gimel nun (= Gan, `garden'), which is Malkhut, and such is the beauty of the melody, for it has in it Hallel (`Praise'), as in the Hallel (Psalms 113:128), as in "It was a night of watching to the Lord for bringing them out of the Land of Egypt" (Exodus 12:42). In other words, not every melody is Ḥesed, but only the beauty of the melody bends down towards Ḥesed, which is the secret of the Hallel of the Exodus from Egypt, which inclines towards Ḥesed. Ashrei (`Happy'), with which the world begins to offer praises, in Keter, since Keter is the beginning of the Sfirot, e.g. "Happy is the people that is in such a case" (Psalms 144:15). Berakhah (`Blessing'), as in "I will bless the Lord at all times" (Psalms 34:2), is Binah, for the emanation of Binah is unceasing. Tehilah (`Praise'), as in "His praise is in my mouth continually" (Psalms 34:2) is Malkhut, for `mouth' intimates Malkhut.

193 Returning now to the verse: "For the Leader, upon Shushan Eduth, Mikhtam of David, to teach" (Psalms 60:1), it has been explained that "For the Leader" is Netzaḥ. "Upon Shushan Eduth" is Netzaḥ, and he goes on, upon Shushan Eduth is Hod, which is in which the red controls the white, while with Netzaḥ the white controls the red. But what is Eduth (Testimony)? This is the righteous one who is the covenant, i.e. Yesod, which is held by the heavens and the earth which are Zeir Anpin and Malkhut. This is as it is written: "I call heaven and earth to witness against you this day" (Deuteronomy 4:26), which implies the unity of Tiferet, Yesod, and Malkhut, for 'I call to witness' is Yesod, while the heaven and earth are Tiferet and Malkhut. What is Mikhtam? [The literal meaning of this word is unclear; it is used as a title in the headings of six psalms, and a possible rendering is "A Psalm of Expiation". — tr.] The letters of Mikhtam [mem kaf tav mem] form the two words makh [mem kaf] and tam [tav mem]; and makh ('humble') is righteous one, i.e. Yesod, while tam ('complete') is the central column, i.e. Tiferet, which is secret of the body, on the level of "Jacob was a complete man" (Genesis 25:27). We consider the body and the covenant, which are Tiferet and Yesod, to be one, which is why makh and tam are written as one word: mikhtam.

'To teach' (in the heading of Psalm 60): This is Ḥesed and Gvurah, for from there was the Torah given "to learn and to teach" (see the "Ahavah Rabba" prayer, the second blessing before the Shema Yisrael, in the Morning Service). And this verse contains all seven of the Sfirot: Ḥesed, Gvurah, Tiferet, Netzaḥ, Hod, Yesod, and Malkhut. For, 'to teach' is Ḥesed and Gvurah, 'Mikhtam' is Tiferet, 'For the Leader' is Netzaḥ, 'Upon Shushan' is Hod, 'Eduth' is Yesod and 'to David' is Malkhut.

194 The Faithful Shepherd said to Rabbi Shimon: What you say is all very well, but Scripture says: "For the Leader; on the Sheminith" (apparently an eight-stringed instrument — tr.) (Psalms Shushan 12:1). This means that Netzaḥ should not move from Hod, which is the eighth Sfirah, and that is why he says: For the Leader [Lamnatzeaḥ = Netzaḥ] on the Sheminith [= Hod], rather than "For the Leader; upon Shushan", as you have it. The Holy Luminary, Rabbi Shimon, responded: If that

is so, if you want to be so pedantic, one can ask an even profounder question. Your level is that of Binah; why, then, was it taught that He gave Hod to Moses (the Faithful Shepherd)? — as it is written: "And you (Moses) shall put some of your honor [Hod] upon him (Joshua)." (Numbers 27:20)?

195 The Faithful Shepherd replied: That is a good question that you have asked. The reason is that the letter hei of the Yah [yud hei] of the Tetragrammaton [yud hei vav and hei] ascends and is multiplied by the yud of Yah [yud hei], making five times ten, which is 50, i.e. the fifty gates of Binah, whose extention is from Ḥesed to Hod, i.e. five Sfirot. And in each of the Sfirot there are ten, making fifty Sfirot, that receive the fifty gates of Binah, and there is, therefore, just one extention from Binah to Hod, in which Binah is included. Subsequently `righteous one', which is Yesod, comes and by itself takes all fifty gates of Binah, it being equivalent to all five, since Yesod incorporates all five Sfirot: Ḥesed, Gvurah, Tiferet, Netzaḥ, and Hod. And it is called `all', kol [kaf lamed, i.e. 20 + 30 = 50] because it takes all 50 gates. And so also does the bride [kallah, kaf lamed hei], which is Malkhut, take all 50 gates, which is why it is called bride [kaf lamed hei], i.e. kol [kaf lamed], as Yesod, hinting at the fifty gates, with the addition of hei, it being feminine.

Said Rabbi Shimon: Now surely everything is falling into place, and I understand.

Commentary

Indeed, one who has not merited *Binah*, but only the five *Sfirot*: *Ḥesed*, *Gvurah*, *Tiferet*, *Netzaḥ*, and *Hod*, has only so merited them in terms of themselves, but has not merited the spread of the fifty gates of *Binah* which is in them.

196 Again. The letters of the word for `For the Leader', Lamnatzeaḥ [lamed mem nun tzadik ḥet] can be re-arranged as mal with Netzaḥ. And what is mal [mem lamed]? mem is the first letter and lamed the last letter of min ḥashmal (from `electrum' — v. Ezekiel Chapter 1), and min ḥashmal can be re-arranged to read mal min ḥash, and ḥash [ḥet shin] is the first and last letters of ḥayot esh (`beasts of fire'), and these are Hod and Netzaḥ, which are parallel to the two lips, Netzaḥ being the upper and Hod the lower lip. Therefore the lips are called the speaking beasts of fire. And in Ḥagigah the question is asked: "Until where is the Work of the Chariot?" (Talmud Bavli, Ḥagigah 13a). And the answer was given: From `And I looked' (Ezekiel 1:4) until `electrum' (Ezekiel 1:27), where the word `electrum' [ḥashmal, ḥet shin mem lamed] forms the initials of speaking beasts of fire. [ḥet for ḥayot = beasts; shin, the last letter of `esh' = fire; mem lamed, two of the root letters of m'mal'lot, `speaking'.] For from the side of Gvurah, Netzaḥ, and Hod are called beasts of fire, and the river that flows from the sweat of these beasts of fire is Yesod, and all three of them, that is Netzaḥ, Hod and Yesod, form a Chariot for the splendor of man, which is Zeir Anpin.

Commentary

The word *Lamnatzeaḥ* (`For the Leader') is here interpreted as referring to *Netzaḥ* and *Hod* together, as the text says: The letters of the word *lamnatzeaḥ* can be re-arranged as *mal* and *Netzaḥ*, where *mal* of *hashmal* (`electrum') means `speaking' [*m'mal'lot*]. And the only speech is by means of the two lips which are `*Netzaḥ* and *Hod*', and therefore when there are the words with *mal* (*mem lamed*) with *Netzaḥ*, *mal* points to *Hod*, for in the joining with *Hod Netzaḥ* becomes a speaker.

He also clarifies, incidentally, that from the side of *Gvurah*, *Netzaḥ*, and *Hod* are speaking beasts of fire, the initials of this phrase being the letters of *ḥashmal* (`electrum'). And *Yesod* is the secret of the river of fire that flows from the perspiration of *Netzaḥ* and *Hod*. And *Netzaḥ*, *Hod*, and *Yesod* are the chariot for *Tiferet*, which is really *Zeir Anpin*.

And where the text says `Until where is the Work of the Chariot?', the answer was: From `And I looked' until `electrum', i.e. until speaking beasts of fire, which are hinted at by the initials *ḥet shin mem lamed* [*ḥashmal*, `electrum'], and which are *Netzaḥ* and *Hod*, with *Yesod* including them.

197 The Work of the Chariot: this is Malkhut, inasmuch as it is made by the Chariot that is Netzaḥ, Hod, and Yesod, and in these three (Netzaḥ, Hod, and Yesod) are Ḥokhmah, Binah, and Da'at of Malkhut, for Ḥokhmah, Binah, Da'at of Malkhut are made from the heads of Netzaḥ, Hod, and Yesod of Zeir Anpin. For this reason the sages of the Mishnah taught: "The Work of the Chariot may not be expounded by one alone, unless he is a sage who understands of his own knowledge" (Mishnah Ḥagigah 2, 1). And who is meant: by a sage (haḥam) who understands (mevin) of his own knowledge (mida'ato)? This refers to one who has merited Ḥokhmah, Binah, and Da'at, since a sage (haḥam) is Ḥokhmah; who understands (mevin) is Binah; and of his own knowledge (mida'ato) is Da'at.

THE CHARIOT OF METATRON

198 And there is a Chariot below, composed of Netzaḥ, Hod, Yesod of Zeir Anpin, who is Metatron, alias the small man; and in his Chariot, which is Pardes, they are hurrying from the sea of the Torah, like a river whose waters are flowing with great speed and force towards the sea, flowing out of his

Orchard, namely: Ben Azzai and Ben Zoma, the other one (Elisha ben Abuyah) and Rabbi Akiva" (Talmud Bavli, Ḥagigah 14b). The first three were injured by the force of the flow of the waters of Ḥokhmah, which are called Pardes, and only Rabbi Akiva entered in peace and "left in peace". (ibid.) And we have already learnt this.

Commentary

The Chariot of Metatron, the secret of the four angels Michael, Gabriel, Uriel, and Raphael, is also called *Pardes*. And they said about it "Four entered Pardes" (*Talmud Bavli*, *Ḥagigah* 14b). The *Ḥokhmah* flowing out of this *Pardes* is called water, and it was in these waters that Ben Azzai, Ben Zoma and Elisha failed, that is with the exception of Rabbi Akiva, "who entered in peace and left in peace" (*Ḥagigah*, ibid.).

199 For he, Metatron, is the bird who espied Rava bar bar Hannah on the beach of the sea of the Torah (Talmud Bavli, Baba Batra, 73b.) when the sea, which is the secret of Malkhut, rose and reached his ankles, i.e. to the end of his Netzaḥ and Hod, called ankles, and his head reached to the top of the heavens, which is Zeir Anpin, and the three of them were faulted in it, which is the secret of the Pardes, as above. And the three of them were not faulted in it because it contains much waters of Ḥokhmah, but because of the force of the flow of the waters of Ḥokhmah in it (Baba Batra, 73b). That is to say that they are sharp and forceful with laws, and so have we learnt.

200 The first three letters of the alphabet, aleph, bet, gimel, include them, that is the components of the Chariot of Metatron, for the numerical value of these three letters is (1 + 2 + 3 =) six, which is the number of letters in the name Metatron [mem tet

tet resh vav nun]. The fourth letter of the alphabet, dalet, is the secret of "a still small voice" (I Kings 19:12), which is the secret of Malkhut, for the King comes there (cf. Talmud Bavli, Berakhot 58a), for it (Malkhut) is a man to sit on the throne, since Malkhut is the secret of a man who sits on this throne of Metatron.

201 The letter aleph is written as a line running diagonally downwards from left to right, with a letter yud to the right above and a letter yud to the left below the line. The upper yud stands for the upper waters, which is the secret of Zeir Anpin, and the lower yud for the lower waters, which is the secret of Malkhut, and there is nothing between them apart from a hairsbreadth, which is the letter vav, written like the line in the middle of the letter aleph; and drawn between the two letters yud is in the secret of the firmament which is the secret of the curtain that "divides the waters from the waters" (Genesis 1:6), so that there should be a distinction between female and male, and that is why it is written "And let it divide..." (Genesis 1:6). And the inner meaning of the matter is as follows: In the combination of the two divine names, the Tetragrammaton [yud hei vav and hei] and 'The Lord' [aleph dalet nun yud], namely: yud aleph hei dalet vav nun hei yud [i.e. taking a letter alternatively from each of them — tr.], the upper or first yud of the combination is the upper, male waters and the lower or last yud of the combination is the lower, female waters. The six letters aleph hei dalet vav nun hei, which come between the two letters yud are as the numerical value of the letter vav (= 6), which is the secret of Metatron, which is the vav between the two yuds in the form of the letter aleph.

Commentary

The Tetragrammaton is the secret of *Zeir Anpin* and the Lord of *Malkhut*. When the two of them are in a mating, the two names combine together to form the combination: *Yud Aleph Hei Dalet Vav Nun Hei Yud.* And then *Zeir Anpin,* is essentially in the first *yud* of the combination, which is the secret of Upper *Ḥokhmah,* and *Malkhut* is essentially in the secret of the final *yud* of the combination, which is the secret of Lower *Ḥokhmah.* The six letters that come between the two letters *yud* hint at *Yesod,* which unites *Zeir Anpin* and *Malkhut* with each other. And it is known that on weekdays, Metatron serves instead of *Yesod* to unite *Zeir Anpin* and *Malkhut,* which is why the text says that the six letters between the first *yud* and the last *yud* hint at Metatron, for he is discussing weekday unification (see Introduction of *Tikunei haZohar,* page 2, bottom).

202 Again, yud is a point, which is the secret of Upper Ḥokhmah. Vav is the secret of wheel, which revolves with the six Sfirot: Ḥesed, Gvurah, Tiferet, Netzaḥ, Hod, Yesod. And there is no movement in the wheel at the six intermediate Sfirot, as the numerical value of vav, but only at the point, for everything that is in Ḥesed, Gvurah, Tiferet, Netzaḥ, Hod, and Yesod is received from this yud. And this point is the unity of everything, and is witness to that unity, which is Ein Sof ('the Infinite One'), who is unique, and about whom the sages taught that one has to proclaim His unity in order to establish His kingship (*224a) over the heavens and the earth and the four directions of the compass. This is the secret of the aleph (whose numerical value is one). Bet (numerical value 2) is the secret of heaven and earth, which are Zeir Anpin and Malkhut. Gimel (numerical value 3) is the secret of the pillar that bears them, which is the secret of Yesod. Dalet (numerical value 4) is the secret of the four beasts of the Chariot. Hei (numerical value 6) is the secret of the six steps up to the throne, which are Ḥesed, Gvurah, Tiferet, Netzaḥ, Hod, and Yesod.

Again. The first nine letters of the alphabet: aleph, bet, gimel, dalet, hei, vav, zayin, ḥet, tet are the secret of man, i.e. the first nine Sfirot of Zeir Anpin. Yud (the tenth letter of the

alphabet) is His Unity, i.e. Malkhut, which is the tenth Sfirah of Zeir Anpin who is called Adam (`man'). This is the secret of the Tetragrammaton filled in with alephs, making the numerical value of Adam [aleph dalet mem, i.e. 1 + 4 + 40 = 45]. The nine Sfirot of Zeir Anpin parallel nine letters. Happy are those of Israel who know the secret of their Master!

SMOKE AND FRAGRANCE AND INCENSE

203 Alternative explanation: "Command the Children of Israel and say unto them: My food which is presented to Me for offerings made by fire, of a sweet savor to Me..." (Numbers 28:2). Rabbi Yehuda said: With an offering there is smoke and there is fragrance and there is a pleasant aroma. Smoke is from the side of Judgment, as it is said: "But then the anger of the Lord shall be kindled" (Deuteronomy 29:19) [The Hebrew idiom is "the nostril of the Lord will smoke" — tr.] "Smoke arose up in His nostrils, and fire out of His mouth did devour" (Psalms 18:9). Pleasant aroma is Mercy, as it is said: "The fragrance of your nostrils is like apples" (Song of Songs 7:9).

204 Said the Faithful Shepherd: Both of them, smoke and fragrance, are in the nostrils, and are called testimony. The former is in the nostrils, as it is written: "Smoke arose up in His nostrils" (Psalms 18:9), and the latter is in the nostrils, as it is said: "The fragrance of your nostrils is like apples" (Song of Songs 7:9). If that is so, if they are both in the nostrils, then why is the former, smoke, called Judgement, and the latter, fragrance, called Mercy? The answer is that in the nose there are two openings, each of which is a nostril. "Smoke arose up in His nostrils" is said about the left-hand nostril, which is Judgement. What is the meaning of "arose up"? It is that the smoke rose up from the heart, which is on the left and is parallel to Gvurah. And from the right a breeze descends to cool him and quiet his anger from the side of ḥesed, which is where the

brain is; i.e. Ḥokhmah, which is to the right, who wishes to aquire wisdom moves to the south. And Binah, which is the secret of Ḥokhmah of the left, is in the heart, opposite the left, and who wishes to enrich moves to the north. And this is why "Smoke arose up in His nostrils", i.e. from Binah, which is on the left, to Ḥokhmah, which is on the right. And Ḥokhmah welcomes it with rejoicing and levitical melody.

205 And this smoke only rises up with fire that is kindled with pieces of wood that are mitzvah-full limbs, which are called "the wood for the burnt offering" (cf. Genesis 22:3). And the Torah of Torah scholars is enkindled by the mitzvot, their fire is by virtue of Gvurah, and the smoke rising up in them, in Binah, is called the smoke of the system.

206 And when the smoke has arisen and reached the nostril, it is called incense, as it is written: "They shall put incense in Your nostrils." (Deuteronomy 33:10). And nothing is as effective as incense for doing away with death in the world, for incense is the connecting of Judgment in Mercy with the pleasant fragrance in the nostril, for the Hebrew root kuf shin resh (meaning to connect or tie together) is in Aramaic kuf tet resh, and this is the Hebrew root for incense. (cf. Midrash Bereshit Rabba 61:4). Said Rabbi Yehuda: Happy is our portion that we have gained hidden matters and can understand them openly. The Holy Luminary added: Since prayer is like a sacrifice, anyone, therefore, who says the prayer "Compounding of the Incense" after "Praise of David" (Psalm 145) does away with death from the house.

Commentary

The Judgment that ascends from the left column before the latter has joined with the right column (see above, Gen. I, 47) is called smoke. However, these Judgments do not ascend and are not recognised from the point of view of the *tikune* (correction), but by the curtain of the *ḥirik* (vowel `i'), that the central column makes to rise up, as above (see *Lekh* 13, where the matter is explained.) For the curtain of this *ḥirik* is termed fire and wood, with which the sacrifice is burnt, which hints at the diminution of the first three of the left, from which the smoke ascends, for they are the judgments of the left prior to its joining with the right. And this is distinguished in the secret of the offering of the sacrifice in two ways:

a) The smoke which is the judgment of the left when it is separate from the right.

b) The pleasant fragrance, which is the secret of the large illuminations that emanate after the unification of the left with the right, in the secret of the six intermediate *Sfirot* of *Ḥokhmah* that give light upwards from below, in the same way as the fragrance rises up into the nose from below, and not as food and drink that enter the body in a downwards direction from above.

The text: With an offering there is smoke and there is fragrance and there is a pleasant aroma. Smoke is from the side of Judgment, as it is said: "But then the anger of the Lord shall be kindled" (Deuteronomy 29:19) (above, 203). For these are the judgments that rise up from the left column before it is joined to the right.

Pleasant aroma is Mercy, as it is said; "The fragrance of your nostrils is like apples" (Song of Songs 7:9) This is the secret of the intermediate *Sfirot* of the left that join up with the right, which is the secret of *Ḥokhmah*'s six intermediate *Sfirot* enclothed in *Ḥasadim*, that cause the pleasant fragrance to ascend.

The Faithful Shepherd then shows a difficulty with this explanation, and says (above, 204): Both of them, smoke and fragrance, are in the nostrils, and are called testimony; that is to say, the smoke, which is the secret of the judgment of the left side when it is separate from the right, is not at its root but in *Binah*, for it is there that the two columns, the left and the right, separated from each other, until *Zeir Anpin* came and united them in the secret of the central column, and when they are with *Zeir Anpin* they exemplify the secret of three came out from one, and one exists in three (see above, Gen. I, 287, Three.) Thus the two columns, left and right, have already come to Him when they are in unity, and it follows that the source of the smoke is only in *Binah*, from which the smoke is emitted by the unity of the central column, and joins with the right, which is the secret of *Ḥokhmah*, for the right column of *Binah* is called *Ḥokhmah*, and is the aspect of *Ḥasadim* (as above, *Tzav*, 151). And after the columns become united with each other and attires itself *Ḥokhmah* of the left in the *Ḥasadim* of the right, and the smoke ceases, they then re-awaken, the smoke with *Ḥokhmah* sweetened in *Ḥasadim* and rise up in the two orifices of the nose, and divide up there. The smoke is in the left orifice, and the fragrance, which is the secret of the *Ḥasadim*-attired *Ḥokhmah*, in the right orifice of the nose. And the smoke which is located in the left orifice of the nose is not considered to be Judgment, for *Ḥokhmah*

and *Ḥasadim* have already been united with each other by *Ḥokhmah* and *Binah*. It is, instead, considered a witness, for the smoke and the fragrance are in the two orifices of the nose by way of two witnesses that testify to the great action of the central column, by whose power the left and the right have been united. The smoke testifies to the harsh Judgments which were on the left before it united with the right; the pleasant fragrance testifies to the extent of the light's greatness and praise, following the unification of the right and the left. In this case the smoke that rests in the nose is not in the aspect of Judgment, but, on the contrary, is as a witness of the action of the central column, by whose testimony this unity is maintained, more than any grasp in the world.

Rabbi Yehuda had said: The smoke is from the side of Judgment (203), but the Faithful Shepherd corrects this, and states: Both of them, smoke and fragrance, are in the nostrils and are called testimony (204), as they are only in the aspect of testimony, as has been explained. See above for the secret of *Zeir Anpin*'s nose (*Idra Rabba*, *Naso*, 223).

The text says: The answer is that in the nose there are two openings, each of which is a nostril. "Smoke arose up in His nostrils" is said about the left, i.e. the left-hand orifice. What is the meaning of "arose up"? It is that the smoke arose up from the heart, etc. The heart is the secret of *Binah*, which is the left column, i.e. *Ḥokhmah* that is on the left.

Ḥokhmah, which is to the right, etc. This is the secret of the right column, which is *Ḥasadim* (see above *Tzav*, 151, q.v.) And this is why "smoke arose up in His nostrils", from *Binah* to *Ḥokhmah*, which is on the right. And the smoke, which is the secret of the judgement of the left column without the right, inasmuch as it is *Ḥokhmah* without *Ḥasadim* (as above in *Tikunei Zohar*, page 17.), whose origin is in *Binah*, as explained above — This smoke ascends and is sweetened by the *Ḥokhmah* of the right, which is *Ḥasadim*.

And welcome it with rejoicing. The right welcomes the left with great rejoicing, for even the right is not perfected without the unification with the left, for right without left is lacking the first three.

Levitical melody. For this unity is effected at the time that the Levities sing their melody over the offering.

And it is known that, just as *Zeir Anpin* ascends to *Binah*, in which it takes on the aspect of the central column, with the power of its curtain of *ḥirik* that diminishes the first three of the left, and unites the two columns in each other — in this way, subsequently, *Zeir Anpin* is considered as right and *Malkhut* as left, and the central column is needed to unite them with each other. And the souls of Israel, by engaging in Torah and *mitzvot*, bring up the female waters in the aspect of the curtain of *ḥirik* and become for them the aspect of the central column, and were it not for the female waters that the souls of Israel cause to rise up, *Zeir Anpin* and *Malkhut* would not become united with each other (as was explained above, Gen. II, page 152, Commentary, q.v.) And these female waters that are brought up, i.e. the curtain of *ḥirik*, are achieved by the *mitzvot* that are performed. But to enkindle it in such a way that it will diminish the first three of the left is undertaken by the Torah; wherefore he says: And this smoke does not rise up...(205), for the smoke only rises up by the action of the central column, as explained above at the beginning of the Commentary. Thus it only rises up by means of the fire that is kindled with pieces of wood that are *mitzvah*-full limbs, which are called "the wood of the burnt offering". The souls are called the limbs of the *Shekhinah* (see above, *Behar*, 33), as the text says: the souls [*nefesh*], the spirits [*ruaḥ*] and the living souls [*neshamah*] are to the Holy One, blessed be He, and His Divine Presence, as limbs are to a body, and by the many *mitzvot* that these limbs perform they raise the curtain of *ḥirik*.

And the Torah scholars whose Torah enkindles the fire with the mitsvot, by virtue of *Gvurah*, and the smoke rises up in them (205). By means of the Torah in which these limbs engage, they kindle the fire in the rising curtain so that it will perform its task in diminishing the three first of the left, and unite it with the right, and thereby the smoke, which is the secret of the judgments of the left column prior to its unification with the right, ascends. For it is not recognized, nor does it ascend prior to the appearance of the central column with the curtain of *Ôirik*, as explained above.

In *Binah*, the wood of the system. And this smoke, while it is still in *Binah*, i.e. Prior to the unity, is called the smoke of the wood of the system. And when the smoke reaches the nostrils, it is called incense (206). After *Binah* has become united with *Ḥokhmah* and the smoke has risen to the nostrils, as above, the smoke is then termed incense.

For incense is the connecting of Judgment in Mercy with the pleasant fragrance in the nostrils (206). For in the nostrils, the smoke is connected to the pleasant fragrance as one, this being the secret of the two witnesses, as explained above.

THREE PRAYERS

207 The Faithful Shepherd said: One has to know how the prayers were arranged to parallel the sacrifices, for the prayers are three. (cf. Talmud Bavli, Berakhot 26b, which the following text parallels.) The morning prayer [Shaḥarit] parallels "And the one lamb you shall offer in the morning" (Exodus 29:39 and Numbers 28:4). As it is

said: "And Abraham rose early in the morning to go to the place where he had stood before the Lord" (Genesis 19:27), and the rabbis have taught that standing means prayer. "And the other lamb you shall offer at dusk" (Exodus 29:39 and Numbers 28:4) parallels the afternoon prayer [Minḥah], which was set by Isaac, as it is said: "And Isaac went out to meditate in the field at the eventide" (Genesis 24:63) — and there is no meditation that is not prayer. The evening prayer (Arvit) parallels the parts and the pieces (of the burnt-offering) which are devoured "all night" (See Leviticus 6:2). And it is said: "And he came upon the place and spent the night there for the sun had set" (Genesis 28:11), and there is no `coming upon' that is not prayer (This verse refers to Jacob, who established the evening prayer).

208 Since we have referred to the story in our discussion, there is a point in asking why Scripture says: "And he (Jacob) took of the stones of the place and put one under his head, and lay down in that place to sleep" (Genesis 28:11). Did he not have pillows and cushions to lie on? The answer is: When the groom comes to the bride, even if he is used to lying on pillows and cushions, should she give him stones to lie on, he will accept everything willingly. And we have already learned this (Zohar, Gen. II, 216), and it is also stated in the First Part. With respect to the verse: "And Jacob said when he saw them" (Genesis 32:3), Rabbi Shimon said: Sit down. And Scripture says. (Continued in 238, below).

Commentary

Jacob is the secret of *Zeir Anpin*, who is called Jacob, and he cleaves to the intelligence of *Ḥasadim* from Mother, whose emanation is incessant. And it is written here: "And he took of the stones of the place and put one under his head", which means that he took the curtain of the Female, that is termed stones, and drew to her the illumination of the left, which is the secret of staying the night. The question is then put as to why *Zeir Anpin* did this, for his way is to be always in the light of day in the *Ḥasadim* of Mother. The answer to this is given: When the groom comes to the bride ... he will accept everything willingly. This means that the diadem of *Zeir Anpin* is completed only by him mating with the Female (as above, *Balak*, 438 in the Commentary). And since this is the way things are, he accepts her bed of stones willingly and with great longing.

209 Said Rabbi Pinḥas: I have been thinking: 'Keeping' certainly means in the heart, which is why it is written: "Keep" (Deuteronomy 5:12), meaning in the heart, which is Malkhut, and nowhere else. 'Remembering' [zekhirah] is a matter of the male [zakhar], i.e. in the brain, which is Zeir Anpin, and it is therefore written: "Remember the Sabbath day" (Exodus 20:8), meaning for the male, which is Zeir Anpin, while "Keep the Sabbath day" (Deuteronomy 5:12) is for the female, which is Malkhut. The brain, which is the male, Zeir Anpin, mounts and controls the heart, which is Malkhut. The heart controls and mounts the liver, and liver is Samael and Serpent intertwined, and they are one. (*224b) And they are the lobe of the liver and the liver, and so it is with the sacrifice. (cf. Exodus 29 and Leviticus 3). The lobe of the liver is Serpent, and the liver is devourer, the male, who is the secret of Samael.

210 Rabbi Shimon said: That is certainly how it is, and it is good, and it is a clarification of the matter and thus are the secret of the hidden matters of the sacrifice. He (the priest) first takes the liver, together with its lobe,

which are Samael and Serpent his mate, and all those arteries that are in the liver are their hosts and encampments, and their receiving is that they devour the fatty parts and the fat of the sacrifice, as it is written: "and the fat that is upon them" (Exodus 29:22). And then everything draws near [same root as 'sacrifice'] to the heart.

Commentary

This is similar to what the Zohar notes above (*Noaḥ*, 130), where he says: The whole desire of the evil forces is in the flesh, which is the secret of the first three of *Ḥokhmah* that enlighten the left column before it unites with the right, for from the lights of the correction they can not receive anything, for the reason that was explained in the commentary on the text there. And therefore, in the sacrifice, will rises up to one place, and the flesh rises up to another place: that is, the flesh of the sacrifice ascends to the evil forces, but the desire of the person offering the sacrifice and of the priest ascend to holiness. The meaning is that the purpose of the sacrifices is to unite *Zeir Anpin* and *Malkhut*, and at the beginning of the mating the illumination of the first three of *Ḥokhmah* of the left is drawn for a moment, and this illumination is in order to feed the evil forces, sufficient just to keep them alive so that they should not fade away. And this illumination is compared to the flesh of the sacrifice that ascends for the evil forces to devour, while the desire of the sacrifice goes up to unite *Zeir Anpin* and *Malkhut*. Consider the secret (*Balak* 441) of the little illumination of the mating that the evil forces and all the nations of the world take.

And it follows that the purpose of offering a sacrifice on the altar is to bring *Malkhut* close to *Zeir Anpin*, but in its initial stage it feeds the evil forces, for at the beginning of the preparation for the mating of *Zeir Anpin* and *Malkhut*, the three first *Sfirot* of *Ḥokhmah* of the left (Separation) awaken, to give light to and nourish the evil forces, whose source is Samael and Serpent, who are called liver and the lobe of the liver.

And when they said: The liver takes first, this refers to the beginning of the preparation for the mating of *Zeir Anpin* and *Malkhut*. Together with its lobe refers to Samael and his mate, who are the roots of all the evil forces. And all those arteries that are in the liver means the evil forces that spread out from them. And these are the first three of the left of Separation that the evil forces receive, which are termed fatty parts.And their receiving is that they devour the fatty parts. This is done in such a way that the sacrifice that ascends to unite *Zeir Anpin* and *Malkhut*, which are termed brain and heart, first nourishes the evil forces, Samael and Serpent, which are termed liver and lobe of the liver, and subsequently they ascend to unite brain and heart, which are *Zeir Anpin* and *Malkhut*. And see below (410, in the Commentary) where the matter is explained at greater length..

211 And the heart does not receive from the whole of the sacrifice, but only from the confession made with it, which ascends with the smoke and the prayer that is made over the sacrifice. Subsequently, the heart offers to the brain the desire of the unification of the priests in it and the rejoicing of the Levities. This brain, which is Zeir Anpin, is the light that comes from the Divine Brain, which is Father and Mother, and the Divine Brain offers to the All-Hidden who is Completely Unknown, that is, Keter, and everything is inter-connected. And the brain, which is Zeir Anpin, offers pleasure to all, to all the heavenly beings.

212 The arteries that are in the liver, these are the personages, i.e. the angels of the evil forces, and all these are their hosts. The liver is as we said, that is Samael, while the lobe of the liver, which is feminine, is his female. And why is it called lobe [yoteret — from a root meaning to be left over — tr.]? It is because it does not join together with the male, which is Samael, unless it has some spare time left over after the prostitution in which it engages. And leaves him. Yoteret means to leave over, for she leaves the male, and makes him into a left-over, after all her fornications. Again, the female is called yoteret, for when she wants to join together with a man to make him sin, she first of all becomes for him as left-overs, without any importance, i.e. without the power to rule over man, for the start of a sin is as the breadth of a hair. Later she draws close to him, little by little, until she is in one union with him, and he can no longer separate himself from her. And from those arteries that are in the liver, other forces of a number of types spread out, and they all take the limbs and the parts that are burnt on the altar at night, and all of them are included in the liver, which is Samael.

213 And the heart which is the main thing in holiness, i.e. Malkhut, takes and offers to the brain as we have learned (211). The heart rules over the two kidneys, which are Netzaḥ and Hod, and they are two Cherubs, who are advisers, in the secret of the advising kidneys. ("A man has two kidneys. One advises him to good, and one advises him to evil, and it appears that the good one is on his right and the evil one on his left." Talmud Bavli, Berakhot 61a, bot.) That is to say: they arrange the emanation that descends from Zeir Anpin and Malkhut in the secret of the heavens that grind the mannah for the righteous, which are righteous one and righteousness, i.e. Yesod and Malkhut. And they are far and near, right and left. For when Netzaḥ, which is right, is in control they are near, but when Hod, which is left, is in control they

are far. And all of them take and eat from the light of the mating which is by the sacrifice, each one as befits him, until everything is tied together as one.

214 "The sacrifices of God are a broken spirit" (Psalms 51:49). This, (i.e. a broken spirit, confession, and prayer) is sacrificed to the heart. For it is certain that: "And the spirit returns to the God who gave it" (Ecclesiastes 12:7), i.e. a broken spirit ascends to (*225a) God who is Malkhut that is called heart. And the liver, which is Samael, offers it to the heart, for he has become a good advocate for him. And everything is one bond in the sacrifice.

Commentary

Since the liver benefits from the offering of the sacrifice, for it receives from the illumination of the first three of the left of Separation from the beginning of the preparation of the mating (as above, 210), the accuser thus becomes the defence and a good advocate for the broken spirit of the man who sacrifices, that he should be acceptable to the heart, which does this for its own good so that the illumination of its mating should not go wrong.

And so the text says: And the liver offers it to the heart, for he is an advocate for him, since the prosecution has become the defence counsel.

215 And from the liver, which represents Samael, come all the diseases and illnesses to all parts of the body and rest in it. But the heart, which represents Malkhut, is the purest of all the parts of the body, and from it are derived all goodness, all health of all the parts, and all the strength and all the joy and all the perfection needed by all the parts.

THE FAITHFUL SHEPHERD

THE SACRIFICES

216 The Faithful Shepherd said: The purpose of the sacrifices is to remove the impure sides and bring the holy sides near. And we learnt in the First Part that amongst the arteries of the liver, which are the soldiers of Samael, as above, there are large ones and there are those that are both large and small, and they spread out from there in a number of directions, and they take the parts and the pieces that are devoured on the altar the whole night, for the whole of the sacrifice belongs to the Lord, and the evil forces take only the parts and the pieces.

217 The Holy Luminary, that is, Rabbi Shimon, said: O, Faithful Shepherd, did you not say before that the only purpose of the sacrifices of the Holy One, blessed be He, is to draw close the yud to the hei and the vav to the hei? Nevertheless all the sacrifices have to be offered before him, before the Holy One, blessed be He, and He distributes the foodstuffs of the sacrifices to all the various camps, to each as befits him. To the intelligent ones, i.e. on the side of holiness, He gives the nourishment of the Torah, and drinks of the wine and water of the Torah, which is the secret of the central column that is called Torah, by which all the lights are corrected. To the natural ones, which are the shades who are like people, i.e. the evil forces, He gives the natural foodstuffs, whose fire descends to devour them, i.e. the illuminations coming from the left column of Separation, without the correction of the central column that is called Torah.

218 And this is as the sages taught. (cf. Talmud Bavli, Ḥagigah 16a and Sanhedrin 109a — shades like people.) If Israel is meritorious, He would descend like a lion of fire to devour the sacrifices, but if they were not meritorious, He would descend like a dog of fire. Likewise, when a man dies, if he has been meritorious, the image of a lion descends to welcome his soul, but if he has not been meritorious, an image of a dog descends, concerning which David said: "Deliver my soul from the sword; my only one from the power of the dog" (Psalms 22:21).

219 And since the Holy One, blessed be He, desired to save the bodies of Israel from them [from the evil forces — tr.], and their souls, too, He commanded that sacrifices be offered of beasts and bodies in their stead (instead of Israel), so that the evil forces should not have control over them (Israel), but should enjoy them (the sacrificed animals). (See above, 210, in the Commentary.) This is according to the verse: "If your enemy be hungry, give him bread to eat, and if he be thirsty give him water to drink" (Proverbs 25:11). And thus will the accuser become counsel for the defence (see above 214). But the Holy One, blessed be He, takes nothing from the sacrifice except the desire of the heart and remorse of the heart, as it is written: "The sacrifices of God are a broken spirit; a broken and contrite heart, O God, You will not despise" (Psalms 51:49). They are like earthenware vessels, about which it is said: "After they are broken, they become clean" (Mishnah, Kelim 2,1).

220 (There are three divisions of the Jewish people; Priests, Levites, and Israelites.) A priest is brain, standing for Zeir Anpin, which is right. Levite is heart, standing for Malkhut, which is on the left. Israelites are the body, i.e. the central column, for when the souls of Israel rise up to the Female Waters, they become the central column, between Zeir Anpin and Malkhut (see above, 206, in the Commentary "And it is known"), and it is said about them: "The priests at their service, the Levites at their teaching-stand, and the Israelites at their post" (cf. Talmud Bavli, Megillah, 3a). And if the liver, which is Samael, wishes to offer fatty parts that are levitically impure to the heart, he takes only the fat of a levitically pure fatty levitically part. That is: the three first of the left of Separation are levitically impure fatty parts and the six intermediate Sfirot of Ḥokhmah of the left that are united with the right by the central column are levitically pure fatty part. For just as in the body there are pure and impure fatty parts, clean blood without waste matter and blood contaminated with waste matter, for the arteries of blood in the heart, which is Malkhut, are the holy hosts, while the arteries of the liver, which is Samael, are the impure hosts. Here also, there are camps of the evil inclination and camps of the good inclination. The latter are appointed over the arteries of the heart and the former over the arteries of the liver. Similarly, too, there are two types of people: Israel, who is like the arteries of the heart, and the other nations of the world, who are like the arteries of the liver.

221 The Faithful Shepherd said to him: What you have said is altogether beautiful, but even the Israelites are not all equal, for there are amongst them the sons of royalty, from the side of the holy Malkhut that is composed of ten Sfirot and all the Havayot and names; and there are those that are like slaves, from the side of the servant, Metatron, who is "his servant, the elder of his house" (Genesis 24:2), i.e. of Malkhut. There are also those who are like animals, about whom it is said: "And you, My sheep, the sheep of My pasture, are men" (Ezekiel 34:31). And the Holy One, blessed be He, commanded those who are like sheep to sacrifice animals in their stead, to make atonement for them. But the sacrifices of those who are like angels are the good deeds, over which are appointed angels who offer the good deeds before the Holy One, blessed be He, in the stead of them.

222 And those who are the sons of the Tetragrammaton, about whom it is written: "You are the children of the Lord (the Tetragrammaton) your God" (Deuteronomy 14:1). It is because of their sins that the letters of the Tetragrammaton become separated, for there is no heavenly mating of yud hei, and there is no mating of Zeir Anpin and Malkhut, which are vav hei. And their correction lies in the Torah, which is the four-letter name of God (the Tetragrammaton), to bring the letters together by means of their sacrifice: yud with hei, which is the secret of the mating of Father and Mother, and vav with hei, which is the secret of the mating of Zeir Anpin and Malkhut.

223 And for all the sacrifices, whether of those who are animal-like, or those who are like the angels appointed over the precepts, or of those who are like royalty, or of those who are like the Tetragrammaton — in all cases the sacrifice has to be offered to the Holy One, blessed be He, in a mating of the four holy letters of the Tetragrammaton, and the Holy One, blessed be He, mounts with the four letters of the Tetragrammaton on the four angelic beings (Michael, Gabriel, Uriel, and Raphael) which are the Chariot that is in the Creation. And the Holy One, blessed be He rides, with the four letters of the Tetragrammaton, on the four prime elements of fire, wind, water, and earth, which are the secret of Ḥesed and Gvurah, Tiferet and Malkhut, that are in the world of Formation, which is the aspect of Yesod. From them were created the four natural beings, i.e. Ḥesed and Gvurah, Tiferet and Malkhut, that are in the world of action. And the Holy One, blessed be He, Himself brings water close to fire, which is the secret of the two columns Ḥesed and Gvurah; and this is the secret of yud hei, and the bringing of wind to the earth (i.e. Tiferet, that is called wind, to Malkhut, that is called earth), this being the secret of vav hei. And this is as it is written: "He makes peace in His high places" (Job 25:2). And so also, He brings together the four beings of the angels, namely: Michael, who is the thought intelligence of water, with Gabriel, who is thought intelligence of fire, which is the secret of right and left, the basis of yud hei; and He also brings close Uriel, who is air, i.e. thought intelligence of wind, with Raphael, who is thought intelligence of earth, which

is the secret of vav hei. For the moment the Holy One, blessed be He, departs from amongst them, they have no strength.

224 Should you suggest that we have here a problem, since it is written about all the sacrifices "to the Lord" (the united Tetragrammaton), and ask how, therefore, can it be said that there is a separation of the letters of the Tetragrammaton, and that the sacrifice now comes to unite them? — I should answer: This is said about those stages that were created and called by His name and not that they are He Himself, as it is written: "Everyone that is called by My name, and whom I have created for My glory, I have formed him, and also made him" (Isaiah 43:7); and there are the four letters of the Tetragrammaton in Atziluth, containing no separation nor cessation, for they are as fountains for all the worlds, watering the trees. And regarding those that were created, i.e. vis-a-vis the Tetragrammaton attired in the world of Creation, the four letters of Atziluth are likened, the yud to a head, the vav to a body, while the two heis are likened to ten fingers (5 + 5 = 10).

225 But the Prime Cause, i.e. the Infinite One (Ein Sof), blessed be He, who is over everything, whose light is attired in the Tetragrammaton is called yud hei vav and hei, about Him it is said: "To whom then will you liken Me, that I should be equal? says the Holy One" (Isaiah 40:25). "To whom then will you liken God, or what likeness will you compare to Him?" (Isaiah 40: 18) "For I, the Lord, change not" (Malakhi 3:6). The sins of the creatures below do not touch Him, nor separate in Him the letter yud from the letter hei, nor the vav from the hei. For there is no separation in Him and it is said about Him. "Evil shall not sojourn with You" (Psalms 5:5). He rules over all and there is none who rules over Him. He comprehends all and there is none who comprehends Him. And He is not called by the Tetragrammaton, nor by all the other names, but is known by His light that spreads over them, over

the levels that are in the four worlds, Atziluth, Briah, Yetzirah, Assiah, and when He departs from them, He has, of Himself, no name at all. "Exceeding deep; who can find Him?" (Ecclesiastes 7:24).

226 And there is no light that can withstand His radiance without appearing dark, even upper Keter, of Atziluth, whose light is stronger than all of the levels and all the hosts of the upper and lower heavens, and it is said about Him, concerning Himself: "He made darkness His hiding place" (Psalms 18:12). Concerning Ḥokhmah and Binah, it is said, "cloud and mist surround him". How much more is it so for the other Sfirot and for the celestial beings, and the prime elements that are dead, without life. He surrounds all the worlds, and none but He surrounds them in any direction, up or down or the four corners of the compass, and no-one has left His domain for the outside, for He fills all the worlds and there is no other that fills them.

227 He grants life to all the worlds, and there is no other god above Him to give Him life, as it is said: "You give life to them all" (Nehemiah 9:6), and for Him Daniel said: "All the inhabitants of the earth are reputed as nothing, and He does according to His will in the host of heaven" (Daniel 4:32). He joins together and unites members of each species above and below, and the four prime elements have no proximity to each other apart from the Holy One, blessed be He, when He is amongst them.

228 Immediately, when those who are called ("You are the children of the Lord your God" [Deuteronomy 14:1]) who are from the side of the Tetragrammaton, sin, He removes Himself from the letters of the Tetragrammaton which are left separated from each other. How is this to be corrected? By bringing together the letters in the Holy One, blessed be He, yud to hei, which is the mating of Ḥokhmah and Binah, vav to hei, which is the mating of Tiferet and Malkhut. So also: those who are his servants, who are from the side of

Metatron, and are from the side of the celestial beings Michael, Gabriel, Uriel and Raphael, whose sins caused His Divinity to leave them, how are they to be corrected? By repenting and bringing the Holy One, blessed be He, down to them, and to bring them close to each other. So also with those who are the four prime elements, fire, wind, water and earth, which are called the flock of the Holy One, blessed be He, who, by their sins, cause the Holy One, blessed be He, to ascend from them — what is their correction? It is to draw them close to the Holy One, blessed be He.

229 And this is why He commanded for all of them a sacrifice to the Lord, i.e. in order to unite the letters of the Tetragrammaton, that were separated and removed, as explained above. "My food which is presented to Me for offerings made by fire" (Numbers 28:2). Also: "The one lamb you shall offer in the morning and the other lamb you shall offer at dusk" (Numbers 28:4). Elsewhere it is written: "Two turtle-doves or two young pigeons" (Leviticus 5:7). In each case, mention is made of two of the same species that are joined together. And the Holy One, blessed be He, brings all together in this place, for He is the cause of all; there is no God beside Him, and none but He is able to bring the forces together.

230 But the forces of the idol-worshipping nations are from the side of Separation. Woe to him that by his sins brings Separation to the letters, beings and prime elements, for the Holy One, blessed be He, immediately removes Himself from Israel, and the idol-worshipping nations come in amongst them (amongst the Jews.). The idol-worshippers have no proximity to the Holy One, blessed be He, since there are no sacrifices outside the Land of Israel, where the idol-worshippers are. In this context, the rabbis taught: "He who lives outside the Land of Israel is as one without God" (cf. Talmud Bavli, Ketuvot, 110b). As the Faithful Shepherd said these things, all the holy

letters from Atziluth, and the holy beings from Briah, and the four prime elements in Yetzirah and Assiah came down to him, blessed him, and said: "By your doing, O Faithful Shepherd, did the Holy One, blessed be He, descend upon us, and each kind was drawn close (*225b) to his own kind. You are blessed to the Holy One, blessed be He, by the four prime elements. Now everything has been clarified in its rightful place."

231 He began by quoting: "Trust in the Lord and do good; dwell in the land and cherish faithfulness" (Psalms 37:3). "Trust in the Lord" — This is as it should be. "And do good" — that is, undertake the correction of the holy covenant, that you should correct it and keep it properly. And if you do this, you will be here in the land, i.e. dwell in the land, and it will receive nourishment at your hand, and will flourish at your hand, i.e. that upper faithfulness which is Malkhut, this being the meaning of "cherish faithfulness".

232 And the following verse: "So shall you delight yourself in the Lord; and He will grant you the petitions of your heart." (Psalms 37:4). All this is remedied in the correction of the covenant, for since the covenant is corrected, everything is corrected. And Pinḥas, because he was zealous for this covenant, merited everything. And not only that but he was defender of all Israel, and the verse "You shall delight yourself in the Lord" was upheld in him, for he ascended and made contact above, with the first light that the Holy One, blessed be He, created and then concealed, that same light that Abraham enjoyed and with which Aaron the priest was bound.

233 After Pinḥas was promoted to the office of high priest, the killing of Zimri is not mentioned in connection with him, for it is not fitting that he should not be caught up in the tentacles of the evil forces, and it is indeed not proper to mention the killing in connection with Pinḥas. Everyone who kills

has extensions of the evil forces in him, but Pinḥas had already become united with the right, which is the priesthood, and had no portion whatsoever in the evil forces, which is why his name is not mentioned here. What might have seemed praise-worthy is really a matter of disgrace for him, for it would mean a descent from the upper level with which he was united. It is, therefore, written: "Now the name of the man of Israel that was slain, who was slain with... And the name of the Midianitish woman that was slain..." (Numbers 25:14-15), without mentioning by whom they were slain.

234 Said Rabbi Pinḥas: Happy is the generation that hears your interpretations of Torah, and happy is my portion that I have so merited. Rabbi Shimon replied to Rabbi Pinḥas: Happy is the generation in which you and your piety are. While they were still sitting and enjoying each other's company, Rabbi Elaz the son of Rabbi Shimon, came and found them there. Commented Rabbi Pinḥas: This is certainly in fulfillment of the verse: "And Jacob said when he saw them: This is God's camp" (Genesis 32:3). Rabbi Shimon said: Elazar, my son, sit you down, my son, and expound to us this verse, and Rabbi Elazar sat down.

235 He began: "And Jacob went on his way and the angels of the Lord came upon him" (Genesis 32:2). What is the meaning of "they came upon him?" The answer to this is that there is a coming upon for good, a coming upon for evil and a coming upon for prayer. When Jacob was on his way to Haran, what does Scripture tell us? "And he came upon the place" (Genesis 28:11), for he prayed the evening service at that place, which is Malkhut that is called place, as it is written: "And the Lord said: Behold, there is a place by Me" (Exodus 33:21). For the evening prayer is proper for that place; that is, the evening prayer is the aspect of correction of Malkhut, and this is in accord with what was said

above (207): "There is no \`coming upon' that is not prayer".

236 Again. "And he came upon the place" (Genesis 28:11). This means that he spoke words of concili-ation, i.e. as he has already noted: There is no \`coming upon' that is not concilia-tion. "Because the sun was set" (Genesis 28:11), the Holy One, which is Zeir Anpin, comes to the moon, which is Malkhut, the husband to the wife. It follows that it is not right for a husband to come to his wife without words of appeasement to placate her, for it is written: "And he came upon the place", which means that he addressed her with words of appeasement. And afterwards (in the continuation of the same verse): "And he stayed there the night". This was when Jacob was on the way from Haran, but what does Scripture tell us about his return from there? "They came upon him" (Genesis 32:11), i.e. Malkhut sent (messengers) to placate him, so that he would come into her.

Commentary

For *Zeir Anpin* is in the aspect of right and *Malkhut* is the secret of left. And just as there is a dispute between right and left (See Gen. I, pp. 56, 44), so was there between *Zeir Anpin* and *Malkhut*. The secret of the waning of the moon is the victory of *Zeir Anpin* over *Malkhut*, for the latter becomes smaller and leaves the left column, and *Zeir Anpin* has, therefore, to placate her, i.e. to return the illumination of the left to her. (See on this, above, Gen. II 215, where the matter was discussed in the Commentary at some length.)

And the text says: It is not right for a husband to come to his wife without words of appeasement, for initially He draws down for her the illumination of the left as an appeasement, and later He mates with her and bestows reliable *Ḥasadim* upon her. Sometimes it is the other way around, and *Malkhut* placates *Zeir Anpin*. This is when *Zeir Anpin* is at the six intermediate *Sfirot* and *Malkhut* placates Him so that He will mate with her, and, thereby, the three first will return to Him, this being the inner meaning of the verse: "A virtuous wife is a diadem to her husband" (Proverbs 12:4).

When Jacob was on the way back from Haran (for He was then in a state of diminution, which is called Haran), what does Scripture tell us? "They came upon him" (Genesis 32:11), that is, she (*Malkhut*) sent (messengers) to placate him, so that he could come in to her and unite with her, and, thereby, the three first would return to him.

237 "And Jacob said when he saw them" (Genesis 32:3). What is the meaning of 'when he saw them'? The answer is that they were the day-

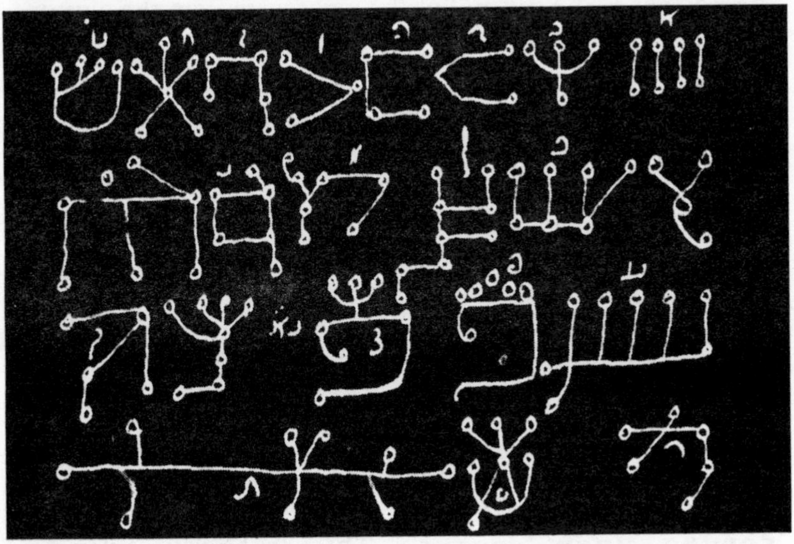

time angels of Zeir Anpin, who is called day, and the night time angels of Malkhut, who is called night. They were hidden from him and subsequently revealed to him, which is why it is written: "When he saw them". The verse continues: "This is the camp of God." From here we know that there were those of the day and those of the night. Concerning those of the night, it is written "the camp of God [Elohim]" and Malkhut is called Elohim, and concerning those of the day, it is written: "This", for Zeir Anpin is called "This". And thus the verse continues: "And he called the name of that place Maḥanaim (literally: two camps)".

Echoing this sentiment, Rabbi Elazar said: And now I see here holy camps, i.e. the camp of Rabbi Shimon and the camp of Rabbi Pinḥas. Happy is my path that brought me here!

Commentary

These angels of the day and of the night were from the illumination of the mating, and, until now, when he was in Haran, he did not see them, but now, in the secret of the mating, he saw them. And this is why it says: They were hidden from him and subsequently revealed to him. On this, Scripture says: "When he saw them."

THE FAITHFUL SHEPHERD

"COMING UPON" IS APPEASEMENT

238 [This is the continuation of Rabbi Shimon's words, 208, above.] But 'coming upon' means words of appeasement. When the groom comes to the bride, the groom does not unite with the bride without words of appeasement, and afterwards he spends the night with her. This is the meaning of

"Because the sun had set" (Genesis 28:11). (See 236 above for explanation.)

239 The Faithful Shepherd said: If this is so, what is the meaning of "Because the sun had set", which is here explained homiletically? [Note: the word order of the Hebrew sentence is: "Because it had set" which in Hebrew is ki va: kaf yud, veth aleph.] Ki va is phonetically close to the word K'viyah [kaf veth yud hei], meaning `extinguishing', and so "Because the sun had set" means when the light of the sun was extinguished. However, what we can learn from this is that whoever unites with the wife must extinguish the lights at night, and that the sages do not advocate sexual intercourse by the light of day (cf. Talmud Bavli, Niddah, 17a, where such is explicitly forbidden), but only by night, with modesty. When, therefore, does one use the term linah (`staying overnight')? Scripture says: When the sun has set, i.e. after the light of the sun has turned away from the world.

240 For this reason, just as one has to cover oneself up from the sun, so does one have to cover oneself from the angels who are the good inclination on the right in a number of camps, as well as from the angels who are the evil inclination on the left in a number of camps. And so it was that after the morning had dawned (Genesis 32:1), Jacob spoke when he saw the angels, for at night he did not see them. And there was no one with Jacob, who was "complete" (Genesis 25:27), which is the central column except for the camps of the King and the Queen, who are called the daytime angels and the night time angels, which is why "And he called the name of that place Maḥanaim (two camps)" (Genesis 32:3). About the daytime angels, who are Zeir Anpin, who is called day, it is written: "...when he saw them: This is the camp of God" (Genesis 32:3), for Zeir Anpin is called day. And when the night time angels came, i.e. those of Malkhut who is called night, who gathered around him to protect him, it is said:(*226a) "And he

called the name of that place Maḥanaim (two camps)." And there is no difficulty here, for the verse "when he saw them" is written about the time after he had returned from Haran, for "there is no `earlier' or `later' in the Torah" (cf. Talmud Bavli, Pesaḥim 6b).

241 [The author here wishes to harmonize what he said initially (207) on "And he came upon the place" (Genesis 28:11) and "there is no `coming upon' that is not prayer (referring to the evening prayer) and what he said later (238), i.e. that `coming upon' means appeasement when a groom comes to a bride, etc., according to which "And he came upon the place" means the unity of bride and groom. And this is what he says:] Since prayer is a bride, i.e. Malkhut, as it is said: "Come with me from Lebanon, my bride, with me from Lebanon" (Song of Songs 4:8), thus Malkhut is here called "with me", and in the written Torah (Pentateuch), it is said about her: "Behold there is a place by Me" (Exodus 33:21) [which also lends itself to the translation: Behold `a place' is `with me' — tr.]. `A place' is Malkhut, as is `with me'. And since Malkhut is called a place in this world, it is said about her: "And he came upon the place and spent the night there" (Genesis 28:11).

Commentary

Because the meaning of "And he came upon the place" is that he came upon *Malkhut*, which is called place, and is also called both `prayer' and `bride', the meaning is, therefore, that the groom who is Jacob, the secret of *Zeir Anpin*, came upon and came in to the bride who is *Malkhut* that is called `place'. It can thus be said that it was the `coming upon' that arranged the evening prayer, since the arranging of prayer is also interpreted as unification of bride and groom, because prayer is the secret of *Malkhut*. And so the two interpretations are really one.

242 And for this reason, she says: "Would that I were in the wilderness, in a wayfarers' lodging-place" (Jeremiah 9:1), for then she would have been independent, without those who impose an obligation on her, and without her groom. And whenever a man prays, the Holy One, blessed be He, precedes him and protects her. And the secret of the matter is to be found in the verse: "And the man looked at her wondering" (Genesis 24:21), for whenever the word 'man' is used the reference is to the Holy One, blessed be He, as it is written: "The Lord is a man of war" (Exodus 15:3). "And it came to pass, before he had done speaking, that, behold, Rebeccah came out" (Genesis 24:15), just as "And His arrow shall go forth like the lightning" (Zekhariah 9:14).

Commentary

Night time is the time of darkness, which is the secret of the control of Judgment, which is the secret of control by the left column, for it is known that control by the left column without the right is darkness (See above Gen. I 47); while control by the right, which is the secret of the light of *Hasadim*, is the secret of the light of day. It is, therefore, necessary to pray the evening service in order to mate her with *Zeir Anpin*, the secret of the central column, for she is then protected from the evil forces and they can not extract the emanation from her, downwards from above. And just as night is control by the left in terms of time, so the wilderness is control by the left in terms of place, as it is written: "...wilderness, wherein are serpents, fiery serpents and scorpions" (Deuteronomy 8:15).

On the text: "Would that I were in the wilderness, in a wayfarers' lodging-place" (Jeremiah 9:1): then she would have been independent. That is to say: the *Shekhinah* is waiting and says: Would that I were in the wilderness, which is a place where the left is in control, and I could mate with *Tiferet* and *Yesod*, who are called wayfarers, and this is the secret of wayfarers' lodging-place. For he who prays the evening service corrects her with this mating, and she is as though independent, i.e. that the emanation of *Ḥokhmah* in her remains with her and is not drawn down from above, for this is the correction of the central column, which is the secret of *Tiferet* and *Yesod* (as above Gen. I, 60).

On the text: "For she would then have been independent." For *Malkhut* waits for the one who makes this correction and says: Would that...

On the text: "Without those who impose an obligation on her and without her groom". For then she is protected and the emanation of *Ḥokhmah* is not drawn down from her, downwards from above, for they mark her down on the debit side, and separate her from her groom, the central column.

On the text: "Whenever a man prays, the Holy One, blessed be He, precedes him and protects her." For by prayer a man unites *Malkhut* with the Holy One, blessed be He, who is the central column, who precedes him and protects her from the external ones and the wicked, so that they should not extract from her, downwards from above.

And the secret of the matter is to be found in the verse: "And the man looked at her wondering" (Genesis 24:21), for the Holy One, blessed be He, is waiting to mate with her.

"And it came to pass, before he had done speaking, that, behold, Rebeccah came out" (Genesis 24:15). This intimates that before he had finished praying, the mating has taken place, which is the secret of "behold, Rebeccah came out", [for Rebeccah is in Hebrew `Rivkah' *resh bet kuf hei*], and the same letters, re-arranged, [*hei bet resh kuf*], spell *haBarak* ('the lightning'), which corresponds to "And His arrow shall go forth like the lightning" (Zekhariah 9:14), where 'lightning' hints at the mating that shoots like an arrow.

243 If you should raise the possible objection to the above that the rabbis taught that in a gathering of ten (a minyan or quorum for religious services) the Shekhinah is amongst them, but does not come for one (a single person praying by himself) until he sits down (to study Torah) (cf. Talmud Bavli, Berakhot 6a), and how did I say? That whenever a man prays, the Holy One, blessed be He, receives him, i.e. even a single person, then I should answer that the explanation is as follows: In the case of ten, there is yud (numerical value 10) before hei; that is to say, if there is yud hei [Yah] (which are the intelligences of Ḥokhmah and Binah, for the yud includes the hei also), then the Shekhinah, which is the secret of hei, comes. In the case of one, which is vav,: if the vav is one without Yah [yud hei], until he sits himself down and receives the intelligences of Yah (the second hei of the Tetragrammaton [spelled: Yud Hei Vav and Hei]) the Shekhinah does not come to him. And the secret of the matter is that the hei that is Malkhut does not come to a place where Yah is not. Whoever wishes to unite the letters yud hei and vav hei must pray with supplications and entreaties, this being the reason for the verse: "And I besought the Lord at that time, saying: O Lord God, You have begun to show..." (Deuteronomy 3:23), for The Lord [Aleph Dalet Nun Yud], which is the Shekhinah, is sought with entreaties, and mercy is sought from the Holy One, blessed be He. And that is the explanation for the evening prayers.

Commentary

Entreaties ('*Taḥanunim*') increase the charm [*ḥen*] of the *Shekhinah*, so that she will be more attractive for the mating, while mercy [*raḥamim*] is the secret of the intelligences of the central column, composed of the two columns, the left and the right, which are *yud hei* [*Yah*]. In order to bring together the letters of the Tetragrammaton in unity, it is necessary to draw down mercy, which is the secret of the intelligences of *Yah*, to the Holy One, blessed be He, and entreaties increase the charm of the *Shekhinah* in His eyes, and then the unity is attained. In other words, it is as explained above: the *Shekhinah* does not come unless the intelligences of *Yah* are with *Zeir Anpin*.

THE ONE LAMB YOU SHALL OFFER IN THE MORNING

244 "The one lamb you shall offer in the morning, and the other lamb you shall offer at dusk" (Exodus 29:39 and Numbers 28:4). [The Hebrew word for 'lamb' is Keves, kaf bet sin, which, in unpointed Hebrew, can be read kaf bet shin, kevesh, a 'secret' — tr.] And about the secrets of the Merciful One, the sages have taught: "Why do you probe into the secrets of the Merciful One?" (Talmud Bavli, Berakhot 10a), the meaning of which is: Matters that are of the mysteries of the world, let them be concealed under your dress (cf. Talmud Bavli, Ḥagigah 13a). Just as clothes cover the body, so also must the secrets of the Torah be kept covered up, and this applies even more to the secret of the sacrifices, which are like a wife drawing near to her husband, which is why a sacrifice is called korban, from the same root as the word kirvah, meaning nearness. And the meaning of the expression 'Mysteries [from the root: kaf bet shin] of the world' is the excessive concealment that there is in the world, and the proof of this is that Jonathan in the Aramaic translation of the

Bible] renders the word 'hide' in the verse "And if the people of the land do at all hide their eyes..." (Leviticus 20:4) by the root kaf bet shin.

245 And just as the proximity of the two of them, of husband and wife, has to be in concealment, so also must the sacrifice be concealed from wicked, impudent incest-practicers, who have no shame and no modesty. And they are bastards of a number of sorts, those who practice incest, those who have intercourse during menstruation [Niddah]. The word for menstruation [niddah, nun dalet hei] can be read as two words [nun dalet and hei] with the meaning that hei, which is the Shekhinah who is called hei, has moved away from her, and in her place is a bondwoman, daughter of a strange god, a prostitute. And this is a secret: "For three things the earthquakes: for a servant who rules; for a churl when he is full of food; and for a bondwoman who inherits her mistress" (Proverbs 30:21). For the hei has moved away from her place, which is Malkhut and is the good inclination, and in her stead has come in a bondwoman, the evil inclination.

246 And the secret of the matter is to be found in the verse: "I seem to have a plague in the house" (Leviticus 14:35), i.e. the impure blood of menstruation. Just as in the one case (of the house) "the priest shall shut up the house seven days" (Leviticus 14:38), so also in the other: "she shall be in her impurity seven days" (Leviticus 15:19). Happy are the organs that are sanctified at the time of intercourse, for they are called the wood (*226b) of the offering, for they are engulfed by holy fires from the Tetragrammaton, which is Zeir Anpin, who takes hold of their fire (see above 205). And for this reason is it written: "Glorify the Lord with lights" (Isaiah 24:15). Thus the mysteries of the Merciful One are: "The one lamb (mystery) you shall offer in the morning, and the other lamb (mystery) you shall offer at dusk."

247 And the scriptural text continues: "And the

tenth part of an efah [a Biblical unit of dry measure — tr.] of fine flour" (Numbers 28:5) That is, happy is he who draws down from his brain a tefaḥ [unit of length, one handsbreadth] of clean fine flour without chaff, at the time of the mating, and this is hinted at in the letter yud of `The Lord' [Aleph Dalet Nun Yud], and that is why it says `a tenth part' [the numerical value of yud being 10] and is inherent in the ten Sfirot. And the flour is to be "mingled with a fourth part of a hin [a Biblical fluid measure] of beaten oil" (Numbers 28:5). That is, it is mingled from four, namely: Bible, Mishnah, Talmud, and Kabbalah, on which the righteous beat themselves and so raise up the Female Waters for her mating.

EZEKIEL'S CHARIOT

248 When Ezekiel saw the Shekhinah amongst the shells [klippot], that is to say, amongst the garments, he saw, with her, ten Sfirot, without any separation whatsoever, and these are the brain that is amongst all of them. He saw them within the earthly river Kevar [kaf bet resh] (Ezekiel 1:1), i.e. the earthly chariot [resh kaf bet, i.e. the letters of Kevar re-arranged] of Metatron. "The chariots of God are myriads, even thousands upon thousands" (Psalms 68:18). Each myriad is ten thousand, so the myriads referred to in the verse are twenty thousand. [This deduction is from the word used for `myriads', which is in the dual form of the plural, implying `two' myriads —tr.] The expression rendered as `even thousands upon thousands' is alfei shin'an, shin nun aleph nun, and the letters of this latter word may be re-arranged: shin aleph (yud) nun nun, meaning: `which are not', while alfei, being plural, denotes two thousands.

The verse is thus understood: The chariots of God are twenty thousand, with two thousand which are not, making eighteen thousand, which is as the number of the worlds. [Eighteen in letters is yud (10) ḥet (8), or ḥet yud or ḥai, `alive' — tr.] This is Yesod, which is called ḥai,

'alive', which includes the ten Sfirot, attired in the tet tet (9 + 9 = 18) of Metatron [mem tet tet resh vav nun], and this tet tet is taken from the word Totafot [tet tet pey vav tav], meaning 'phylacteries' [tefillin], about which it is said: "And they shall become totafot between your eyes" (Deuteronomy 6:8). Who are the eyes? They are those above, about which it is said: "The heavens were opened and I saw visions of God" (Ezekiel 1:1). Who are the visions? "They are the ten visions of Metatron, whom Ezekiel saw as a candle within a lantern, nine of the visions being clear, with one being vague.

Commentary

Although Ezekiel saw the *Shekhinah* attired in garments of *Briah*, *Yetzirah*, and *Assiah*, as it is written in Ezekiel, he nevertheless saw the secret of the unity of the ten *Sfirot*, namely *Zeir Anpin* and *Malkhut*. That is to say: he saw the *Shekhinah* untied with *Zeir Anpin*.

On the text: "When Ezekiel saw the *Shekhinah* amongst the shells [*klippot*], that is to say, amongst the garments, he saw, with her, ten *Sfirot*, without any separation whatsoever". For *Zeir Anpin*, which is the secret of the first nine *Sfirot*, was joined together with *Malkhut*, without any separation whatsoever. And these ten *Sfirot* are the brains attired within, but he saw them when they were attired with Metatron. For in time of exile the mating of *Zeir Anpin* with *Malkhut* is enclothed in Metatron.

On the text: "And these are the brain that is amongst all of them. He saw them within the earthly river Kevar..." That is, he only saw them when they were attired with the river Kevar, which is Metatron, for Metatron is called the river Kevar (see Introduction to *Tikunei Zohar*, page 4a). The letters of *Kevar* [*kaf bet resh*] re-arranged [*resh kaf bet, rekhev*] make the word for Chariot, and it is, therefore, said about Metatron: "The chariots of God are myriads" (Psalms 68:18), which, as explained in the text, makes eighteen thousands, which is as the number of the eighteen worlds. When *Zeir Anpin* and *Malkhut* are in a mating by means of *Yesod*, then *Yesod* is called eighteen worlds, where, as explained in the text, eighteen is the numerical value of the word `alive', and *Yesod* is, therefore, the life of the worlds. And the author explains that the ten *Sfirot* of direct light then descend from *Yesod* to *Malkhut*, and ten *Sfirot* of reflected light ascend from *Malkhut* to *Zeir Anpin*. And since the mating is in the secret of *Ḥokhmah*, whose *Sfirot* are in the secret of two thousand, two myriads are therefore discerned, ten thousand of direct light and ten thousand of reflected light, which are included in Metatron, as noted above. It is, therefore, then said: "The chariots of God are myriads", for Metatron, who is the chariot of God, contains twenty thousand lights. However, although the mating is with *Malkhut*, the essence of *Malkhut* is missing from *Malkhut*, for *Malkhut* is the secret of concealed lock, and so *Yesod* of *Malkhut*, which is the secret of key, serves in its place. (See above, Introduction to *Sefer haZohar*, 45.) And so, if we wish to be accurate, two of the twenty *Sfirot* are missing, namely: *Malkhut* of the ten *Sfirot* of direct light, and *Malkhut* of the ten *Sfirot* of reflected light, and there are no more than eighteen *Sfirot* there. This is intimated by Scripture, as explained in the text, where the letters of *shin'an* are re-arranged to read *she'enan*, `which are not'; i.e. two *Sfirot*, which are two thousand, are not there, for they have been concealed.

On the text: "Less the two thousand which are not, making eighteen thousand, which is as the number of the worlds." This refers to *Yesod* at the time of the mating, which, for this reason, is called the life of the worlds, and is attired with Metatron.

On the text: "Attired in the *tet tet* of Metatron" The first *tet* hints at the nine of direct light, and the second *tet* at the nine of reflected light, for the numerical value of *tet* is nine. And this is also the secret of the *tet tet* in the word *totafot* [phylacteries, *tefillin*], about which it is said: "And they shall become *totafot* between your eyes" (Deuteronomy 6:8), which is the secret of the illuminations of *Ḥokhmah* which are in *Malkhut*, which are called eyes.

On the text: "Who are the eyes? ...visions of God". This is because visions are the secret of the illuminations of *Ḥokhmah* and are called eyes.

On the text: "Who are the visions? They are the ten visions of Metatron". That is to say: the ten *Sfirot* of *Malkhut* that are attired with Metatron are called visions, for there is vision and seeing in *Malkhut* only, since there is no revelation of the illumination of *Ḥokhmah* in any of the *Sfirot* except *Malkhut*. (See above, Gen. I, 276). However, he did not receive the visions of *Malkhut* from *Malkhut* herself but only when enclothed in Metatron.

On the text: "He saw a candle within a lantern." That is, as a candle resting within a lantern whose sides are made of glass, and one sees the illumination of the candle through the glass sides. This is how Ezekiel saw the visions of the *Shekhinah*, which is the secret of the candle, from within the tools of Metatron, which is the secret of the lantern. However, although we say that he saw the ten visions of *Malkhut*, to be accurate, he saw only nine, for *Malkhut* of *Malkhut* was concealed, and illumination of *Yesod*, called key, served in its stead, as was explained above.

On the text: "Nine of the visions being clear and one being vague." He saw no more than nine visions, the nine first *Sfirot* of

Malkhut, but he did not see the vision of the *Malkhut* of *Malkhut*, for it is hidden and concealed.

249 One vision that he saw at the beginning of those ten visions was the one about which it is said: "And above the firmament that was over their heads was the likeness of a throne, as the appearance of a sapphire stone" (Ezekiel 1:26). Although this verse has already been explained above, new things have to be said about it.

250 The Holy One, blessed be He, said to the heavenly encampments: Anyone who prays, whether he be a hero, a wise man, or a rich man (a hero, that is, in privileges because he overcomes his inclination; a wise man means wise in Torah; and a rich man is rich in Mitzvot) — does not allow his prayer to enter this temple until there is seen in him these signs: that he has applied My corrections to himself. For this reason, the sages of the Mishnah taught: If the rabbi is like an angel of the Lord of Hosts, let people come to consult him in matters of the Torah (Talmud Bavli, Ḥagigah 15b). In other words, you may accept the prayer of anyone who is noted by these signs in his dress: One sign is that he should be noted in his prayer by the blue on the four corners of his fringes, for blue is like the color of the firmament, which is Metatron, and it would then follow that he would be like an angel of the Lord of Hosts, whose form is the blue that is in the fringes. (cf. Talmud Bavli, Sotah 17a.)

251 And for this reason the rabbis taught: A cloak that a minor wears and which covers his head and most of his body must have fringes attached (Talmud Bavli, Menakhot 40b), and this is the same as was said about it: "And a little child shall lead them" (Isaiah 11:6), for Metatron is called a little child, and he which is Metatron leads the four beasts, the four being dalet, and includes the six steps up to the throne, i.e. Ḥesed, Gvurah, Tiferet, Netzaḥ, Hod and Yesod,

which are vav (numerical value 6); and since he is composed of ten (four being and six steps), the ten Sfirot of Zeir Anpin and Malkhut of Atziluth attire themselves in him, for they, too, are ten, yud. And through him does the Holy One, blessed be He, appear in His Divine Presence [Shekhinah] to the prophets, for He is composed of ten Sfirot. And from the side of the Shekhinah, which is enclothed with Metatron, for it is the tenth Sfirah and the blue of the fringes, Metatron also appears as the blue of all colors, that is to say: all the colors included in this blue.

252 For it, Malkhut that is called blue [t'khelet], is the ultimate [takhlit] of the ten Sfirot, and in it "all the work of the tabernacle of the tent of meeting was finished [tekhel]" (Exodus 39:32), since it is the ultimate [takhlit] perfection. And the word t'khelet [blue] comes from the root: kaf lamed hei, meaning to finish, as it is written: "And it came to pass on the day that Moses finished setting up the tabernacle" (Numbers 7:1). This is why the Shekhinah is called t'khelet [blue], which is the blue flame in a

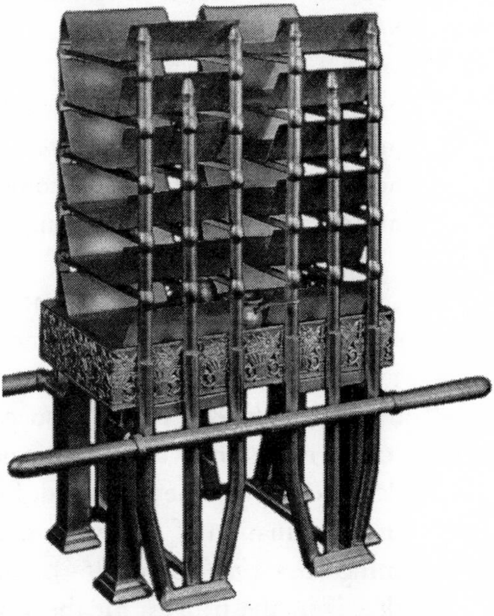

burning candle, which devours the fatty parts of the burnt offerings. (See above Bereshith Beth, 254.)

Commentary

The light of the left column which is in *Malkhut*, which is the secret of the illumination of *Ḥokhmah*, is termed 'blue' [*t'khelet*], and the reasons for it being so called, he gives as follows:

a) Because it is the ultimate [*takhlit*] of the ten *Sfirot*, as in the verse: "And searches to the furthest bound [*takhlit*]" (Job 28:3); or, as in the saying: "The ultimate in wisdom is repentance and good deeds" (*Talmud Bavli, Berakhot* 17a), where the meaning of `ultimate' is result or end purpose, objective. The illumination of *Ḥokhmah* that is in *Malkhut* results from all nine of the first *Sfirot.*

b) In the verse, "And all the work of the tabernacle of the tent of meeting was finished [*tekhal*]" (Exodus 39:32), it should be noted that *t'khelet* (`blue') comes from the same root as *tekhal*, meaning `finished' for it's illumination culminates all the *Sfirot.*

c) Also, *t'khelet* (`blue') comes from the word *kallah* (`bride') since *Malkhut* is *Zeir Anpin*'s bride.

d) And *t'khelet* (`blue') is so called from the root `to finish', `come to an end', as the fatty parts and the burnt offerings are devoured and come to an end, for the Judgments that come with the illumination of *Ḥokhmah* that is in it destroy and burn everything (*Bereshith Beth*, 254). And this is the secret of the blue that is in the fringes, for the white threads are the secret of the lights of *Ḥasadim*, while the blue thread is the secret of the illu-

253 And about it, i.e. about the light of Ḥokhmah in it, that is called t'khelet (`blue'), Ezekiel said: "...the likeness of a throne, as the appearance of a sapphire stone" (Ezekiel 1:26); and the particular virtue of this stone is that, whoever inherits it, the light of Gehenna has no control over him, and there is no flame in the world that can damage it, nor any type of metal, for if one hits this

sapphire stone with a hammer, the hammer will break but the stone will be undamaged, as the sages said (Shabbat 88a, Tosefot). It is, therefore, quite obvious that water can not harm it. Thus, for whoever inherits it the verse "When you pass through the waters, I will be with you" (Isaiah 43:2) will be upheld, and all the upper and lower evil forces are fearful before him. It was also for the blue [t'khelet] that it was said: "When you pass through the waters, I will be with you," for with this special attribute, the blue light of Malkhut that is called sapphire stone, "The horse and his rider has He thrown into the sea" (Exodus 15:1), for it is the one appointed over Egypt, who drowned in the sea in the strength of this blue light.

254 From this blue color the upper and lower beings are fearful; the encampments of the sea are fearful of it, and the encampments of the firmament, which is blue, hold it in awe, as do the encampments of the blue fires of Gehenna, i.e. the blue of the evil forces.

Commentary

For at the same time as is revealed the blue light that is in *Malkhut*, which is the secret of the illumination of *Ḥokhmah*, very harsh judgments are revealed with it, and they cast terror and trembling over all the external ones. (As above, *Idra Rabba*, 219, q.v.)

255 And this blue (*227a) is Judgment, for the name of Malkhut is `The Lord' [aleph dalet nun yud], the letters of which can be rearranged: dina [dalet yud nun aleph], making the Aramaic word for Judgement, and this is the secret of the ruling: Dina d'malkhuta dina. [This famous ruling is mentioned frequently in the rabbinic literature, and is usually understood to mean that the law of the

secular government is supreme, i.e. supersedes the Jewish law in civil affairs; here, however, interpreted to mean that, when the Sfirah Malkhut is termed `The Lord' [aleph dalet nun yud], the reference is to Judgment [dalet yud nun aleph — tr.]

The tallit (prayer-shawl) has two colors: white and blue, and in respect to these two colors it is said: "And there was under His feet a kind of paved work of sapphire stone" (Exodus 24:10). Livnat (paving brick) is the white [lavan] of the sapphire, because the sapphire is composed of two colors, which are Mercy and Judgement, i.e. white, which is Mercy, and black, from which comes the darkness of the blue [t'khelet]; and the sages hinted at these two colors when they asked: "From what time in the morning may the Shema Yisrael be recited?" and answered "As soon as one can distinguish between blue and white" (Mishnah, Berakhot 1,2). For the daughter of the king, which is Malkhut, which is the secret of the recital of the Shema Yisrael, which is the unity of the Holy One, blessed be He, is composed of these two colors, white and blue, which are the Tetragrammaton `The Lord'. The Tetragrammaton [Yud Hei Vav and Hei] is the secret of white, while `The Lord' [Aleph Dalet Nun Yud] is the secret of blue, thus combining Mercy and Judgment. Similarly, the Holy One, blessed be He, who is Zeir Anpin, is composed of two colors, which is the secret of the Tetragrammaton `The Lord', being Mercy and Judgment, i.e. the Throne of Mercy and the Throne of Judgment.

256 If the sapphire stone is the blue of the fringes, what, then, is "The likeness of a throne" (Ezekiel 1:26)? The answer is that it is to parallel the throne that has 72 bridges, i.e. 72 lights from the 72-letter name of God (the Tetragrammaton filled out with yuds). So should a person be noted for the 72 knots and links in his fringes, paralleling the 72 bridges of the throne, for there are Ḥai [`life' = ḥet yud, i.e. 8 + 10 = 18] knots and links on each of the four corners of his gar-

ment, that is, 5 knots and 13 links, and 5 + 13 = 18 and 18 times 4 is 72. For the throne which is hei (= 5), i.e. Malkhut, has on each corner the four being of the throne, and these four parallel the four corners of his raiment.

257 And the six steps of the throne which are vav (numerical value 6), which is Metatron, include 4 beings, as it is said: "And a little child shall lead them" (Isaiah 11:6), they being Michael, Gabriel, Nuriel, Raphael. And Metatron is the six stages to the throne which are Ḥesed, Gvurah, Tiferet, Netzaḥ, Hod, Yesod, each of which is composed of a hundred, totalling six hundred in all. Tzitzit ('fringes'), when written out full, tzadik yud tzadik yud tav, has the numerical value of six hundred (90 + 10 + 90 + 10 + 400 = 600). And if the word tzitzit ('fringes') is written in the abbreviated spelling, with one yud omitted, then the ḥirik (vowel "i") is like a yud and makes up for its omission. And on each of the four corners of his garment there is a fringe with the numerical equivalent of 600, which, together with the 13 links, makes six hundred and thirteen. And 613 [Taryag = tav resh yud gimel, i.e. 400 + 200 + 10 + 3 = 613] is the number of the precepts in the Torah.

258 Again, the six steps to the throne are vav (numerical value 6), and when the name of the letter 'vav' is spelt out in full, namely vav aleph vav, its numerical value is 6 + 1 + 6 = 13. And this vav is hinted at in three words of the combination of 72 names included in the three verses: "And the angel of the Lord, who went before the camp of Israel, removed and went behind them; and the pillar of cloud removed from them, and stood behind them; and it came between the camp of Egypt and the camp of Israel; and there was the cloud and the darkness there, yet gave it light by night there; and the one came not near the other all the night. And Moses stretched out his hand over the sea; and the Lord caused the sea to go back by a strong east wind all the night, and made the sea dry land, and the

waters were divided" (Exodus 14:19-21). Each of these verses contains (in Hebrew) exactly 72 letters. (See above Beshallaḥ, page 51, para. 173.)

And these three words are v'ho [vav hei vav, and hei], Ani [aleph nun yud, I] and v'ho [vav hei vav, and hei], the initial letters of which are: vav, aleph, and vav, which spell the name of the letter vav (= 6). And there are five knots on the fringe, i.e. on each of the four corners of the garment, that is hei (= 5) on each corner, and the completion of hei, which is aleph, is the garment [habeged: hei bet gimel dalet, i.e. 5 + 2 + 3 + 4 = 14] itself, which is one for all of them. And when the letter hei (= 5) is joined with the letter vav (written out in full: vav aleph vav, i.e. 6 + 1 + 6 = 13), the total comes to (5 + 13) eighteen [yud ḥet, 10 + 8, or ḥet yud, Ḥai = life], which is the tet tet (9 + 9 = 18) of Metatron [mem tet tet resh vav nun]. And eighteen, Ḥai, hints at Ḥayah, a celestial being, one of which is on each of the four corners, and which is made up of four beings, for the four corners belong together in the one garment, each being having four countenances and four wings, making a total of thirty-two (4 countenances + 4 wings per being, times four beings, 8 x 4 = 32) countenances and wings, all of which are dependent on the fourth of the four beings that has the face of a man, i.e. a man wearing fringes.

259 And these, the fringes, are 32 in number, as explained above, as is the numerical value of yud hei hei, which, when written out in full, is vav, i.e. 13 links of each of the four corners (as above, 257). And the vav [vav aleph vav] unites with all the four beings of the four corners, and completes the name Yud Hei Vav and Hei (the Tetragrammaton) above in Zeir Anpin and Malkhut of Atziluth, and completes it below in the beings. For the central column, which is Metatron, is to complete above like Tiferet of Atziluth, for Metatron's name is as that of his master, Tiferet, in whose image and according to whose likeness he was created, for he,

Metatron, includes all the stages downwards from above, since Tiferet and Malkhut of Atziluth are attired in him, and also upwards from below, i.e. including all four of the holy beings, Michael, Gabriel, Nuriel, Raphael and is held in the center, as it is said: "And the middle bar in the midst of the boards, which shall pass through from end to end" (Exodus 26:28).

260 And he, Metatron, is made up of the four countenances and the four wings of each of the beasts above in Zeir Anpin and Nukvah, which are Yud Aleph Hei Dalet Vav Nun Hei Yud, i.e. the combination of the two names: the Tetragrammaton [Yud Hei Vav and Hei] and 'The Lord' [Aleph Dalet Nun Yud], which are Zeir Anpin and Malkhut.

"Then sang Moses" (Exodus 15:1), for Zeir Anpin, which is the secret of Moses, has in each of his beasts four countenances and four wings (4 + 4 = 8), which is as the numerical value of the word 'then' [az: aleph zayin, i.e. 1 + 7 = 8]. In like manner, az (= 8) of lion, az (= 8) of ox, az (= 8) of eagle, az (= 8) of man, make up thirty two (8 x 4 = 32) wings and countenances.

261 And the four countenances are the four letters of the Tetragrammaton [Yud Hei Vav and Hei], and the four wings are the four letters of 'The Lord' [Aleph Dalet Nun Yud], that stand for the four garments of gold (which is the secret of 'The Lord') and the four garments of white (which is the secret of the Tetragrammaton) that the priest wore to make atonement for Israel. And they stand for "O Lord, open my lips" (Psalms 51:17), which is said at the beginning of the Amidah prayer [also known as Shemoneh Esreh, 18, as it originally contained 18 now 19 blessings — tr.], and each of the blessings terminates with "Blessed are You, O Lord, who..." Thus the Tetragrammaton occurs eighteen times, and as each Tetragrammaton has four letters, this makes a total of seventy-two (18 x 4 = 72) letters, which is the same as the numerical value of "And

(they) were finished" (Genesis 2:1), i.e. Vaykhulu [vav yud kaf lamed vav, i.e. 6 + 10 + 20 + 30 + 6 = 72.] And this is the secret of Yesod, which is called kol [kaf lamed, 'all'], for the eighteen beasts are included in the Righteous One, the Life (18) of the Worlds, which is the secret of "And (they) were finished" [Vaykhulu].

262 And each one of the four beings contains the Tetragrammaton and 'The Lord', i.e. a total of eight letters each, in each of the four directions, that is, a total of thirty-two (8 x 4 = 32) letters. And there are thirteen letters in the initials of v'ho ani v'ho (see above, 258), which are vav written out full, i.e. vav aleph vav, having the numerical value of 13 (6 + 1 + 6 = 13). And thirteen, since the upper and lower ones are included in this vav, as above, completes man [adam: aleph dalet mem, i.e. 1 + 4 + 40 = 45], which is the central column. For the 32 letters of the Tetragrammaton and 'The Lord' (eight on each of four sides), together with the 13 of the vav, (32 + 13 = 45) come to forty-five, the numerical value of adam (man).

FOUR SHELLS (KLIPPOT) THAT SURROUND FOUR BEINGS

263 At the top of the Tree of Life, which is Zeir Anpin, there are no shells, "for none might enter within the king's gate clothed with sackcloth" (Esther 4:2). Lower down, around Metatron, there are shells, for he, Metatron, is in the form of the central column, which is Zeir Anpin, for when the Holy One, blessed be He, is deprived of his Malkhut, i.e. when Malkhut is in exile, He covers himself with the countenances and wings of His servant, who is Metatron, as it is written: "And He rode [root: resh kaf bet] upon a cherub [root: kaf resh bet] and did fly" (II Samuel 22:11), for Metatron is called both cherub and chariot [root: resh kaf bet].

264 And these shells that surround the four beings of Metatron are:

a) Tohu ('unformed' — see Genesis 1:2), about which is written: "A great and strong wind rent the mountains, and broke in pieces the rocks before the Lord" (I Kings 19:11).

b) Vohu ('void' — see Genesis 1:2), about which is written: "And after the wind an earthquake, but the Lord was not in the earthquake" (I Kings 19:11). These are two shells, which are the secret of the green shell and the white shell of the shells of the walnut. The former, Tohu, is the green column, while the latter, Vohu, is smooth stones (see above Bo, p. 34), and is a shell as hard as a smooth stone. These two shells are also represented by the chaff and the straw of wheat.

265 The third shell that surrounds the four beings of Metatron is Dakah ('ground thin' — see I Kings 19:12) and is represented by the bran of the wheat, for here it sticks to the wheat and cannot be separated from there without grinding it in the millstones, which are represented by the molar teeth in a man's jaw, with which matters of Torah have to be ground until they are as flour, as clean flour. And in a sieve, which is the lips, the waste matter, which is the bran of the Torah, is sorted out, until the Halakhah is as clean flour. At that time, the heart and the brain and all those parts of the body through which the soul spreads, take that Halakhah which is as clean flour, and the soul lives on it just as the body lives on things from the material world, for God made the one against the other: just as there is food for the body, so is there food for the soul, as it is written: "Come, eat of my bread" (Proverbs 9:5).

266 And this shell is like the shell that sticks to the kernel of the nut, for when the nut is soft the shell separates from the kernel without difficulty, but when the nut is (*227b) dry, it is difficult for man to remove it from there, and the problem remains. For this reason, the Holy One, blessed be He, commanded man to return in repentance during his youth, before the evil inclination makes him (prematurely) old, as it is written: "You shall rise up before the hoary head" (Leviticus

19:32), that isto say: Rise up in repentance before you own old age. And this shell is fire, about which is written: "And after the earthquake a fire, but the Lord was not in the fire" (I Kings 19:12). The fourth shell surrounding the four beings of Metatron is Tehom (`the deep'; see Genesis 1:2, "and darkness was upon the face of the deep"). And this is the secret of the space that is in the nut, about which is written: "a still small voice" (I Kings 19:12), for this is where the King comes, and about it is written: "and out of the midst thereof as the color of electrum, out of the midst of the fire" (Ezekiel 1:4).

267 And these four shells have their signs in four parts of the body: in the lung, in which is moisture from which come the adhesions of the lung that attach the lobes of the lung to each other and enfeeble it, about which it is written: "Her feet go down to death; her steps take hold of the netherworld" (Proverbs 5:5) and also there is a "strong mountain-rending wind" (cf. I Kings 19:11) that stirs up a man's body. This refers to the first shell, which, in Ezekiel, is called "a stormy wind" (1:4), and this is the wind that Elijah subjugated and on which he ascended on high, as it is written: "And Elijah went up by a whirlwind into heaven" (II Kings 2:11). And this wind bangs against the lung that imbibes all manner of drinks, concerning which is written: "And the spirit (same Hebrew word as `wind') hovered over the face of the waters" (Genesis 1:2). This is a shell for the holy spirit, for the left, a stormy wind, about which is written: "A wise man's heart is at his right hand, but a fool's heart at his left" (Ecclesiastes 10:2).

C o m m e n t a r y

Scripture says: "And I looked, and, behold, a stormy wind came out of the north, a great cloud, with a fire flashing up, so that a brightness was round about it; and out of the midst thereof as the color of electrum, out of the midst of the fire. And out of the midst thereof came the likeness of four living creatures..." (Ezekiel 1:4-5). Scripture here enumerates four shells, namely: stormy wind, great cloud, fire flashing up, and brightness, and then says that within these four shells are four beasts: lion, ox, eagle, man. The author's problem is: Why are the four holy beasts inside the four shells? What he says is (263): At the top of the Tree of Life, which is *Zeir Anpin* of *Atziluth*, there are no shells around his four beasts. Lower down, around Metatron, there are shells, because the four beasts of Metatron are within four shells, as above.

In order to explain the matter of these four shells to us, the author compares them to the four shells *Tohu*, *Vohu*, Darkness, and the Spirit of God from the Creation Story (Genesis 1:2); and to the four of Elijah, namely: a great and strong mountain-rending wind, earthquake, fire and still small voice; as well as the four shells of wheat: chaff, straw, bran, crushed grain, and to the four shells of a walnut in which are the four kernels, for the kernel of a walnut is split into four sections. He mentions all these comparisons so that one may teach about the other.

And we have already clarified the content and compared the four of the Creation, of Ezekiel, and of Elijah (above *Bereshith Aleph*, 17-28, q.v. thoroughly) and there is no point in repeating the matter here at length. Briefly, however: Just as at the beginning of the Emanation, the worlds came forth in four aspects, namely: the first contraction and the curtain of the first contraction, and the second contraction and the curtain of the second contraction, so too every item that is purified of the seven kings of the world of points came forth in the same four aspects, and they are: the four of Creation, the four of Ezekiel, and the four of Elijah. For the first contraction is called *Tohu* in the Creation Story, a stormy wind in Ezekiel, and a great and strong mountain-rending wind by Elijah, all corresponding to the chaff of the corn, and the green of the walnut. The curtain of the first contraction is called Vohu in the Creation Story, a large cloud in Ezekiel, earthquake by Elijah, corresponding to the straw of the wheat and the white shell of the walnut. The second contraction is called Darkness in the Creation Story, a fire flashing up in Ezekiel, fire by Elijah, corresponding to the bran of the wheat, and the shell that sticks to the kernel of the walnut. The curtain of the second contraction is called *Tehom* (the deep) and the spirit of God hovering over the face of the waters in the Creation Story, brightness and electrum in Ezekiel, corresponding to the crushed grain that is the very thin waste matter (*Halah B'*), and the space in the walnut. With Elijah it is called a still small voice, which is where the King comes.

We shall here clarify only those matters that were not clarified previously (*Bereshith Aleph*, 17-28). On the text: These two shells, which are *Tohu* and *Vohu*, are the chaff and the straw of the wheat, for they are the shells of the first contraction and the curtain of the first contraction, which have no contact with the first nine *Sfirot*, just as the chaff and the straw have no contact with the kernel of the wheat. And also on the text: The third shell, which is the aspect of the second contraction, for *Malkhut* has already ascended to *Binah* and been sweetened with the attribute of Mercy, is, therefore, *Dakah*, having been sweetened, and is represented by the bran of the wheat, for it here sticks to the wheat, for here *Malkhut* has ascended to *Binah*, and for this reason is engraved in all nine of the first *Sfirot*, which are the kernel of the wheat, and it can be noticed that the Judgments stick to the very wheat. On the text: It cannot be separated from there without grinding it in the millstones... the waste matter, which is the bran, is sorted out until the *Halakhah* is as clean flour: i.e. the Female Waters have to be raised to draw down the illumination of 72 and 63 of the Tetragrammaton letters of Primordial Man, to bring *Malkhut* down to her place from *Binah*, for then the first three of *Binah* are revealed, this being the secret of pure flour. On the text: When the nut is soft, i.e. when the light of *Ḥasadim*, termed `water', shines in it. The shell separates from the kernel without difficulty, but if it has no *Ḥasadim* it is difficult to bring *Malkhut* down from *Binah*. On the text: When the nut is dry, i.e. without *Ḥasadim*, it is difficult for man to remove it from there, although the *Ḥasadim* are drawn down only in the secret of the curtain of the second contraction, which is the fourth shell. And on the text: The fourth shell is *Tehom* (`the deep'), the space that is in the nut, a still small voice, for there the King comes, for the fourth shell is the secret of the curtain of the second contraction, when *Ḥasadim* are already drawn down, for it is then possible to bring *Malkhut* down from *Binah*, whose first three are revealed, this being the secret of the King. On the text: This is where the King comes, for it is fitting that the first three be revealed there. And this is the secret of the four holy beings, which are termed the four kernels of the walnut.

And so it is that the four shells are the four stages termed revelation of the first three since in the first contraction all the lights disappear and the curtain, called *Vohu*, draws down *Ḥasadim* on the first contraction. And there is not yet any beginning for the existence of the worlds (as above, Gen. I., page 7.), until the arrival of the third shell, which is of the secret of the ascent of *Malkhut* to *Binah*, thus effecting a beginning and a possibility for the first three to come out; and, subsequently, when the curtain of the second contraction has come forth in *Ḥasadim*, it being called a still small voice, it is then possible to bring *Malkhut* down from *Binah* and reveal the first three, this being the secret of "this is where the King comes". And then, after *Malkhut* descends from *Binah*, the first three are revealed in the secret of the three columns, and *Malkhut* welcomes them, they being termed four beings. Thus the four shells are none other than the four stages, one after the other, of the revelation of the beings, and the four shells are enclosed one inside the other, and at the very center the four beings are disclosed.

And on the text: And these four shells have their signs in four parts of the body, namely: lung, heart, liver, and spleen. The lung is the upper shell, the secret of the curtain of the second contraction, which is the secret of the adhesions of the lung, for there is dampness in the lung that imbibes all manner of drinks, which is the secret of *Binah*, on which the stormy wind of the first contraction bangs; and *Malkhut* of the stormy wind becomes combined with *Binah* and becomes adhesions in *Binah*, this being the secret of the curtains of the second contraction. And on the text: In the lung in which there is humidity from which come the adhesions of the lungs: "Her feet go down to death; her steps take hold of the netherworld" (Proverbs 5:5); that is to say, at its end is *Malkhut* of the Lock, from which comes death, but the adhesions themselves are sweetened with the quality of *Binah*, and he goes on to explain that there is a "strong mountain-rending wind" and that this is the "stormy wind", i.e. that a stormy wind is the secret of *Malkhut* of the first contraction. And this wind bangs against the lung that imbibes all manner of drinks, and this wind intermingles with water of *Binah* and becomes adhesions. And on the text: Concerning which it is written: "And the spirit ('wind') of God hovered over the face of the waters": this is the secret of the curtain of the second contraction (as discussed above, Gen. 17-28). This is a shell of the holy spirit, that is to say, after the removal of this shell, the holy spirit is revealed, this being the secret of the first three. And the location of the shell of *Malkhut* of the first contraction, which is called stormy wind, is the heart, as the text says: For the left, i.e. the heart which is to the left of the lung. A stormy wind, i.e. the stormy wind of the first contraction, dwells in it, about which is written: "A wise man's heart is at his right hand", which accepts the aspect of the curtain of the second contraction, which is the secret of "the spirit of God hovering", from the lung which is to the right of the heart. "A fool's heart at his left", for it has a stormy wind and is not fitted to accept light.

268 David removed it, the stormy wind, from his heart and killed it, as it is written: "And my heart is wounded within me' (Psalms 109:22). That is, he removed the stormy wind and remained with a wounded heart in its stead. And for this reason, he was privileged that a north wind should blow, i.e. the illumination of Ḥokhmah from the left, on his lyre, which is Malkhut, and it is said: "Thus says the Lord God: Come from the four winds [ruaḥ], O breath [ruaḥ]" (Ezekiel 37:9). And he used to play four types of melody on his lyre: a simple song, which is the secret of yud; a double song, which is the secret of yud hei; a triple song, which is the secret of yud hei vav; and, a quadruple song, which is the secret of the four letters Yud Hei Vav and Hei (the Tetragrammaton). These, together, are ten letters, against which David composed ten types of psalm: Ashrei, Maskil, Mizmor, Mikhtam, etc. [see the headings of the psalms — tr.]. And they ascend to the 72 countenances, which is the Tetragrammaton spelled out with yuds.

269 And when do they rise to 72 types of melody, this being the secret of the first three of the 72-letter name of God? It is when the rule of sin, destruction, anger, and wrath passes, for in them does the stormy wind bang, this being the secret of Malkhut of the first contraction on the four sides, as explained above adding up to yud (10) crowns, as above. The four letters of the Tetragrammaton, in the double, triple, and quadruple song, are ten letters adding up to a total of 72, and they then subjugate 72 nations, which are

the seventy nations, together with Edom and Ishamel, as it is written: "When the wicked perish there is joy" (Proverbs 11:10) since, when the four shells of sin, destruction, anger, and wrath perish, the first three are revealed, which is the secret of joy, i.e. 72 types of melody.

270 For Michael, Gabriel, Nuriel, and Raphael, who are the beings of the Chariot, control man's four good elements, which are water, fire, wind and earth, which are the secret of Ḥesed and Gvurah, Tiferet and Malkhut, each one of them having four countenances: lion, ox, eagle, man. And sin, destruction, anger, and wrath are dependent on white gall, which is the lung in which they make an adhesion, and on the red gall that is in the liver that turns red with Mars [the Hebrew name for which comes from the root meaning `red' — tr.]; and on the green gall that is attached to the liver, which is the sword of the Angel of Death, about which it is said: "Her end is bitter [same root word that means `gall'] as wormwood, sharp as a two-edged sword" (Proverbs 5:4); and on the black gall which is Lilith, which is the planet Saturn, which is controlled by the spleen, which is melancholia, lower netherworld, poverty and darkness, weeping and mourning and starvation.

C o m m e n t a r y

Man's four good elements — water, fire, wind, and earth are in the aspect of the four beasts — Michael, Gabriel, Nuriel, and Raphael — which are inside the four shells: stormy wind, large cloud, fire flashing up, and brightness. And just as the four beings are enwrapped inside the four shells, so are the four elements of man enveloped by the four shells of sin, destruction, anger, and wrath, where sin parallels brightness, destruction fire flashing up, anger a stormy wind, and wrath a large cloud.

On the text: Michael, Gabriel, Nuriel, and Raphael control man's four good elements, which are water, fire, wind, and earth; that is to say that the four elements fire, wind, water, and earth are aspects of the four beings in man like these four angels. And each of them has four countenances, just like the four beasts on high, each of which has four countenances: and like the beasts above who are enveloped in four shells, namely: stormy wind, large cloud, fire flashing up, and brightness. So also, the four beasts in man, which are fire, wind, water, and earth, are enveloped by four shells, namely: sin, destruction, anger, and wrath. And on the text: Are dependent on white gall, which is the lung in which they make an adhesion: for in the lung resides the shell of brightness, which is the secret of the curtain of the second contraction (as above, 267) that, in man, is called sin, and from which come the adhesions that are in the lung. And the red gall that is in the liver that turns red with Mars stands for the shell of fire flashing up, which is from the second contraction, whose Judgments are not of itself but from its intermixing with *Malkhut*, which is why it is called fire flashing up, for it flashes up from another fire, and thus he says: turns red with Mars, because its reddishness comes to it from another redness, and, in man, this shell is called destruction. And the green gall that is attached to the liver which is the sword of the Angel of Death. This is parallel to the shell of stormy wind that is drawn down from *Malkhut* of the first contraction, from where comes death (as above, *Vayetze*, 13). And on the text: Which is the sword of the Angel of Death, in man this shell is called by the name anger. The spleen, which is melancholia, lower netherworld, poverty and so on — this is the secret of the shell of large cloud, which is drawn down from the curtain of the first contraction, and is, in man, called wrath. And within these four shells of sin, destruction, anger, and wrath are enveloped the four elements of fire, wind, water and earth that are in the aspect of the four beasts that are in man.

271 Immediately, when these four shells move away from man, the Tree of Life takes control over him with 72 countenances of the illumination of Malkhut, namely: The Tetragrammaton in a square, thus: yud, yud hei, yud hei vav, and yud hei vav and hei, the numerical value of which is 72, the number of actual letters totalling ten, being dependent on the four winds, which are the four letters of the Tetragrammaton, about which it is said: "Thus says the Lord God: Come from the four winds, O breath ('wind')" (Ezekiel 37:9). This is the spirit of the Messiah, about whom it is said: "And the spirit of the Lord shall rest upon him" (Isaiah 11:2). The spirit of the Lord is that of Malkhut, while He, the Tetragrammaton, which is Zeir Anpin, blows in the right auricle of the heart, where is Ḥokhmah from the side of Ḥesed, in which one who wants to gain wisdom will move to the south with Ḥokhmah (wisdom). And Ḥesed blows in Binah, and then in Zeir Anpin, and then in Malkhut. When it blows in Ḥokhmah, it is yud; when in Binah, hei; when in Tiferet, vav; and when in Malkhut it is hei. The Tetragrammaton, which is Zeir Anpin, knocks on all four of these Sfirot and becomes four combinations. When on Ḥokhmah, He is yud; when on Binah, yud hei; when on Tiferet, yud hei vav; and when on Malkhut, yud hei vav and hei, making a total of ten letters, paralleling the ten Sfirot. And their numerical value is 72, which is Ḥokhmah, i.e. the thought of the heart.

272 The letters of the Tetragrammaton, Yud Hei Vav and Hei, spelled out with an aleph, have the numerical value of 45 (20 + 6 + 13 + 6 = 45), names of the letters of Yud Hei Vav and Hei have the numerical value of 45 (10 + 5 + 6 + 5 = 26), which is Zeir Anpin, whose right is water, and is the large hand, i.e. Ḥesed and the right column. His left is fire, which is the strong hand, i.e. Gvurah and the left column. In the central column that is between them, He is the uplifted hand, i.e. Tiferet, which is the central column, which is the holy spirit. And He has altogether Yud Hei, for he has the intelligences of the first three from Yud Hei.

273 "For the spirit of the living creature was in the ofnaim (angelic beings). What so ever the spirit was to go, so they went" (Ezekiel 1:20). Water and fire are directed by the spirit, for it grips both of them and bangs on the arteries of the brain, which is water, and is Ḥokhmah, and on the arteries of the heart, which is fire, and is Binah. And the place of the spirit (wind) is in the lobes of the lung, as above.

274 In every part of the body are to be found these four, namely the wheels of the sea of the Torah, which is water, and the wheels of the firmament, which is fire, all of them ascending and descending in it, in the bodily part, for the water, which is right and Ḥesed descends, while the fire, which is the left and Gvurah, ascends. For the left illuminates only upwards from below (as above Gen. I, page 60), while it, the spirit, which is Tiferet and the central column, has its place in the center between the firmament and the sea, which are the left and the right. And the tool of the spirit, which is Tiferet, is the Earth, which is dust, which is the Shekhinah, the Divine Presence.

275 And just like the birds, who open their wings against the wind so that they can fly with it, so also all the parts of the body are open at a number of sources, at a number of joints, a number of arteries, a number of compartments of the heart and a number of areas of the brain, in order to welcome the spirit which is the central column. Were it not to blow in the compartments of the heart, the fire that is in the heart, which is the secret of the left column, would burn up the whole body. That is to say: Were it not for the central column which is called spirit wind, uniting the right and the left with each other, the Judgement of the left side, which is the secret of the fire that is in the heart, would burn up the whole body. For the illumination of the left without the right is harsh and bitter judgment. And a number of ladders, i.e. steps and compartments from the arteries of the aorta and trachea, are all corrected with it, with the wind which is the central column.

VOICE AND SPEECH

276 When speech ascends, that is to say, at the beginning of the formation of speech in a man, to the lobes of the lung, it there becomes a voice. At that time, it is said: "For birds of the sky shall carry the voice" (Ecclesiastes

10:20). "The voice of the Lord is upon the waters" (Psalms 29:3) because it ascends from the side of the water, which is the right, which is the brain, that there ascends on the lobes of the lung. "The voice of the Lord hews out flames of fire" (Ecclesiastes 10:7) from the side of the heart, which is the left, which is fire. And when the voice emerges from the mouth, which is the secret of Malkhut, it is called speech.

277 And just as there are two lobes to the lung, i.e. the two halves of the lung that open up to welcome the voice as it is written: "their countenances and their wings were stretched upwards" [Ezekiel 1:11], for the lobes of the lungs are separated from each other — so also are the lips two in number that take the speech and cast it upwards.

278 And just as there are five lobes to the lung, i.e. five divisions in the two halves of the lung, all of them being open without an adhesion to receive this voice, so must there be five corrections in the mouth, all of them open without adhesions, and the five corrections are: (*228a) the guttural letters

aleph ḥet hei ayin that are formed in the throat; the labial letters bet vav mem pey that are formed with the lips; and the palatal letters gimel yud kaf kuf that are formed in the roof of the mouth; dalet tet lamed nun tav that are formed on the tongue; and zayin samekh shin resh tzadik that are formed by the teeth.

279 And speech will be in them, in the five emissions of the mouth, without any adhesion or hindrance, as it is written: "And it came to pass, before he had done speaking, that, behold, Rebecca came out" (Genesis 24:15), where Rebecca is prayer, which is speech. And for this reason have we learned: If the prayer is fluent in my mouth, I know that it has been accepted (Mishnah, Berakhot 5,5). But if there is an adhesion and it comes out with a hindrance, I know that my prayer is in disorder, because there is an adhesion in the lung, which is impure.

280 And voice refers to the Shema Yisrael, i.e. the unity of the six words of the Shema Yisrael [Hear, O-Israel, the-Lord our-God, the-Lord (is) One.], which is the unity of Zeir Anpin, is called voice. On this: "And I heard the noise [same Hebrew word as "voice"] of their wings" (Ezekiel 1:24), i.e. the Tetragrammaton, or Zeir Anpin, who is voice, when He emerges to welcome the Shekhinah with whispered prayer, which is speech, i.e. Malkhut that is called speech. Thus it is said: "O Lord, open my lips" (Psalm 51:17 — said silently by the reader before the Shemoneh Esreh). All the parts, i.e. all the 248 lights of Ḥesed of Zeir Anpin, which are called the 248 parts of the body, their wings, i.e. Malkhut which is in each part, are all of them opened by the 248 words in the four sections of the recital of the Shema Yisrael, in which the voice descends.

C o m m e n t a r y

The first section concerns the sentence "Hear, O-Israel, the-Lord our-God, the-Lord (is) one", together with the silent response thereto "Blessed-be the-name-of the-glory-of His-kingdom for-ever and-ever", making a total of 12 words. The second section is from Deuteronomy 6: 5-9, consisting of 42 words. The third section, from Deuteronomy 11:13-21, has 122 words, while the fourth section, from Numbers 25:27-41, contains 69 words. Together (12 + 42 + 122 + 69), they make 245 words, to which must be added the three words The-Lord your-God (is) true, that the cantor recites aloud on completion of the *Shema Yisrael*, making a total of 248 words. This is why, when not praying in a congregation, i.e. when there is no cantor to add these three words at the conclusion of the recital, the individual has to preface his recital of the *Shema Yisrael* with "God, faithful King!" — thus keeping the number of words at 248. (See also *Zohar Ḥadash Ruth*, page 80a.)

281 And when the voice descends to welcome the Shekhinah in the Amidah (Shemoneh Esreh) prayer, a number of birds chirp with it, they being the secret to the 248 lights of the Shekhinah, which is the secret of speech, and for this reason they chirp, all of them, in a number of types of melody on the parts of the body, which are the 248 lights of Zeir Anpin, which are the branches of the tree, and on all the wings that are on all the parts, i.e. of on Malkhut which is in each part and which is called 'wing', for there is the lodging-place of the bird that is called 'The Lord' [aleph dalet nun yud], i.e. Malkhut. For the 248 lights of Malkhut dwell on the aspect of the wing that there is in each of the 248 lights of Zeir Anpin, for each aspect receives from the one that is parallel to it above. For on each of the branches of Zeir Anpin, Malkhut is available to her husband, this being the secret of "O Lord open my lips" (said at the commencement of the Amidah or Shemoneh Esreh prayer), which is opening to Zeir Anpin with the Amidah prayer, for there is not one of the 248 parts of the Shekhinah that is not

open to receive Zeir Anpin. This is why the Shekhinah is called "the talk of the ministering angels" (cf. Talmud Bavli, Sukkah 28a, where Rashi comments on the phrase with 'I do not know what this is'!) — because it is the aspect of speech, and it is the chirping of the birds, who are the souls resting on the limbs of the Shekhinah, which are called birds, and it is "the talk of palm trees" (cf. Sukkah 28a), which are the branches of the tree that are the limbs of Zeir Anpin, which are in the aspect of pinions in each branch, for there rests 'The Lord' [aleph dalet nun yud], who is speech.

Commentary

Every *Partzuf* is divided to the left and the right, which is the secret of the 248 parts that are the tools of *Ḥasadim* on the right, and the 365 sinews which are the tools of the lights of the left, which is the secret of the illumination of *Ḥokhmah*, which is on the left. And *Zeir Anpin* is called voice and is mainly the illumination of *Ḥasadim*, and thus His unity in the recital of the *Shema Yisrael* is in the 248 words that emit the *Ḥasadim*. Afterwards, during the *Amidah* prayer, He is united with *Malkhut*, called speech, which is mainly the illumination of *Ḥokhmah*. And when *Malkhut* receives the *Ḥasadim* from *Zeir Anpin* during the *Amidah* prayer, she so receives in the tools of her *Ḥasadim* which are called the 248 parts of the *Shekhinah*. And the secret of the unification of voice and speech is the secret of the unification of *Ḥasadim* and *Ḥokhmah*, that are similar to voice and speech, for just as there is no speech without voice so is there no reality to the illumination of *Ḥokhmah* without *Ḥasadim*. For *Ḥokhmah* is unable to illuminate without being enclothed in *Ḥasadim* (see above, Gen. I, page 47). Thus the *Shekhinah* is thirsty for the *Ḥasadim* from *Zeir Anpin*, so that her speech, which is the secret of *Ḥokhmah*, may be revealed.

On the text: "And voice" refers to the *Shema Yisrael*, etc. (280).

For the unity of the *Shema Yisrael* is for *Zeir Anpin*, so that He may draw down the *Ḥasadim* with His 248 parts, which are the tools of *Ḥasadim* in order to give emanations to the *Shekhinah*. Later, He emerges to welcome the *Shekhinah* with whispered prayer (280), i.e. the *Amidah* prayer (that is said silently). For there He welcomes her and emits *Ḥasadim* to her. And he says (281) that every aspect above gives emanations to the parallel aspect below, for, although we say that the 248 parts of *Zeir Anpin* receive and emanate *Ḥasadim*, the meaning is in respect to the aspect of *Malkhut* that is in every part of *Zeir Anpin*, for it has a relationship with all of *Malkhut*.

And on the text: All the parts open, all of them, their wings, by the 248 words: `their wings' refers to the *Malkhuts* in each limb of *Zeir Anpin*, which accept the *Ḥasadim* and emanate to the 248 parts of *Malkhut*.

And on the text: And when the voice descends: this is in the *Amidah* prayer. A number of birds chirp with it (281) — that is, the 248 parts of *Malkhut* which are called the 248 birds that dwell on the 248 wings in the 248 parts of *Zeir Anpin* and receive *Ḥasadim* from them, in such a way that each part of *Malkhut* receives from the parallel aspect of the *Malkhut* that is in each part of *Zeir Anpin*.

282 And at the time when the Tetragrammaton descends to `The Lord', in every one of the parts of the Tetragrammaton which is Zeir Anpin, it emits to the parallel part of Malkhut which is `The Lord', and it is said about them: "And when they stood they let down their wings" (Ezekiel, 1:24). "When they stood" hints at the unity of the Amidah prayer (said in a standing position), for then the wings, which are parts of Malkhut, are at rest. And this is the secret of `electrum' [Ḥashmal: ḥet shin mem lamed], which is

the letters of silent and speaking beasts of fire. [`Silent', Ḥashot: ḥet shin vav tav, whose root letters are the first two letters of Ḥashmal, `speaking': memal lot, mem mem lamed lamed vav tav, whose first two root letters are the remaining letters of Ḥashmal]. Thus electrum is beasts of fire who are sometimes quiet and sometimes speaking, and the sages of the Mishnah said: "As we learnt in the Mishnah: When speech comes forth from the mouth of the Holy One, blessed be He, they are silent and when no speech comes forth from the mouth of the Holy One, blessed be He, they speak" (Talmud Bavli, Ḥagigah, 13b top). The meaning of this is that at the time when speech and voice are united together (that is, Zeir Anpin and Malkhut, which are the combination: Yud Aleph Hei Dalet Vav Nun Hei Yud) [formed by taking alternate letters of the Tetragrammaton: Yud Hei Vav and Hei and of `The Lord': Aleph Dalet Nun Yud — tr.] during the Amidah prayer, they are silent. But when their countenances, which is the secret of Zeir Anpin, and their wings, which is the secret of Malkhut, are separated (v. Ezekiel 1:11) — that is, when the Tetragrammaton is separated from `The Lord', He, the Tetragrammaton, is to be found in the four countenances of the beasts, which are the aspect of `The Lord' and the aspect of speech, speak, requesting nourishment from Zeir Anpin, for "in it was food for all" (Daniel 4:18). `The Lord' who is Malkhut is to be found on the wings of the beasts, and all of them are open to receive from the beasts.

Commentary

When *Zeir Anpin* and *Malkhut*, which are voice and speech, are in the secret of mating, i.e. during the *Amidah* prayer, then the main control belongs to *Zeir Anpin*, which is the aspect of *Ḥasadim*; and speech, which is the secret of the illumination of *Ḥokhmah* and `The Lord', although it also illuminates, nevertheless is by way of whispered speech, that is to say, without having control. But at a time when there is no mating, then the control of *Malkhut* is discernible, *Malkhut* being the secret of speech and the illumination of *Ḥokhmah*. And on the text: "At the time that speech and voice are united together, which makes *yud aleph hei dalet vav nun hei yud*, they are silent" (282), for then the *Ḥasadim* of *Zeir Anpin* are in control. But when "their countenances and their wings are separated" (Ezekiel 1:11) to receive, they speak, for then the control of *Malkhut*, which is the secret of speech, is discernible.

283 The beasts that are in Yetzirah roar with a voice that is Zeir Anpin, called Yud Hei Vav and Hei (the Tetragrammaton). And they are all on the right, i.e. with Ḥasadim. The wheel, which are in Assiah, squeak in speech, which is Malkhut, called Aleph Dalet Nun Yud ('The Lord'), and they are on the left. In the seraphs, which are in Briah, voice and speech become joined, being Zeir Anpin and Malkhut, and they are in the center, and they attire themselves in one unity in the two names: the Tetragrammaton and 'The Lord', and combine one with the other: Yud Aleph Hei Dalet Vav Nun Hei Yud. About them it is said: "And let fowl fly" (Genesis 1:20), and also: "Then one of the seraphs flew to me" (Isaiah 6:6), the reference being to Metatron. And it is said about them: "For the birds of the sky shall carry the voice, and that which has wings shall tell the matter" (Ecclesiastes 10:20), where the voice is from the side of the Tetragrammaton attired with Metatron, and the "matter" is from the side of 'The Lord' attired with Metatron. "Above Him stood the seraphs; each one had six wings" (Isaiah 6:2) is from the side of the letter vav (numerical value 6), which is attired in them, and is the central column, incorporating right and left, including the six Sfirot of Ḥesed, Gvurah, Tiferet, Netzaḥ,

Hod, Yesod, and it includes the six words of the unity as expressed in the Shema Yisrael (Hear, O-Israel, the-Lord our-God, the-Lord (is) One). And the sign of this is: "With two he covered his face, with two he covered his feet, and with two he did fly" (Isaiah 6:2).

284 From "And I looked" (Ezekiel 1:4) to "appearance of a man" (Ezekiel 1:26) is considered to be one correction, for there are four shells, within which are the four beings, and the secret of Metatron is that vis-a-vis the beings he is the inner meaning of the firmament which is above their heads and leads them, while vis-a-vis Malkhut he is the inner meaning of throne. And all of this is the first correction. The second correction is: "And upon the likeness of the throne was a likeness as the appearance of a man upon it above" (ibid.), where by man is meant the imprint of the scroll of the Torah, i.e. Malkhut that is the imprint of Zeir Anpin, who is called the Torah scroll. And this is: "According to (Tiferet) the beauty of man, to dwell in the house" (Isaiah 44:13). In other words, Malkhut is the Tiferet of man, with a good helping of imagination, and not really Tiferet itself. So also here where it is said "the appearance of a man", which is applied imaginatively to Malkhut, for whom Metatron is a throne.

RECITAL OF THE SHEMA YISRAEL, PHYLACTERIES AND STRAPS

285 The sages taught: "Anyone reciting the Shema Yisrael morning and evening is as though he had observed the saying that "This book of the Torah shall not depart out of your mouth, but shall meditate therein day and night" (Joshua 1:8 and Talmud Bavli, Menakhot 99b). This is because the recital of the Shema Yisrael encompasses right and left, which are the secret of day and night [as he demonstrates below — 290], for a prayer-shawl is white, that is to say, the prayer-shawl with fringes from the point of view of the white that is in it and not the blue that is in it, and is to the right from the side of Ḥesed; and it is

said about it: "Almighty King, who sits on the throne of mercy, governs with kindness [Ḥasidut]" (from the Sliḥot service) And also: "And a throne is established through mercy [Ḥesed]" (Isaiah 16:5). The numerical value of Ḥesed [ḥet samekh dalet, 8 + 60 + 4 = 72] is seventy-two, which hints at the 72 links and knots of the prayer-shawl, i.e. four times eighteen (see above 256).

286 And there is a prayer-shawl from the side of Metatron, which is the tet tet (9 + 9 = 18) of Metatron [mem tet tet resh vav nun] which includes the 18 links and knots on each corner of the prayer-shawl, i.e 5 knots paralleling the five books of the Pentateuch (Genesis, Exodus, Leviticus, Numbers, Deuteronomy), and 13 links, i.e. the 13 loops that are wound around the fringes, which parallel the 13 attributes of Divine Mercy mentioned in the Torah (Exodus 34:6-7), about which it is said: "There are thirteen exegetical principles by which the Torah is expounded" (Boraitha d'Rabbi Ishmael), which is the secret of the 13 attributes of mercy that are drawn down from the 13 emendations of the beard of Arif Anpin.

287 About Malkhut it is said: "As the appearance of a man upon it above" (Ezekiel 1:26), i.e. that Malkhut has the form of Tiferet, which is "the beauty [Tiferet] of a man [Adam]" (Isaiah 46:13) upon it from above, and is called by the name of Tiferet, which is yud hei vav and hei (the Tetragrammaton), which is the inner meaning of the verse: "Every one that is called by My name, and whom I have created for My glory, I have formed him, yea, I have made him" (Isaiah 43:7). So, therefore, "as the appearance of a man from above" is the Shekhinah, which is as the form of the central column, which is Tiferet, with four countenances and ten Sfirot, that make Adam (man). That is, the names of the four letters of the Tetragrammaton [yud, yud vav dalet, 10 + 6 + 4 = 20; hei, hei aleph, 5 + 1 = 6; vav, vav aleph vav, 6 + 1 + 6 = 13; hei, hei aleph, 5 + 1 = 6] have the numerical

value of forty-five (20 + 6 + 13 + 6 = 45), which is the same as the numerical value of the letters of Adam [aleph dalet mem, 1 + 4 + 40 = 45]. And the four faces of Adam are the four simple letters of the Tetragrammaton, which together (i.e. the 10 letters of the Tetragrammaton, its four letters spelled out) make 14 letters, about which it is said: "And by the hand [yad, yud dalet, 10 + 4 = 14] of the prophets have I used similitudes" (Hosea 12:11).

288 Again, the fringe is called 'life' [Ḥai, ḥet yud, 8 + 10 = 18], namely the 13 links and 5 knots, from the side of the righteous one, which is Yesod, in which, i.e. by whose unity, the Holy One, blessed be He and His Divine Presence (Shekhinah) are called by the name Adam. That is, the Tetragrammaton, written out in full by the names of the four letters,when spelled out with Alephs (see 287), has the same numerical value (45) as the word adam where He, the central column that is Zeir Anpin, is yud hei vav (the first three of the four letters of the Tetragrammaton) and has the numerical value of 39, while His Divine Presence is the final hei (the fourth letter of the Tetragrammaton) with the numerical value of 6, making 45 in all, such that this hei completes the name Adam. And this, the righteous one called life, is He who "causes the dew to fall" (inserted in the second paragraph of the Shemoneh Esreh during the summer months), the word for 'dew' being tal [tet lamed, 9 + 30 = 39], and He is yud hei vav (= 39, as above) spelled out with alephs, onto the hei, aleph which is the Shekhinah, for Yesod is the knot of the prayer-shawl, which is 18 (life) worlds on each side, i.e. 5 knots and 13 links that bind together and unite the Holy One, blessed be He, and His Divine Presence (Shekhinah) on all sides, with the four corners of the prayer-shawl, which are Ḥesed and Gvurah, Tiferet and Malkhut.

289 Phylacteries are the aspect of the left column, as it is said: "The Lord has

sworn by His right hand and by the arm of His strength" (Isaiah 62:8), where `by His right hand' refers to the Torah and `and by the arm of His strength' refers to phylacteries. The four passages on the phylacteries (Deuteronomy 6:4-9; 11:13-21; Exodus 13:1-10, 11-16) are the four letters yud hei vav and hei of the Tetragrammaton. `The Lord' is a palace for the four letters, which are the four passages in the four receptacles of the phylacteries. The knot of the hand phylactery is the righteous one, life of the worlds, which is Yesod, and is the bond between the two of them, between the Tetragrammaton and `The Lord', on the left arm. The knot of the head phylactery is the central column, i.e. Tiferet, by which are united together on high the Tetragrammaton and `I am', which are Ḥokhmah and Binah, for Zeir Anpin ascends and unites Ḥokhmah and Binah, which is called the Tetragrammaton and `I am', there Da'at is made.

290 The recital of the Shema Yisrael is the unity that is at the center, i.e. the unity that is in Ḥesed, Gvurah, and Tiferet, and it is held between the fringes and the phylacteries, for the fringes in aspect of the white that is in them are on its right, and the phylacteries are on the left, for all of the passages of the fringes and phylacteries are included in the unity of the recital of the Shema Yisrael. And from the side of the central column, i.e. Prayer-shawl and phylacteries, it is said: "And it shall be for a sign upon your hand and for frontlets between your eyes" (Exodus 13:16), and it is also said: "And they will make themselves fringes" (Numbers 15:38).

Commentary

There are three unities:

a) The unity that is in *Ḥokhmah*, *Binah*, *Da'at* is the

Tetragrammaton with `I am', *Ḥokhmah* and *Binah*, which are united by *Da'at*, which is the knot of the head phylactery.

b) The unity of *Netzaḥ*, *Hod*, *Yesod* is the Tetragrammaton with `The Lord', which are united by *Yesod*, which is the knot of the hand phylactery.

c) The unity of *Ḥesed*, *Gvurah*, *Tiferet*, which is the Tetragrammaton with *Elohim*, which are united by *Tiferet*. And on the text: The recital of the *Shema Yisrael*, which is the secret of *Tiferet*, is the unity that is at the center — i.e. between the upper unity of the Tetragrammaton with `I am' and the lower unity of the Tetragrammaton with `The Lord', for it is in their center, in *Ḥesed*, *Gvurah*, *Tiferet*. And *Tiferet* is the secret of the central column that includes right and left. Recital of the *Shema Yisrael*, therefore, is the secret of the prayer-shawl andphylacteries, where the former is on the right and the latter on the left.

291 (*228b) The letter shin of the phylacteries is ancient Mosaic tradition, as it is written: "And all the peoples of the Earth shall see that the name of Tetragrammaton is called upon you, and they shall be afraid of you" (Deuteronomy 28:10). And it has been taught: What is `the name of the Tetragrammaton'? — It is the head phylactery [this being visible, while the arm phylactery is covered by the sleeve — tr.] (cf. Talmud Bavli, Berakhot 6a). And the shin shin of the phylacteries, that are visible on them from the two external sides, have the numerical value of 600 (shin = 300). shin shin are the six stages Ḥesed, Gvurah, Tiferet, Netzaḥ, Hod, Yesod that are in Zeir Anpin, where the right shin is Ḥesed, Gvurah, Tiferet, and the left shin is Netzaḥ, Hod, Yesod. And the letters shin have seven branches, for the right shin has three heads and the left four, making seven heads or branches. These

seven branches, together with the six stages and the 600, add up to 613, that is Tariag (tav resh yud gimel, 400 + 200 + 10 + 3 = 613) [this being the number of precepts, both positive and negative, in the Torah. — tr.] And there is no precept that is not equivalent to the whole of the Torah, it being, therefore, said about it: "And all the peoples of the earth shall see that the name of Tetragrammaton is called upon you..." (Deuteronomy 28:10).

292 Likewise, just as Tariag is implied in the phylacteries, so each precept is the Tetragrammaton, as follows: The first two letters of the Tetragrammaton [yud hei, 10 + 5 = 15], together with `My name' [Shemi, shin mem yud 300 + 40 + 10 = 350] have the numerical value of 365, this being the number of the negative precepts in the Torah. Again: The last two letters of the Tetragrammaton [vav hei, 6 + 5 = 11], together with `My memorial' [Zikhri, zayin kaf resh yud, 7 + 20 + 200 + 10 = 237] have the numerical value of 248, this being the number of the positive precepts in the Torah. The total number of precepts is 365 + 248 = 613, Tariag. (See above, 175, and also "This is My name for ever and this is My Memorial to all generations" [Exodus 3:15].) This is why each precept is equivalent to Tariag. And the sages have taught that the recital of the Shema Yisrael, incorporating phylacteries and fringes (as above, 290) contains 613 precepts in the fringes, for the numerical value of `fringes' [tzitzit, tzadik yud tzadik yud tav, 90 + 10 + 90 +10 + 400 = 600] is six hundred, which together with the 13 links thereof makes 613, Tariag. And also 613 in the phylacteries, like the numerical equivalent of the two letters shin on them (see preceding paragraph) — and so it is throughout.

293 One phylactery or frontlet is, in Hebrew, totefet, which can be split into two tet tet and pey tav. The numerical value of tet tet (9 + 9) is eighteen, which is `life' [Ḥai, ḥet yud, 8 + 10], the life of the worlds, which is the right-

eous one, i.e. Yesod, parallel to which is Metatron, for Yesod is attired with Metatron. Pey tav refers to Tiferet [tav pey aleph resh tav] whose letters may be re-arranged as tav aleph resh, pey tav (i.e.a description of pey tav). And Metatron is Tiferet's horse; that is to say Tiferet rides upon him. For all the Sfirot dress up in Metatron. At one time it might be Tiferet that wears him, at another Yesod and at another Malkhut, while at other times all three might be attired with him. And so it is that his rela-tionship to them is as that of body to soul, and when the Holy One, blessed be He, removes Himself from him (from Metatron), Metatron is left dumb, having neither voice nor speech. For the Holy One, blessed be He, and His Divine Presence (Shekhinah) are the voice and speech of every angel, and they are in every voice and speech of Torah, and in every voice and prayer, and in each single precept. And in every place of His rule, in the upper worlds and in the lower worlds. He is the life of everything. He carries everything.

294 Just as there is no speech without voice and no voice without speech, so is there no 'The Lord' without the Tetragrammaton. And this is true for the world of Atziluth, for there is no separation between Zeir Anpin and Malkhut, who are voice and speech. But in the world of separation, i.e. in the three worlds of Briah, Yetzirah, and Assiah, there is voice without speech. But in Atziluth they are united, and the knot of the phylacteries, which is Shaddai (the Almighty), which is Yesod, is held by them from above and from below, and this is the righteous one, the life of the worlds, who is held between voice and speech and unites them.

295 At this point, the Faithful Shepherd happened upon the old man, and said: Old man, Old man, the phylacteries and the fringes and the section on the mezuzah are three precepts that are incorporated in the recital of the Shema Yisrael, and the recital of the Shema Yisrael is the fourth precept. And the four are parallel to Ḥesed and Gvurah,

Tiferet and Malkhut, where fringes and phylacteries are Ḥesed and Gvurah (as above, 290), recital of the Shema Yisrael is Tiferet that unites them, and mezuzah is Malkhut. Fringes are mentioned three times (Numbers 15: 38-39), paralleling the three columns, and regarding phylacteries the word 'sign', which is Yesod, is mentioned twice (Deuteronomy 6:8 and 11:18), once for the knot of the head phylactery and once for the knot of the hand phylactery. In respect to the fringes, the letter zayin of the word tizk'ru ("So that you will remember", Numbers 15:40 — the fourth section of the Shema Yisrael) has to be well stressed, for this letter zayin (numerical value 7) implies Malkhut, which is the seventh Sfirah, and is the secret of the blue that is in the fringe, on which the remembering depends (see above 252). And on the mezuzah, which is Malkhut, the name Shaddai (the Almighty) is on the outside, while the Tetragrammaton is on the inside. This is because there are two matings, the external mating with Yesod, and the internal mating with Tiferet. The Faithful Shepherd clarified all this to the old man for him to understand on his own.

296 The Faithful Shepherd answers the various questions that face us. Why are there open and closed sections? (answered below, 310). Why does the fringe have a fixed length and width, for the length of each fringe was determined as the size of 12 fingers? (answered below, 297). Why was the precept of the blue fixed at one-third twisted threads and two-thirds untwisted threads? (answered below, 297). Why between each pair of knots in the fringes does there have to be a space of a full thumb's breadth? (answered below, 301). And why should each link be triple, i.e. three loops? (answered below, 298). Also, why are phylacteries on the brain and against the heart? And why is the length of the straps to the heart on the left and to the navel on the right? (answered below, 456, and see Tikunei Zohar, page 9b)

And why does the strap of the hand phylactery have to be wound three times round the middle finger? (answered below, 299).

297 The answer is as follows: But certainly the garment is not important unless it has three on three for each side of the four sides, making 12. And they represent the four garments of white that parallel Zeir Anpin, which is the secret of the four letters of the Tetragrammaton; and the four garments of gold that parallel Malkhut, which is the secret of the four letters of 'The Lord'; and the four garments of the ordinary priest, which is the secret of Metatron. In terms of the blessing of an ordinary priest, it is implied "Let not the blessing of an ordinary man be considered lightly in your eyes" (cf. Talmud Bavli, Berakhot 7a). And, therefore, the blue is one-third twisted thread, i.e. 13 links are wound around the fringe for it is parallel the four garments of white, which is the secret of Zeir Anpin, who is the root. And two-thirds are untwisted thread, for it has to hang loose, like the branches on a tree.

Commentary

The answer is as follows: the length of the fringe has to be twelve thumb-breadths parallel to the twelve types of garments: the garments of white, which are the four of *Zeir Anpin*, and the garments of gold, which are the four of *Malkhut*, and the garments of an ordinary priest, which are the four of Metatron. It is also explained why the blue is one-third twisted and two-thirds free-flowing. The third that is twisted is against the garments of white, which is the four of *Zeir Anpin*, who is the root. And the two-thirds free-flowing are against the eight garments of *Malkhut* and of Metatron, who are *Zeir Anpin*'s branches. And he explains below (301) why the measurement is by thumb-breadths and not with any of the other fingers.

298 And every link must be triple, made up of three, i.e. of three loops. And the reason is that each tripling is from the side of holiness, which is the secret of the three columns, as it is written: "They proclaim you holy three times" (Mussaf Amidah — Sephardi version only) And Israel is made up of three parts, i.e. priest, levites, and Israelites in order to subjugate the officers (same Hebrew root as the word `three') of the evil forces, as it is written: "And officers (same Hebrew root as the word `three') over all of them" (Exodus 14:7). For the fringe is from the side of the central column, which is Tiferet, which is the third of the patriarchs, for the patriarchs are Ḥesed, Gvurah, and Tiferet. And everything that comes in threes has its root in the 72-letter name of God that starts vav hei vav, yud lamed yud (as above, Beshallaḥ, page 51), in which every word consists of three letters. From its point of view, every link is composed of three triple loops, and the link is the Shekhinah, which is the secret of "They proclaim you holy three times", and is tripled in the central column, for it receives from the central column the three columns that are in it. Thus is it made up of the three branches of the patriarchs, i.e. of Netzaḥ, Hod, and Yesod, which are the branches of Ḥesed, Gvurah, and Tiferet, which are called the patriarchs. And they are the letter shin from the word `sabbath' [Shabbat, shin bet tav], which has three heads [the arms of the letter — tr.], which is the secret of Netzaḥ, Hod, and Yesod. The bet tav from the word Shabbat make the word bat (daughter) and hint at the Shekhinah, who is an only daughter, which is the secret of the link, and the secret of the blue that is in the fringe.

299 Happy is the body who is thus marked with the Shekhinah and the Holy One, blessed be He, on the wings of a precept, i.e. with the 13 links in the precept of the fringe, and also with the strap of the hand phylactery, on the middle finger with three loops, which is like a link, wound around with three loops round the finger.

This also parallels the three columns, just like the link of the fringe, and there are 14 links. And is marked with the knot of the phylacteries that consists of two knots, the one on the head and the other on the arm, for they also are triple. And altogether there are fifteen triplets, for two knots in one knot is also considered a triple, making, therefore, 15 triples.

Commentary

The thirteen links of the fringes are thirteen triples, which, with the one triple of the hand strap on the middle finger, makes fourteen triples. And with the triple of the knot of the phylactery, which includes two knots within it, and which is like the central column that also is considered a triple because it includes two columns in it, there are 15 triples.

300 The 13 triple links contain 39 loops, i.e. the numerical value of the word `dew' [tal, tet lamed, 9 + 30 = 39], which, together with the 13 links themselves that have the numerical value of the word `one' [eḥad, aleph ḥet dalet, 1 + 8 + 4 = 13], adds up to `the son of' [ben, bet nun, 2 + 50 = 52 = 39 + 13]. And this hints at Ben Yah (the son of Yah), which is the central column, Zeir Anpin.

301 Each knot is in the form of a right palm. Each link is in the form of a finger with three joints, paralleling the three loops, and so it is that all the fingers have three joints except the thumb that has just two. And it is thumb that gives the distance between each pair of knots in the fringe, for there has to be a space between them of a full thumb-breadth, and this is the same measurement as the nose, the width of the right and left eye, the distance between the eyes, the measurement of the right and left ear, and of each lip, and of the tongue. "All the curtains shall have one measure" (Exodus 26:2).

Commentary

After the central column has united the two columns, the right and the left, with each other, and the *Ḥokhmah* on the left has been included in the *Ḥasadim* on the right, and the *Ḥasadim* on the right have been included in the *Ḥokhmah* on the left, two columns are discernible in the central column itself, namely: the two columns, the right and the left, of which it (the central column) took possession since it caused their illumination, and the act of their unification one with the other, which is the form of the central column. However where it is unable to reveal the action of their unification with each other in, for example, the head, because the first three of *Ḥokhmah* are reduced by the central column to the point of their disappearance, and the act of the unification of the two columns is not discernible at all there, but only vis-a-vis the six ends of *Ḥokhmah*, which are in the body, not in the head. Consequently, the central column has in the head only the two columns of which it took possession from above, but its own action, that of the central column, is missing there, and it consists of no more than two columns.

There are thus two aspects in the fingers:

a) The thumb that has only two joints, paralleling the central column in the head that has only two columns.

b) The other fingers that have three joints, paralleling the central column in the body, where it has three columns.

On the text: Each knot is in the form of a right palm, i.e. contains only *Ḥasadim*, which are right. Each link is in the form of a finger with three joints, i.e. *Ḥokhmah* also illuminates there, and the action of the central column is discernible, for it has three columns, which is the secret of the three joints and the three loops. And so it is that all the fingers have three joints except the thumb, for the thumb has only two joints, which teaches that the action of the central column itself is not discernible at this place, for the distance between each pair of knots in the fringe is a full thumb-breadth. Just as the knot of the fringe is in the form of a right palm, so between each pair of knots is in the form of a right palm, and the action of the central column is not discernible there, which is why its measurement is according to the thumb, which has only two joints. He thus answers the question (posed above, 296) and says that the measurement of the thumb is used for all of the *Sfirot* of the head because the action of the central column is not discernible in them. And on the text: This is the same measurement as the nose, etc., i.e. of all the *Sfirot* that are eyes, ear, nose, mouth and tongue. And this is the secret of "All the curtains shall have one measure" (Exodus 26:2), for a single measure teaches of the right column which is the secret of *Ḥasadim*, and this measure is used for all the *Sfirot* of the head. And it should be known that in the *Idra Rabba* Rabbi Shimon explained the matter differently. For he differentiates between Father and Mother that are in the head and Israel Grandfather and Understanding that are in the head. And he says there that the central column has just two columns only in the aspect of Father and Mother in the head, but that, in the aspect of Israel Grandfather and Understanding in the head, the central column has three columns. And this is how he explained the matter in most places (v. *Idra Rabba*, *Nasa*, 189).

302 Ammah (cubit) is the measure of the body in four directions and up and down, making six cubits. And each cubit (= forearm) has three joints, i.e. the aspect of three columns (as explained in the previous section), making 18 joints in the six cubits, being the secret of the 18 wavings with which we wave the Lulav in six directions, three in each direction. And about them it is said: "This your stature is like a palm-tree" (Song of Songs 7:8). For a palm-tree amounts to seventy years,

which is the secret of the seven lower Sfirot that are in the body, where Ḥokhmah, which is the secret of the stature, is revealed, and not in the head, as explained above. And therefore the stature,which is the secret of the first three, is likened to a palm-tree, and this is the size of the stature, that it is only in the body, that the gathering [mikveh] of Israel emanates to the Shekhinah, for the letters of the word mikveh [mem kuf vav hei], re-arranged, spell `stature' [komah, kuf vav mem hei]. That is to say, Zeir Anpin emanates this stature of body to the Malkhut. And we wave the Lulav four times when we recite Hallel [Psalms 113-128, inserted into the Morning Service during the pilgrimage festivals, etc.— in this case the reference is to Sukkot — tr.] This makes four times eighteen (see above), which is 72, for the 72-letter name of God is the root of the three columns, and is the secret of the three verses: "And the angel of the Lord, who went before the camp of Israel, removed and went behind them; and the pillar of cloud removed from them, and stood behind them; and it came between the camp of Egypt and the camp of Israel; and there was the cloud and darkness here, yet gave it light by night there; and the one camp came not near the other all the night. And Moses stretched out his hand over the sea; and the Lord caused the sea to go back by a strong east wind all the night, and made the sea dry land, and the waters were divided" (Exodus 14:19-21), each verse of which contains [in Hebrew] exactly 72 letters). (See above Beshallaḥ, page 50.)

303 And the secret of the beasts, their stature (*229a) is the secret of the verse: "As for their rims, full of eyes round about" (Ezekiel 1:18). `Their rims' refers to the four beasts of the lower Chariot, which are from Malkhut. `They were high' refers to the four beasts of the central Chariot, which is the secret of Zeir Anpin. `And their rims' refers to the four beasts of the third Chariot, that from Binah, all of them together being 12 beasts. And the four beasts of the third Chariot are full of eyes round about the four of them, i.e. round about the four beasts of the third upper Chariot, which is the

secret of Tetragram-maton, Tetragrammaton, Tetragrammaton, that is to say, the secret of the three Tetragrammatons in "The Lord is King, the Lord was King, the Lord will be King forever"; and these three Tetragrammatons have a total of 12 letters between them. `The Lord is King' refers to the central Chariot; `the Lord was King' to the third upper Chariot; and `the Lord will be King' to the lower Chariot.

BOWING AND STANDING UPRIGHT

304 **And those of stature are marked with these three chariots during prayer. Where would that be? The answer to this is: "When one bows, one should bow at `Blessed' (the first word of each blessing), and when returning to the upright position, one should do so at the mention of the Divine Name (the third word in each blessing)" (cf. Talmud Bavli, Berakhot 12a, bot.). During the prayer, i.e. the Shemoneh Esreh, there are four occasions when one has to bow and four when one has to stand upright. One has to bow and then stand upright at the beginning and end of `Avot' (the first blessing of the Shemoneh Esreh), and also at the beginning and end of `Modim' (the penultimate blessing of the Shemoneh Esreh). By so bowing and standing upright, one suggests the imminent arrival of He to whom the four directions belong, and they ascend and descend for Him to whom the heaven and the earth belong. I.e. it is the same as with the Lulav, which one shakes in six directions: towards heaven and towards the earth and to the four points of the compass, which parallel the first three blessings (of the Shemoneh Esreh), which are Ḥesed, Gvurah, and Tiferet, and the last three blessings, which are Netzaḥ, Hod, and Yesod, making a total of 8 bowings and standings upright. And there are four in "May He who makes peace in His high places make peace for us and for all Israel" (said at the conclusion of the Shemoneh Esreh), namely: bowing and standing upright to the left and bowing and standing upright to the right, and this is like one who stands opposite his Master. His right will be his master's left, and his left will be his master's right. He thus**

offers peace to his left and his right, where his right is opposite his master's left and his left is opposite his master's right.

305 This makes a grand total of 12 bowings and standings upright, i.e. four bowings and standings upright at the beginning and end of `Avot'; four bowings and standings upright at the beginning and end of `Modim'; four bowings and standings upright to the right and left during "May He who makes peace". And they contain 72 eyes, for there are six directions, i.e. for Him to whom the four points of the compass belong, together with the heavens and the earth, as above, and six times twelve is 72. And because they draw down Ḥokhmah in the secret of the standings upright, they are, therefore, called eyes. The six bowings contain 18 movements, there in each bow, for one has to bend the head, the back, and the tail, loosening the 18 [ḥet yud, Ḥai] vertebrae in the backbone, thus alluding to Yesod, which is called life, and the implication is that one has to include Yesod in these six bowings. And the twelve bowings and standing upright (multiplied by the six directions) come to 72 (as above), and these 72 eyes of the Holy One, blessed be He, that are emanated to Malkhut, illuminated the 72 wings of the Shekhinah that rises up over them and is called Amidah (literally: standing), which is the secret of the Amidah prayer (otherwise known as the Shemoneh Esreh), for, initially, Malkhut was a state of prostration, which is the secret of the bowing, and has to be raised up through the Name of the Tetragrammaton, and has to be stood upright through the Divine Name, through the Life of the Worlds, which is Yesod, that is called life. And four in the standings upright in six blessings, which is Tiferet, including the first three blessings and the last three blessings.

306 And one has to bow at the Life of the Worlds, i.e. at the attribute of Yesod which is called life. And this is vav vav vav (6 + 6 + 6 = 18), for when one bows, one should bow at `Blessed', which is Yesod that is called `Blessed', and

when returning to the upright position, one should do so at the mention of the Divine Name (cf. Talmud Bavli, Berakhot 12a bot.), which is the central column, that is Tiferet, which is called the Tetragrammaton [yud hei vav and hei], and the Righteous One that is called 'Blessed'. And they are vav vav vav, for Tiferet is the secret of the letter vav written with two vavs: vav vav, while Yesod is the secret of the letter vav written as a single vav. And these three vavs allude to the initial letters of the three verses: Exodus 14:19-21 [each of which starts with a vav, — tr.]. And they are the secret of the three columns of the 72-letter Name [for each of these three verses has exactly 72 letters in the Hebrew-tr.] (as above, Vayishlaḥ, page 51). The upper vav (written vav-vav), which is Tiferet, is connected with standing upright and with bowing down, and is therefore with two vavs. But Yesod, which is connected with bowing only, has just one vav. And all of them, all the three vavs, add up to 18, corresponding to the 18 blessings of the (Shemoneh Esreh) prayer.

307 Four bowings are at 'The Lord' [Aleph Dalet Nun Yud], and four standings upright are at the Tetragrammaton (Yud Hei Vav and Hei). And the central column is called the Tetragrammaton, while the Shekhinah is called 'The Lord'. The life of the worlds, which is Yesod, unites them, i.e. 'The Lord' and the Tetragrammaton, one with the other, making: Yud Aleph Hei Dalet Vav Nun Hei Yud, which is the letters of 'The Lord' and of the Tetragrammaton interwoven. The numerical value of these letters (10 + 1 + 5 + 4 + 6 + 50 + 5 + 10) is 91, which is the same as the letters of Amen (aleph mem nun, 1 + 40 + 50 = 91), that is said at the conclusion of each of the 18 blessings of the Shemoneh Esreh. Each blessing contains the Tetragrammaton. There are 18 blessings and four letters in each Tetragrammaton [Yud Hei Vav and Hei], and 18 x 4 = 72, which are the 72 eyes that illuminate in the 72 pinions, which are 18 times the four letters [Aleph Dalet Nun Yud] of 'The Lord'.

Commentary

Although he states in the adjoining paragraph that the bowings are in Yesod, i.e in the aspect of unity, for Yesod always cleaves to Malkhut, bowing nevertheless means the prostration of Malkhut, i.e. it lacks the upper three Sfirot, just as the one who bows lowers his head, and has to lift it up for the head is the upper three Sfirot. And this is achieved with the emanation of Zeir Anpin, which is the Tetragrammaton. And thus he says: Four bowings are at 'The Lord', wherein is the prostration, and four standings upright are at the Tetragrammaton, wherein is Malkhut's strength to stand upright. The life of the worlds connects them, i.e. Yesod is the one to unite them with each other.

308 And the secret of the matter is in the verse: "As for their rims, they were high... and their rims were full of eyes..." (Ezekiel 1:18) that refers to the beings (see above, 303). As for 'and their rims' refers to the pinions, which is Malkhut; 'they were high' refers to countenances, which is Zeir Anpin; 'and their rims', which are in the aspect of Binah, are "full of eyes round about for the four of them", for all of them are surrounded on the four sides by the four letters. And there would seem to be a contradiction here, for he has said that the 72 eyes are in Zeir Anpin. He thus adds: And everything is Emet ('true'), that is to say, all three aspects, pinions, countenances, eyes, are all included in Zeir Anpin, which is called Emet. And the proof of this is to be found in the saying "There are 70 faces to the Torah". [70 is the letter ayin, which also means 'an eye' - tr.] Thus the Torah, which is Zeir Anpin, which has eyes and faces but in the particular aspects, the wings are considered the Lord, (Adonai), which is Malkhut. The faces are the Tetragrammaton which is Zeir Anpin, has eyes and faces, but in the particular aspects the wings are considered the Lord which is Malkhut. The faces is the Tetragrammaton which is Zeir Anpin and the eyes are 'I am', which is

Binah. The sum total of the numerical value of the letters of the three names `The Lord' (1 + 4 + 50 + 10 = 65), the Tetragrammaton (10 + 5 + 6 + 5 = 26), and `I am' (1 + 5 + 10 + 5 = 21) is 112 (65 + 26 + 21), i.e. yud bet kuf (10 + 2 + 100 = 112), and these three letters are the initial letters of the words Yiḥud (`unity'), Berakhah (`blessing') and Kedushah (`sanctification'). The name `The Lord' hints at the aspect of action, the Tetragrammaton at the aspect of speech, and `I am' at the aspect of thought.

309 Each and every eye is of the size of a thumb, and this is the middle vav, i.e. the aspect of the central column, of the only two joints, which are the secret of yud yud. In respect to the nose, the thumb is called vav, i.e. middle vav. And in respect to the two orifices that are in the nose, which are right and left and not as one (see above, 301), they are called yud yud. The numerical value of the vav, together with the two letters yud (6 + 10 + 10) is 26 and is equal to yud hei (written out in full: yud-vav-dalet hei-aleph, 10 + 6 + 4 = 20; 5 + 1 = 6; and 20 + 6 = 26). And this is as in "Then the Lord God formed [vayiytzer, vav yud yud tzadik resh] man" (Genesis 11:7), where the beginning of the word `formed' is vav and two yuds, which teaches about the size of the thumb and is the secret of the control of Ḥasadim (see above 301), which is a thumbsbreadth, the size of each measure of yud hei, which is the upper three Sfirot, whenever the upper three Sfirot have control in each and every part of the body. That is to say, in every limb there is a head and a body, and the measure of thumb which is Ḥasadim controls the measure of the head that is in the limb. Every limb here means every whole limb, such as in "Spreading abroad its wings, takes them, bears them on its pinions" (Deuteronomy 32:11). There are `wings', which are the lower aspect of the limb, which is the aspect of a three-jointed finger, and there is also in the verse the word evrato (`pinions'), whose first three letters are aleph bet resh, evar: `limb', and there is there the aspect of a thumb of two joints, because it is the upper aspect which is the secret of yud hei that is in it.

310 And there is no limb in the whole of his chariot that does not have the form of a complete limb, i.e. aspect of head and of body, as above, in the preceding paragraph, and in every place "Their faces and their wings are stretched upwards" (Ezekiel 1:11), i.e. in the aspect of the upper three Sfirot of the limb, for there a thumb's measure is in control as the right and the left of the central column are separated, as above. And this parallels the open sections (i.e. the Biblical text leaves the line open and continues on the subsequent line) in the phylacteries (i.e. Exodus 13:11-16), which parallels the aspect of the upper three Sfirot, which are separated. To welcome the Torah, which is Zeir Anpin, which is the upper three Sfirot, i.e. the eyes and the countenances, as above. And when they are below, in the aspect of the six ends, there is then a mating between right and left of the central column, as well as between Zeir Anpin and Malkhut and the sections of the phylacteries (e.g. Deuteronomy 6:4-9; 11:13-21; Exodus 13:1-10) are closed (i.e. the next verse in the Biblical text continues on the same line.), paralleling the Yud Aleph Hei Dalet Vav Nun Hei Yud (the combination of the Tetragrammaton and `The Lord') that are on them. With their faces and their wings, which are Zeir Anpin and Malkhut, who are here united in each other, and thus the sections are closed. And here their faces and their wings are not separated, because it is from below, which is the six intermediate Sfirot. (And this settles the question that was posed above, 296.)

311 And the Holy One, blessed be He, keeps notes on Israel in respect thereof, i.e. in respect to the countenances and pinions of the beings in the prayer, in order that Israel should be comrades of the beings, i.e. to bow with the whole body in the 18 blessings of the prayer, so that He should rule over them in each and every one of their limbs, Amen, which is the secret of Yud Aleph Hei Dalet Vav Nun Hei Yud (for this, the combination of the Tetragrammaton and `The Lord', has the same numerical value as the letters of `Amen', namely 91, see above, 306). For, by bowing one draws down `The Lord' and by standing upright one draws down the Tetragrammaton, and later, by the life of the worlds, the two of them unite and interweave together in the secret of Yud Aleph Hei Dalet Vav Nun Hei Yud (as above, 307). And the Holy One, blessed be He, said to the angels, who are the four beings: Whoever is not on record before you as bowing at 'Blessed' and standing up erect at the Tetragrammaton to the full stature of his body, his prayer will not enter into My palace, which is 'The Lord', and you should not accept his speeches on your wings and your faces. For everyone who prays with 'The Lord' and combines this with the Tetragrammaton, which is the faces of the angels, i.e. of the four beings, it is then said about the beings "and their faces and their wings were stretched upwards" (Ezekiel 1:11), in the aspect of their first three Sfirot in order to welcome afterwards the unity of Yud Aleph Hei Dalet Vav Nun Hei Yud, in their six intermediate Sfirot, which are the words of the prayer that issues forth from the mouth of man.

312 And the one who answers 'Amen' is greater than the one who says the blessing, for, regarding 'The Lord' combined with the Tetragrammaton said in just any prayer of man, it is said "their wings and their faces were stretched upwards", for 'faces' parallels the Tetragrammaton and 'their wings' parallels 'The Lord'. And this is the secret of "And make one cherub at the one end" (Exodus 25:19), which is the Tetragrammaton, "and one cherub at the other end" (ibid.), which is 'The Lord'; and the two cherubim are separated, for the unity of 'The Lord' and the Tetragrammaton interweave in the combination (of the letters of the two words) is not achieved in the prayers in general but only in the Amidah (Shemoneh Esreh). But when the leader of the service repeats the prayer (the Shemoneh Esreh), and he responds 'Amen', which unites and combines the Tetragrammaton with 'The Lord', the numerical value of 'Amen' being the same as that of the two names combined, he is thus greater than the one who says the blessing. For he is in the second joining, i.e. in the lower joining of the six inter-

mediate Sfirot, for it is here that the two names, the Tetragrammaton and `The Lord' join together. At the beginning, i.e. at the first joining, which parallels the first three Sfirot, the saying "And the loops are opposite each other on the boards", which is the connection of the fingers with the word `board' [keresh, kuf resh shin], is composed of the letters of `connection' rearranged [kesher, kuf shin resh], for their continuation is not then one in the secret of Yud Aleph Hei Dalet Vav Nun Hei Yud. But in the repetition by the leader of the prayers, which is the secret of the Amidah (Shemoneh Esreh), he answers `Amen', which is the unity of the combination Yud Aleph Hei Dalet Vav Nun Hei Yud, whose total numerical value is as that of the letters of the word `Amen', and then it says: "and the Tabernacle was unified" (Exodus 26:6), for in it "they are coupled one to the other" (Exodus 26:3).

SILENT TIMES AND SPEAKING TIMES

313 The third correction is the arrangement of the speech in prayer, in which the beings of fire speak. And this is: "And I saw as the color of electrum as the appearance of fire round enclosing it" (Ezekiel 1:27). This is the secret of the electrum: that those beings of fire sometimes are silent

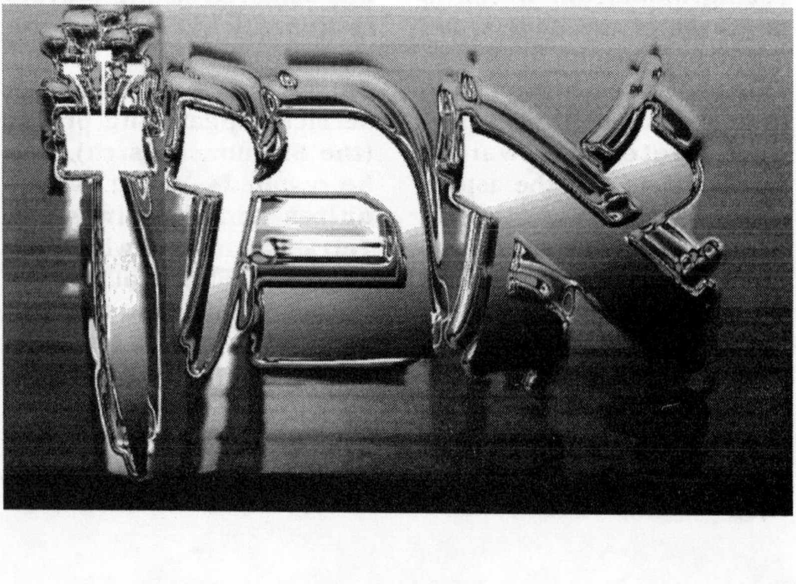

and at other times speak (as above, 282). And they are the secret of the congregation listening to the reading from the scroll of the Torah, for they are silent to the Torah scroll at this time when speech emerges from the mouth of the reader, for it is as important for them as though they were receiving the Torah on Mount Sinai. And when the Holy One, blessed be He, said: "I am the Lord God..." (Exodus 20:2), nothing but His speech was heard, no other sound nor speech of the beings. And therefore, since the one who reads in the Torah is in the place of the Holy One, blessed be He, on Sinai, it is necessary then to be quiet.

314 And just as we have said regarding "I am the Lord your God", so is it always when the speech emerges from the mouth of the Holy One, blessed be He: the beings of fire are quiet, for that is the time of the unity of voice and speech, and Ḥokhmah ceases, and the control of Ḥasadim begins, this being the secret of being silent. And when He is silent, i.e. before there is yet unity of voice and speech, then, the beings of fire are speaking (as above, 282). This is as it is written: "And all the people perceived (*229b) the thunderings" (lit. voices) (Exodus 20:18), i.e. the voice of the beings who were roaring. And these beings also emitted lightnings in their speech (ibid.), that is, a number of types of melody before the King, for this was before the Holy One, blessed be He, started to speak. And when He said: "I am the Lord your God...", the beasts fell quiet and nothing was to be heard except His voice, as explained above. And those (i.e. in the listening congregation) who are quiet at the time of the reading from the scroll of the Torah (during the synagogue service) have the same form as those beings who are quiet at the time of speech of the Holy One, blessed be He, as explained above. And the Holy One, blessed be He, commanded that the beings be brought into the room "as the appearance of fire enclosing it" (Ezekiel 1:27), for this is the secret of harsh Judgement that is revealed at the time when Ḥokhmah is revealed (as above, in the Idra Rabba, 219), and these Judgments were ordained by the Holy One, blessed be He,

that they should enclose them as does a house to protect them from the external bodies that these latter should not suckle from them.

315 Again: Those who are quiet during the prayer, during the 18 blessings, for that is where the unification is, will enter into the room of this vision, i.e. "as the appearance of fire enclosing it"; this will be their reward for the future. And also those who are quiet in practice, i.e. those who are silent in order to hear and understand the practical law as expounded by their rabbi, about which it is said: "The merit of listening to the exposition of the Law is in the understanding obtained thereby" (cf. Talmud Berakhot 6b). They will enter into the room, which is the palace of this vision, of the Torah, which is fire, about which it is said: "Is not My word like as fire? says the Lord; and like a hammer that breaks the rock in pieces?" (Jeremiah, 23:29). And the rock mentioned here is that about which it is said: "And you shall speak to the rock before their eyes that it give forth its water" (Numbers 20:8), which is Malkhut. For those who engage in the study of the Torah for its own sake, the waters of the Torah come forth for them corrected, and it is said about them: "And you shall give the congregation and their cattle drink" (Numbers 20:8). But those who do not engage in the Torah for its own sake shall find that the waters emerge for them bitter, and about them it is said: "And they made their lives bitter with hard service, in mortar and in brick" (Exodus 1:14). The meaning of the verse is as follows: `with hard [kashah] service' is with internal contradictions [kushya]: `in mortar' [homer] refers to the exegetical principle of inference from minor to major [kal vahomer]; and, `in brick' [Hebrew root: lamed bet nun libun] means the elucidation [Hebrew root: lamed bet nun] of the Halakhah.